A History of the
AMERICAS

A History of the AMERICAS

From Prehistory to the 21st Century

Anthony McFarlane
and William Potter

SIRIUS

About the authors

Anthony McFarlane is Professor Emeritus of Latin American History at the University of Warwick and has held the post of Honorary Professorial Fellow at the UCL Institute of the Americas. He has written several books, including *The British in the Americas 1480–1815* and *War and Independence in Spanish America*. He is a member of the Royal Historical Society, the Academia Colombiana de Historia and works on the editorial boards of several academic journals.

William Potter is a Leeds University graduate and has been a writer and editor of reference books for more than two decades. His published works include a history of the world, railway and science museum handbooks, titles on prehistoric life, Vikings, and the environment.

This edition published in 2025 by Sirius Publishing, a division of
Arcturus Publishing Limited,
26/27 Bickels Yard, 151–153 Bermondsey Street,
London SE1 3HA

ISBN: 978-1-3988-5799-5
AD008000UK

Printed in Malaysia

CONTENTS

TIMELINE

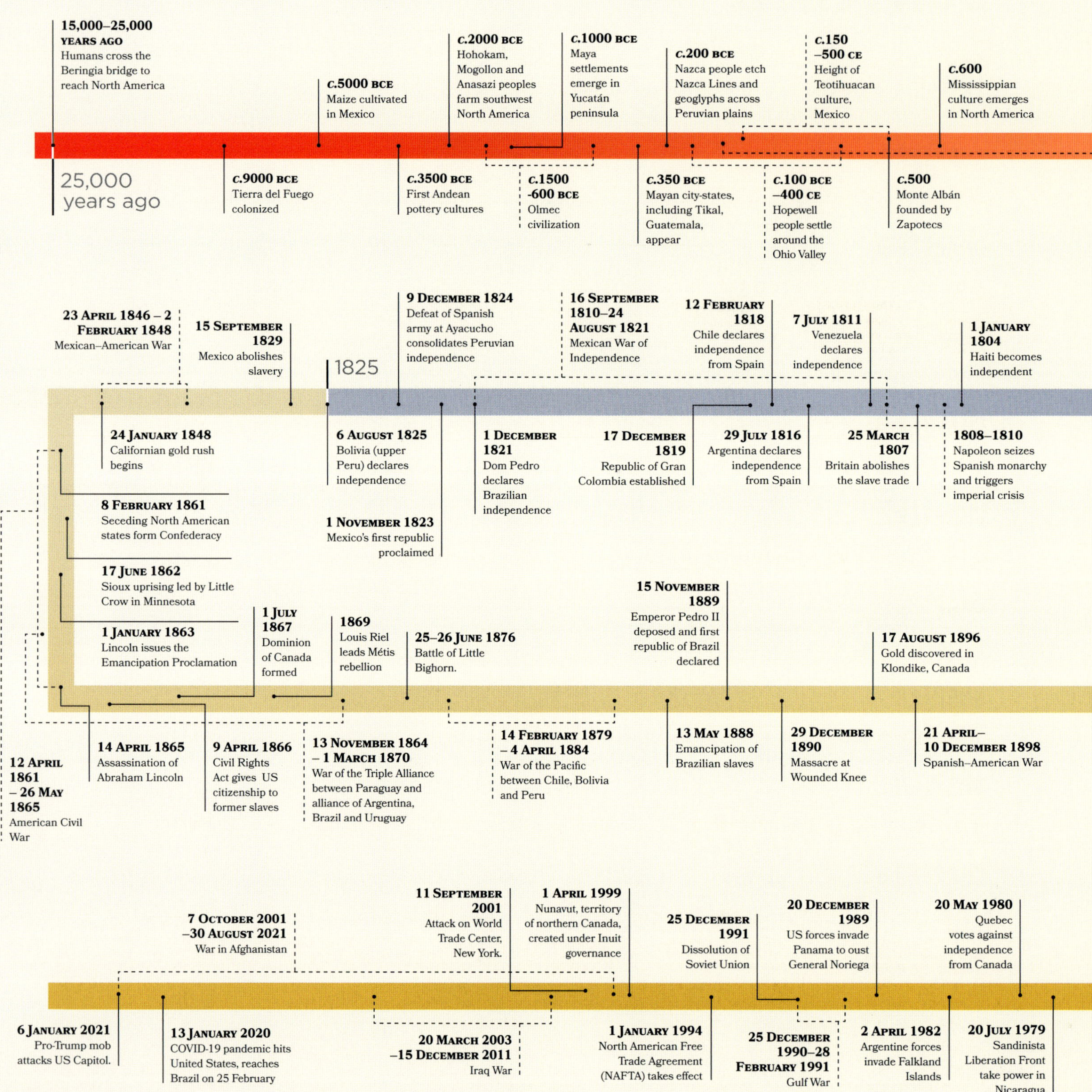

15,000–25,000 YEARS AGO Humans cross the Beringia bridge to reach North America
25,000 years ago
c.9000 BCE Tierra del Fuego colonized
c.5000 BCE Maize cultivated in Mexico
c.3500 BCE First Andean pottery cultures
c.2000 BCE Hohokam, Mogollon and Anasazi peoples farm southwest North America
c.1500 -600 BCE Olmec civilization
c.1000 BCE Maya settlements emerge in Yucatán peninsula
c.350 BCE Mayan city-states, including Tikal, Guatemala, appear
c.200 BCE Nazca people etch Nazca Lines and geoglyphs across Peruvian plains
c.100 BCE –400 CE Hopewell people settle around the Ohio Valley
c.150 –500 CE Height of Teotihuacan culture, Mexico
c.500 Monte Albán founded by Zapotecs
c.600 Mississippian culture emerges in North America
1 January 1804 Haiti becomes independent
1808–1810 Napoleon seizes Spanish monarchy and triggers imperial crisis
25 March 1807 Britain abolishes the slave trade
7 July 1811 Venezuela declares independence
29 July 1816 Argentina declares independence from Spain
12 February 1818 Chile declares independence from Spain
17 December 1819 Republic of Gran Colombia established
16 September 1810–24 August 1821 Mexican War of Independence
1 December 1821 Dom Pedro declares Brazilian independence
1 November 1823 Mexico's first republic proclaimed
9 December 1824 Defeat of Spanish army at Ayacucho consolidates Peruvian independence
1825
6 August 1825 Bolivia (upper Peru) declares independence
15 September 1829 Mexico abolishes slavery
23 April 1846 – 2 February 1848 Mexican–American War
24 January 1848 Californian gold rush begins
8 February 1861 Seceding North American states form Confederacy
17 June 1862 Sioux uprising led by Little Crow in Minnesota
1 January 1863 Lincoln issues the Emancipation Proclamation
12 April 1861 – 26 May 1865 American Civil War
14 April 1865 Assassination of Abraham Lincoln
9 April 1866 Civil Rights Act gives US citizenship to former slaves
1 July 1867 Dominion of Canada formed
1869 Louis Riel leads Métis rebellion
13 November 1864 – 1 March 1870 War of the Triple Alliance between Paraguay and alliance of Argentina, Brazil and Uruguay
25–26 June 1876 Battle of Little Bighorn.
14 February 1879 – 4 April 1884 War of the Pacific between Chile, Bolivia and Peru
13 May 1888 Emancipation of Brazilian slaves
15 November 1889 Emperor Pedro II deposed and first republic of Brazil declared
29 December 1890 Massacre at Wounded Knee
17 August 1896 Gold discovered in Klondike, Canada
21 April– 10 December 1898 Spanish–American War
20 July 1979 Sandinista Liberation Front take power in Nicaragua
20 May 1980 Quebec votes against independence from Canada
2 April 1982 Argentine forces invade Falkland Islands
20 December 1989 US forces invade Panama to oust General Noriega
25 December 1990–28 February 1991 Gulf War
25 December 1991 Dissolution of Soviet Union
1 January 1994 North American Free Trade Agreement (NAFTA) takes effect
1 April 1999 Nunavut, territory of northern Canada, created under Inuit governance
11 September 2001 Attack on World Trade Center, New York.
7 October 2001 –30 August 2021 War in Afghanistan
20 March 2003 –15 December 2011 Iraq War
13 January 2020 COVID-19 pandemic hits United States, reaches Brazil on 25 February
6 January 2021 Pro-Trump mob attacks US Capitol.

Precolumbian 25,000 years ago to 1492

Colonial 1492–1825

Modern 1825–Present

c.250–900
Golden age of Maya in Mexico, Guatemala and Belize

1003
Norse settlement in L'Anse aux Meadows, Newfoundland

1150
Height of Cahokia, period's largest North American settlement

1168
Fall of Toltec Empire, Mexico

1325
Aztecs settle on site of Tenochtitlán, Mexico

c.1450
Machu Picchu built by the Inka in Peru

1492

12 October 1492
Christopher Columbus reaches the Bahamas

7 June 1494
Treaty of Tordesillas signed. Spain and Portugal agree division of New World

22 April 1500
Portuguese Pedro Álvares Cabral discovers Brazil

13 September 1521
Army of Hernán Cortés breaks siege of Tenochtitlan, Mexico

1532-1535
Army of Francisco Pizarro overthrows Inka empire

1534
Jacques Cartier claims Gulf of St Lawrence for France, names area 'Canada'

1549
Bahia becomes capital of Brazil and centre for sugar production based on African slavery

April 1607
Jamestown, Virginia founded in North America

3 August 1610
English explorer Henry Hudson discovers Hudson Bay, Canada

1612
Dutch establish Manhattan Island as North American base for fur trade

21 November 1620
Pilgrim Fathers arrive at Cape Cod, New England

17 February 1627
First English settlement in Barbados

29 August 1664
British take New Amsterdam from Dutch, rename it New York

10 February 1763
Treaty of Paris

16 December 1773
Boston Tea Party protest at British taxes

19 April 1775–3 September 1783
American Revolutionary War

4 July 1776
Declaration of Independence and creation of United States of America

1780 – 1782
Tupac Amaru leads indigenous rebellion against Spanish in Peru

3 September 1783
Britain signs treaty recognizing United States of America

30 April 1789
George Washington made first US president

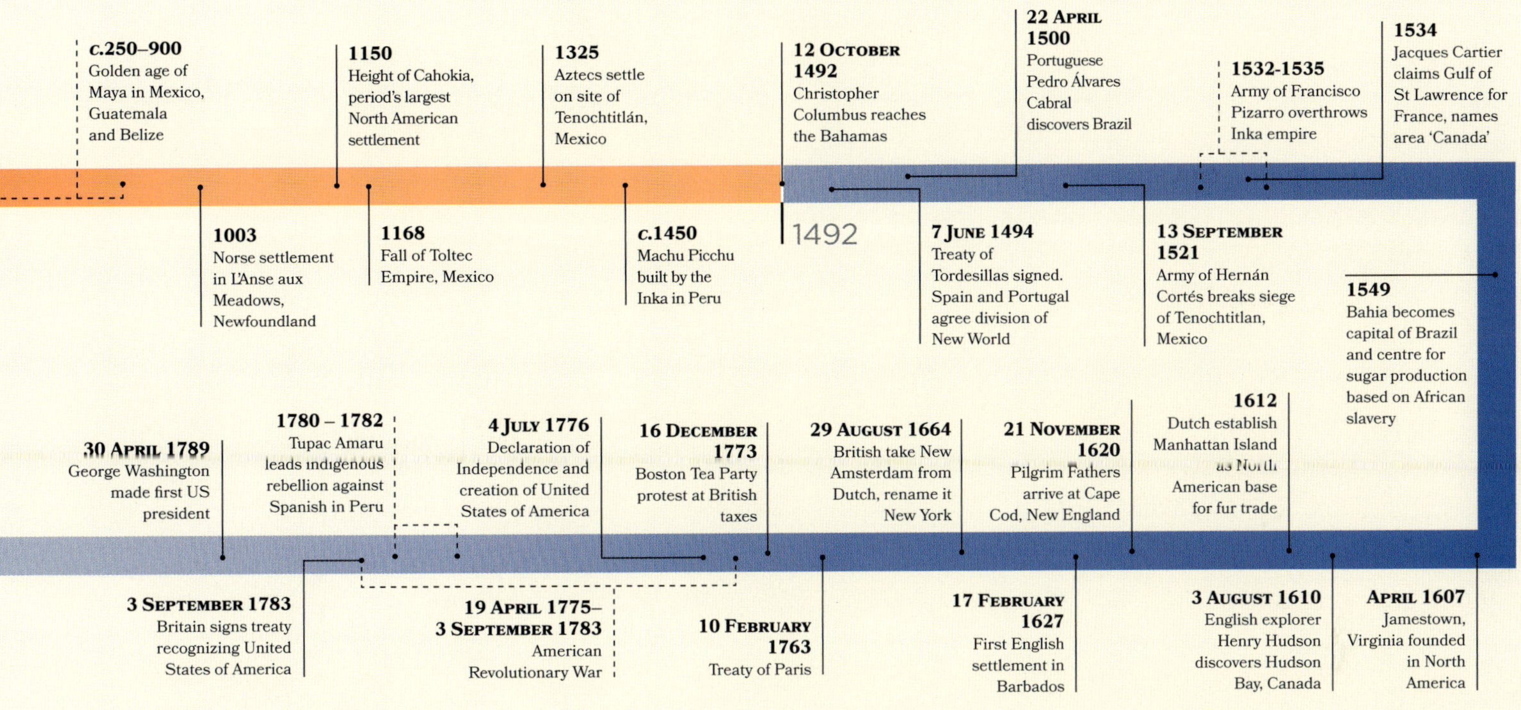

17 October 1899–21 November 1902
Colombian Thousand Days' Civil War

20 May 1902
Cuba becomes independent republic

3 November 1903
Panama asserts independence from Colombia

12 February 1909
National Association for the Advancement of Colored People (NAACP) founded

20 November 1910–1 December 1920
Mexican Revolution

15 August 1914
Opening of the Panama Canal

6 April 1917
US Congress declares war on Germany

16 January 1919
Prohibition in the United States

26 August 1920
Women gain the vote in the United States

24–29 October 1929
Wall Street Crash and beginning of Great Depression

11 December 1931
Statute of Westminster grants Canada autonomy

2 June 1936
General Anastasio Somosa takes over Nicaragua

10 November 1937
Brazil's Estado Novo (New State) begins.

7 December 1941
Japanese attack on Pearl Harbor, Hawaii.

6 August 1945
US drops atomic bomb on Hiroshima, Japan

24 February 1946
Juan Perón elected president of Argentina

31 march 1949
Newfoundland joins Canada as 10th province

4 April 1949
North Atlantic Treaty Organization (NATO) launched with signing in Washington, DC

25 June 1950–27 July 1953
Korean War

3 January 1959
Fidel Castro's guerrillas take power in Cuba

17 April 1961
CIA lands 1,600 Cuban exiles at Bay of Pigs, Cuba, in failed attempt to oust Castro

6 August 1962
Jamaica becomes independent from Britain

15–28 October 1962
Cuban Missile Crisis

28 August 1963
Civil Rights march on Washington, DC

22 November 1963
President John F. Kennedy is shot dead

8 June 1965
US Congress approves use of American ground troops in Vietnam War

9 October 1967
Ernesto 'Che' Guevara is killed

4 April 1968
Assassination of Martin Luther King, Jr in Memphis, Tennessee

21 July 1969
US Apollo 11 makes first Moon landing

31 December 1970
US President Richard Nixon signs Clean Air Act

21–28 February 1972
Nixon visits People's Republic of China

11 September 1973
Augusto Pinochet takes power in Chile, by military coup

9 August 1974
Nixon resigns over Watergate scandal

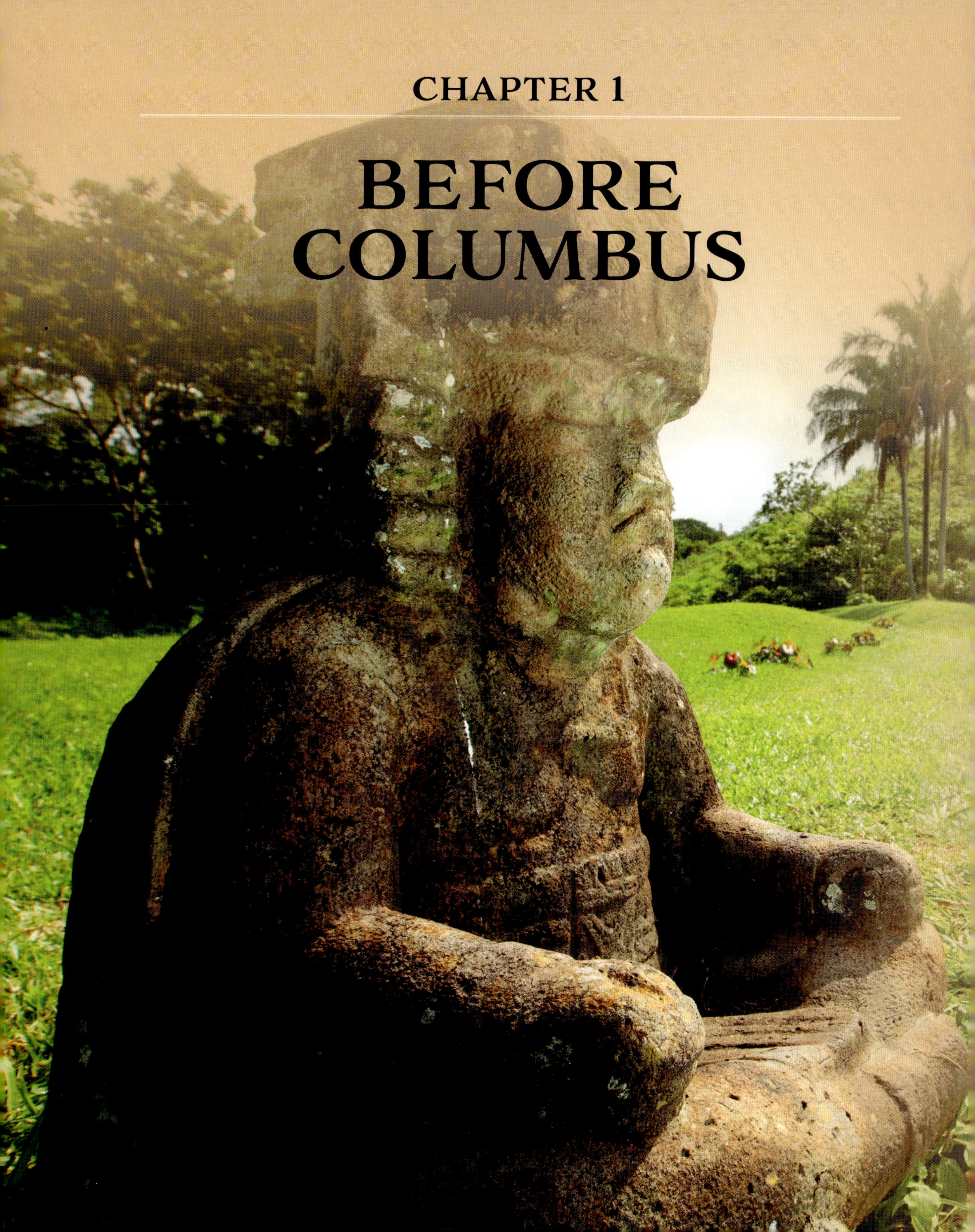

CHAPTER 1

BEFORE COLUMBUS

When Europeans first arrived, the Americas were home to a large variety of peoples and cultures. From Alaska to southern Chile, human settlements had developed in many environments, ranging from sub-arctic tundra to tropical forest. Their peoples spoke dozens of different languages and ranged from nomadic hunters to subjects of powerful states. The most impressive experiments in urbanization and state-building were clustered in southern parts of the western hemisphere, in Mesoamerica (roughly modern Mexico and Central America) and in the northern and central Andes (roughly Colombia, Peru, Ecuador and Bolivia).

Mesoamerican civilization arose in both lowland and highland settings. The Olmec people of the Gulf coast were early city-builders, creating ceremonial centres which spread their goods, styles and religious ideas throughout Mexico. Later, the pace of urbanization accelerated, when city building and state formation developed in the central plateau of Mexico. There, the rise of Teotihuacan prefigured the development of other powerful city-states, ranging from Toltec Tula to the great Aztec city of Tenochtitlan. To the south, city states also appeared around Monte Albán in the Valley of Oaxaca, and in the Maya lowlands of the southwest, where several city-states of great structural complexity nurtured distinctive forms of intellectual life.

Ancient America's other major cultural centres were in western South America. On the Peruvian coast, the Mochica, Nazca and Chimu peoples built large cities with sophisticated cultures. When the Spaniards arrived, the major centres of power had shifted deep inland, to the high Andean valleys and plateaux where the people of Tiwanaku, Wari and Cusco created extensive, tribute-collecting states. Of these, the Inka empire centred on Cusco was the most remarkable, distinguished by its cultural magnificence, extensive road networks, complex political organization, and extraordinary ability to deploy military force.

PEOPLING THE AMERICAS

Europeans were uncertain about where the 'Indians' – as they called them – had originated, and how they fitted into the framework of Christian history. They tended to assume that American peoples had Old World origins of one kind or another. Some insisted that indigenous peoples were descendants of the Ten Lost Tribes of Israel. Others portrayed them as migrants from the supposedly lost continent of Atlantis, or as descendants of ancient Egyptians, or Chinese migrants – all myths which persist today. Modern scientific evidence from physical anthropology, genetics and geology indicates, however, that the Jesuit missionary José de Acosta was right when, in 1590, he suggested that Native Americans came from Asia. Now, the mainstream view is that the first Americans were small groups of nomadic hunters who migrated into North America from northeast Asia, during periods when glaciation and falling sea levels created a continuous land mass between Siberia and Alaska. Called Beringia by geologists, this provided a broad bridge across which animals and their human hunters entered the North American continent.

The timing of human arrivals is uncertain. Some archaeologists think that small numbers might have crossed the Beringian bridge some 40,000 years ago; most think that the evidence points to 15,000–25,000 years ago. Discoveries of early stone and bone tools suggest that Paleo-Indians hunting big game had spread across North America at least 14,000–15,000 years ago, before extending across South America in the thousand years that followed.

The timing of arrivals and dispersions is still open to debate, and speculation continues about possible migrations at other times and from other directions, such as Melanesia, Polynesia or Australia. However, archaeologists generally agree that America's indigenous cultures developed independently of the rest of the world. Norsemen briefly settled in Newfoundland around 1000 CE but withdrew without leaving any lasting mark. Asians had possibly reached America too, but likenesses of ancient Japanese pottery styles in Ecuadorian ceramics, for example, or traces of Chinese architectural patterns and styles in Mexico and coastal Peru are inconclusive evidence of trans-Pacific cultural transmission. It is more likely that Native American societies developed within local and regional frameworks, without any continuous connections with or knowledge of other continents.

For many millennia, American peoples lived in small nomadic bands of hunter-gatherers, without hierarchies of wealth and power. This kind of society persisted in sub-polar regions, where extreme environments constrained population growth but more complex forms of social organization evolved in tropical and temperate zones where abundant resources favoured population growth. There, the development of early horticulture started with the selective cultivation of wild plants more than 10,000 years ago. For thousands of years, communities gathered wild plants to supplement hunting and fishing. Then, as plant cultivation became increasingly central to dietary needs, so people set up permanent settlements to raise their crops, thereby creating village communities that were the basis for later towns and cities. Settled agriculture emerged slowly in regions rich in game, such as the temperate woodlands of North America, where

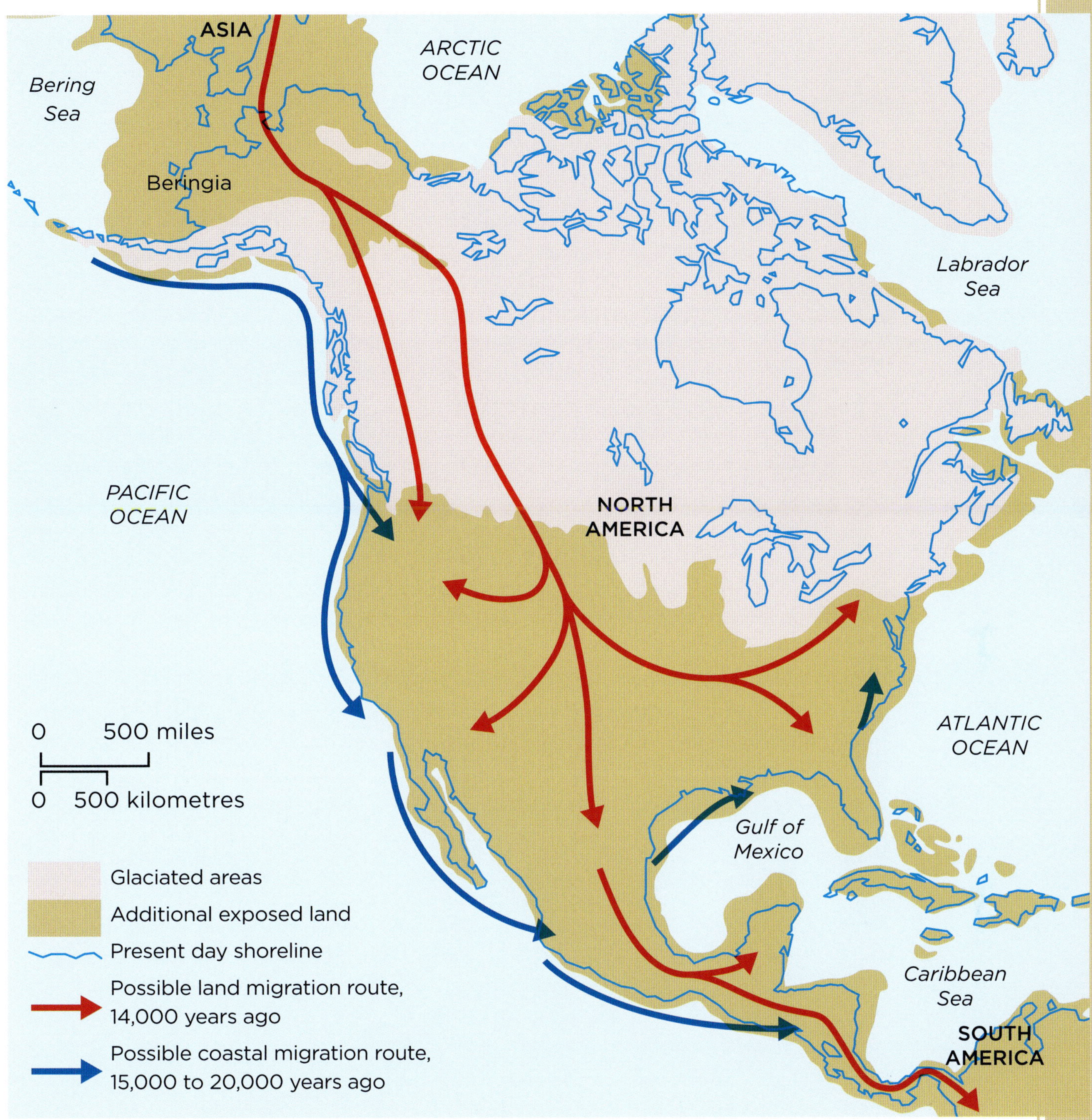

ABOVE *The first routes of human migration into the Americas.*

nomadic hunters long sustained their way of life. But elsewhere, the transition began around 5000 BCE, with gradual but profound effects especially in some South American and Mesoamerican regions (Mesoamerica comprising what is today central and southern Mexico, and northern Costa Rica, Nicaragua, Honduras, El Salvador, Guatemala and Belize).

In Mexico, early cultivars included squashes, beans, amaranth, chilli peppers and avocados, while maize, which became the only cereal widely cultivated in the Americas, first appeared in central Mexico around 5000 BCE. By 2000 BCE maize had become an important food throughout Mesoamerica and, combined with beans and squash, a foundation for population growth. It was also quickly adopted in Central and South America, reaching the Peruvian highlands around 3000 BCE. For Andean peoples, maize was a vital addition to the range of plants they had cultivated for centuries, including potatoes, squashes and beans. In tropical lowland areas, manioc was more important. Cultivated from around 2000 BCE and also known as cassava, it became a key element of the diet in the Amazonian lowlands, along the coasts and rivers of Brazil, and on the islands and shores of the Caribbean Basin, where manioc complemented the proteins provided by hunting and fishing.

Notably absent were the cattle, sheep, goats, pigs, chicken and horses that were so important in the Old World. Native Americans had some livestock. In Mesoamerica, hairless dogs and turkeys were domesticated for food, while in the southern Andes llamas and alpacas provided meat, wool and a means of light transportation. These small camelids were, however, no substitute for horses or other heavy draft animals which were used in Europe, Asia and parts of Africa for transport and in agriculture. Nor did Native Americans use the wheel. The survival of four-wheeled toys shows that some were aware of the concept but they did not exploit it. For the energy needed in large-scale building and irrigation works, indigenous peoples mobilized large numbers of workers, a circumstance which invariably coincided with the growth of urban centres under hierarchical and centralized leadership.

Ongoing agricultural development underpinned social change. A more secure and plentiful food supply allowed populations to grow and, through a positive feedback loop, encouraged the adoption of intensive farming techniques, such as irrigation and terracing. While many farming communities long remained in small villages, population growth made new forms of social organization possible. A key innovation is captured by the concept of the 'chiefdom'. Archaeological research shows that larger communities of thousands, even tens of thousands of villagers sometimes coalesced under the authority of a single chief, who managed collective rituals, defence and the redistribution of goods. The chief typically resided in a large central community, set apart from a hinterland of villages and distinguished by the presence of ceremonial structures for the worship of local deities. Chiefdoms of this kind appeared throughout the Americas during the first millennium BCE; in some parts of Mesoamerica and the Andes they evolved into states, a few of which built empires. States were distinguished by their larger-scale, more complex social hierarchy – with divisions into classes of royalty, nobles, commoners and slaves – and by the tendency of the central community to become a dominant city that housed a ruling elite.

ABOVE *A 7th–9th century Mayan sculpture of the Maize God emerging from an ear of corn.*

RIGHT *A Mesoamerican wheeled toy.*

Such states were unusual but were built on forces similar to those behind the growth of large chiefdoms. They emerged because centralized political authority offered advantages for controlling growing populations and for defence and warfare. Religion also played an important part. Throughout the Americas, religion was polytheistic and based on belief in gods and spirits related to nature; ritual burials and ancestor worship were also ancient practices, nurtured in small communities. In larger societies and in cities, such practices grew in scale, as greater resources allowed for more elaborate and large-scale religious rites, managed by a priestly caste who organized a calendar of ceremonies and festivals. By helping to unite peoples in shared beliefs, they played a key role in tightening social bonds and reinforced the power of leaders, who often held priestly positions or claimed divine descent.

MESOAMERICA

OLMEC CIVILIZATION

The first chiefdoms emerged in Mesoamerica, starting on Mexico's Gulf coast. There, the Olmecs (*c.*1500 BCE–600 BCE) built large ceremonial centres at San Lorenzo, La Venta and Tres Zapotes, containing large earthen mounds, stone platforms and pyramids, and gigantic basalt heads – some weighing up to 40 tonnes – which perhaps portray their chieftains.

With populations of a few thousand, these were sites of modest size, much smaller than later Mesoamerican cities. Nonetheless, their stone building, jade carving and sophisticated ceramics reflect the presence of a stratified society organized in a powerful chiefdom, perhaps an incipient state, united under a central political authority and capable of production and trade on a large scale.

Explanations of Olmec growth point to a high agricultural productivity, which yielded the surpluses needed to sustain the elite who organized ceremonials and ordered social life, as well as the artisans and traders who produced and exchanged key products. Why the wider population accepted elite rule is unknown. Material advantages brought by intensive agriculture and trading networks played their part, but religion probably had a central role. Priests and rulers promoted a religious cult that focused on a jaguar deity and was reflected in the motif of a half-human, half-feline figure which recurs throughout the work of Olmec artists.

ABOVE *An Olmec head from the San Lorenzo archaeological site.*

Their jade figurines were widely coveted and became the most valuable of Mesoamerican wealth symbols, spread widely through long-distance trade. The Olmec priestly caste also created hieroglyphics and a calendar, which enhanced their role as intermediaries with the gods and interpreters of the world, natural and spiritual. And, as

LEFT *A seated Olmec figurine.*

RIGHT *The Kunz Axe, one of the first artefacts of Olmec civilization discovered. This jade figurine likely had a ritual function.*

their elaborate ceremonials attracted large numbers of pilgrims, the elites' authority grew, allowing them to create an incipient state in which government was sanctified by a state religion.

The Olmecs have been called the 'mother culture' of Mesoamerica because they were the first to develop major ceremonial centres, monumental architecture and a complex art style, and because their religion, writing and calendrical systems prefigured those of the Maya and other Mesoamerican societies. They were also the first to engage in long-distance trades that projected cultural influence. Traces of Olmec culture are found across a huge area, stretching from central Mexico into Central America, and continued after the demise of its centres. The nature of their decline also foreshadowed that of other Mesoamerican cultures. When San Lorenzo was abandoned around 900 BCE and La Venta about 600 BCE, it was probably because their agriculture was unable to sustain growing populations. Food shortages generated social crises that undermined the power of religious and political authorities and eventually triggered their overthrow, a fate that affected several later Mesoamerican cities.

After the Olmec decline, other Mesoamerican urban centres developed during the first millennium CE. The most prominent were Teotihuacan in the central Valley of Mexico, Monte Albán in Oaxaca (*c.*600 BCE–800 CE) and the various Maya cities in the Yucatán Peninsula, southern Mexico and parts of Guatemala, Honduras and El Salvador (*c.*2000 BCE–900 CE).

RIGHT *Map of the Olmec heartland.*

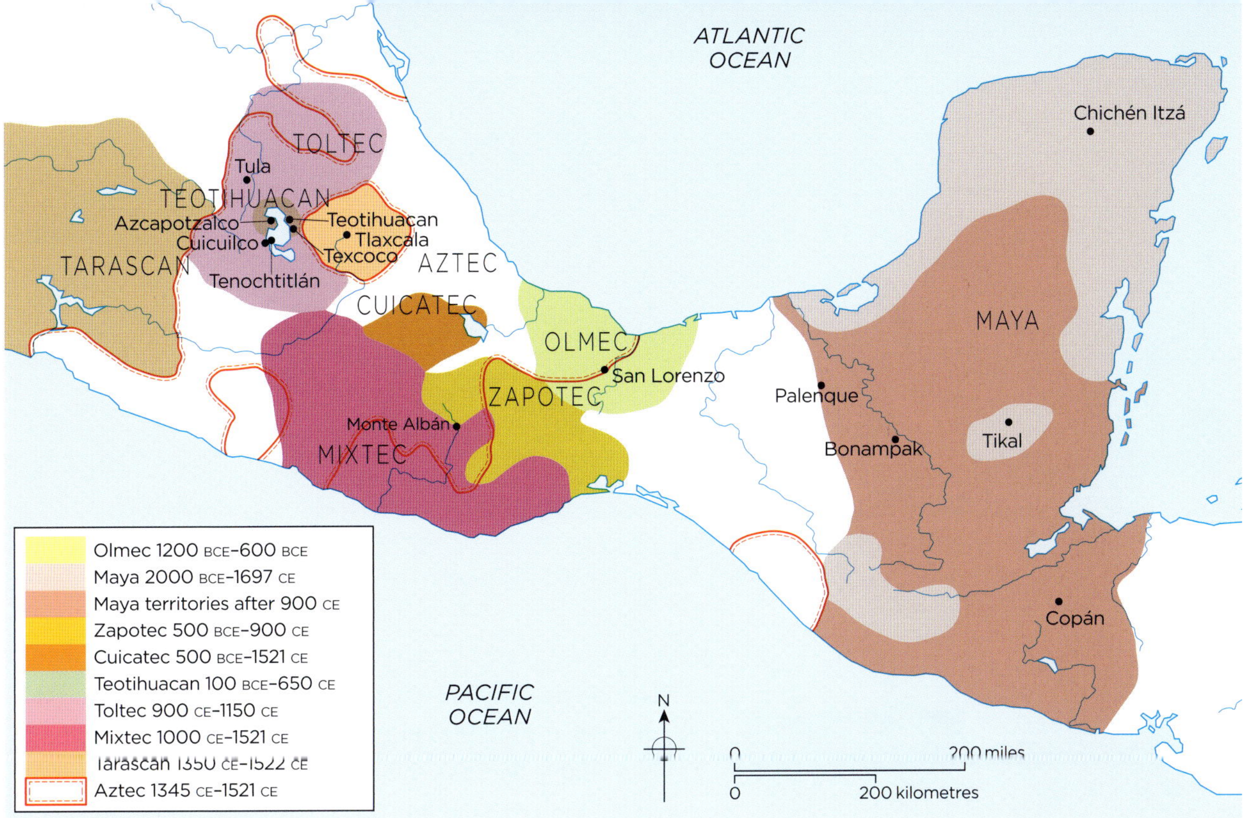

Although in some ways quite distinct from each other, these urban centres shared salient features. They depended on intensive agriculture supported by sophisticated systems for water management, and used maize and beans as staple foods. Their societies were ranked in hierarchies and governed by centralized political authorities, controlled by small elites of priests and secular leaders. These elites displayed their power in monumental works of stone architecture, including pyramids, temples, palaces and ball courts, buildings which reflected their ability to mobilize large numbers of workers. They all had some variant of the Mesoamerican ball game, played with rubber balls on special courts at events of religious and ritual significance. The elites' power rested partly on their control of trade, which provided goods that were redistributed to select groups in order to win their loyalty. In some cases, their power was reinforced by military means, but religion was a more important force. Everywhere, cities were the spaces where ruling elites conducted rituals and ceremonies, including human sacrifices, to appease their deities and keep cosmic order. Priests developed complex calendar systems related to their religious practices, and several Mesoamerican cultures had writing systems that used hieroglyphs or pictographic writing to record religious texts, historical events and astronomical data.

LEFT *Pre-Columbian Mesoamerican civilizations.*

BELOW *The Avenue of the Dead in the city of Teotihuacan.*

Teotihuacan, located in the north of the Valley of Mexico (near modern Mexico City), entered a phase of rapid growth in 1–350 CE, when it became the largest metropolis in Mesoamerica. Its growth was underpinned by raising agricultural productivity using canals and chinampas (cultivated beds raised on

ABOVE *The site of Monte Albán, Oaxaca, Mexico.*

swampy grounds) but its rise accelerated after the nearby rival city of Cuicuilco was destroyed by volcanic eruption. At its height (150–500 CE), Teotihuacan covered more than 26 sq km (10 sq miles) and had about 150,000 inhabitants, and perhaps as many as 250,000.

At its heart were two huge stone pyramids, positioned on a broad avenue with an array of temples, palaces, public buildings and homes for the elite, all of which show the elite's capacity to mobilize mass labour from the lower echelons of a stratified society. In the city's environs, artisans produced a range of functional and luxury goods, from common pottery and utensils to rich decorative clothing and jewellery. The city was also a major producer of obsidian arms and tools, which enhanced its ability to create far-reaching and enduring trading networks.

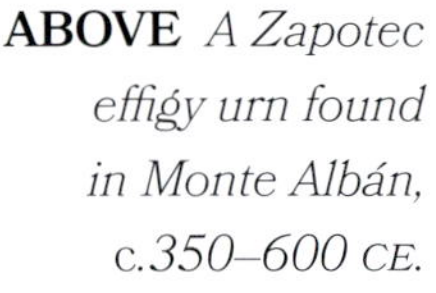

ABOVE *A Zapotec effigy urn found in Monte Albán, c.350–600 CE.*

Renowned as 'the place where the gods reside', Teotihuacan became the greatest religious centre in Mesoamerica. Its priests drew up calendar systems, divided time into 52-year cycles, and worshipped gods that were adopted by other Mesoamerican cultures, including the Aztecs. Some scholars believe that Teotihuacan became militaristic under elites who imposed themselves by force. Others stress the importance of cultural diffusion and trade, and the formation of alliances with smaller cities which became client states ruled by collaborating elites. What is not in doubt is that Teotihuacan left a strong imprint across Mesoamerica, reflected in the forms of religion, trade and governance of successive city-states. Teotihuacan's long-lived power finally waned between 650 and 750 CE, when problems over the distribution of resources sparked conflicts within the city and its destruction from within.

MONTE ALBÁN

In southern Mexico, the Zapotecs founded Monte Albán around 500 BCE. By 200 BCE it was the largest city in southern Mexico, with about 17,000 inhabitants, thanks to the resources provided by the supply of foods from temperate highlands and hot tropical lowlands. At the city's core was a great ceremonial centre with large temples and palaces, and an observatory for scanning the stars, suggesting that a powerful priestly elite presided over a highly stratified society. Perched on a hill, the city grew by making conquests and alliances within the Valley of Oaxaca. Then, when its resources came under pressure from excessive population, it expanded outwards in the aggressive acquisition of territory beyond the Valley. The city lost its political pre-eminence by around 800 CE, revived later but was defeated by the Aztecs in the early 15th century.

THE MAYA

In the southeast of modern Mexico and the neighbouring regions of Central America, another pattern of urban growth took place, as Maya civilization (*c.*2000 BCE–900 CE) emerged in an environment of tropical rainforests. Mayan people employed slash and burn farming and irrigation techniques for the cultivation of maize, beans and squashes, and on this agricultural foundation built their first temple-palace complexes around 750 BCE. By 500 BCE, their number had multiplied and in cities such as Tikal, Palenque and Bonapak priestly elites organized peasant labour to create large pyramidical temples, with elaborate façades and exquisite decoration.

During their golden age (*c.*250–900 CE), Maya cities were linked by a trade network which also extended into central Mexico, and they enjoyed a long period of peace and prosperity. Though generally smaller than those of central Mexico, such cities displayed great skills in art and architecture, shown in carved stone stelae, polychrome ceramics and the use of the corbel arch. Their hieroglyphic writing, sophisticated mathematics, astronomy and extraordinary calendrical systems (much more accurate than those of contemporary Europe) also show exceptional intellectual prowess, ahead of other American cultures.

Maya fortunes changed in the 9th century, however, when the lowland cities in the Yucatán Peninsula were undermined by drought and soil exhaustion. Peasants withdrew

ABOVE *Tikal Temple of the Masks.*

BELOW *El Castillo, the Temple of Kukulcan in Chichén Itzá.*

ABOVE *A Toltec pyramid.*

their support and, without labour to sustain them, many cities were abandoned by about 900 CE. Their future was also threatened by invasions from central Mexico, spearheaded by Toltecs who established a city on Maya terrain at Chichén Itzá. There was a later resurgence of Maya culture, but in a new form. By about 1200 CE, cities revived in the Guatemalan highlands and the Yucatán but were now fortresses ruled by competing warrior elites, rather than religious and trading centres.

THE TOLTECS

While Maya civilization contracted, a new power emerged in central Mexico. The rise of the Toltecs (*c.*950–1150) marked the start of several phases of change, associated with the arrival of migrants who moved from drought-ridden northern areas in search of new lands. They overran existing cities, built new ones, and generally assimilated into pre-existing ways of urban life. Imitating Teotihuacan, the Toltecs created their own city at Tula, installing a militaristic polity dominated by warrior orders and religious practices that included human sacrifice. Toltec power was subsequently displaced by new migrants. In 1200, the city fell to plundering invaders and turmoil followed as competing groups vied for land and power. Several established competing city-states in the Valley of Mexico, around the fertile shores of Lake Texcoco, under rulers who justified their position by claiming descent from the Toltecs.

THE AZTECS

One of these migrant tribes was the Mexica (later known as the Aztecs) who, in *c.*1325, founded a settlement called Tenochtitlan on an island in Lake Texcoco. Their society broadly resembled that of their neighbours, with an economy based on intensive, irrigated maize cultivation and horticulture, and a culture centred on the worship of nature divinities. However, the Aztecs' dedication to war gave them a crucial edge. In 1438, they allied with two neighbouring city-states to defeat their major competitor, the city of Azcapotzalco, and this Triple Alliance became the dominant power in central Mexico, able to draw tributes from its neighbours. During the latter half of the 15th century, the Aztecs' aggression took them further afield, until they had extended their hegemony into parts of southern Mexico. Expansion was driven by material and religious imperatives. Tenochtitlan needed food and other goods to sustain its growing population and ruling elites, and Aztec priests demanded thousands of victims for human sacrifice to appease their deities, taken from captives of war. War therefore became a driving force in Aztec society, more than in any other in the Americas.

With about 200,000 inhabitants, Tenochtitlan was the most spectacular concentration of wealth and power in Mesoamerica and, indeed, in the entire North American continent. The city's artisans produced an impressive array of crafts and its elite used a system of pictographic writing which, inscribed on deerskins, recorded events and tribute payments. The social order was steeply hierarchical, ruled by a centralized monarchy. Lords chose a king from the royal family and imbued him with semi-divine status, while nobles, priests and warriors enforced

ABOVE *Aztec jewellery – a golden ornament of a snake,* c.*15th century.*

ABOVE *The city of Tenochtitlan, the capital of the Aztec empire.*

his mandate. The 'empire' had a distinctive character, for the Aztecs did not seek to hold territories or govern peoples conquered in war. They exercised power by intimidating rather than co-opting the conquered, and, as their hegemony depended on military strength, it tended towards instability. The arrival of Europeans after 1500 was to reveal even more serious weaknesses, when Spaniards used steel swords, guns and mounted men to attack Aztec warriors who wielded stone-age weapons and operated only on foot.

THE CARIBBEAN REGION

When the Spaniards landed on the Caribbean islands and the adjacent shores of Panama, Venezuela and Colombia, they encountered peoples who were organized in 'tribes', each linked by a common language, customs and political leadership. Most lived in groups or villages of hundreds of inhabitants or in chiefdoms of thousands of people, linked for defensive or religious purposes. The first chiefdoms which confronted the Spanish invaders were in the Caribbean region, where they made their first contacts with so-called 'Indians'. The majority were Taino people, descended from mainland migrants who arrived after 500 BCE. Migrating from the lower Orinoco and the coasts of Venezuela, a substantial population of agricultural and pottery-making people settled in the Greater Antilles, where they lived by cultivating maize, manioc, sweet potatoes and various fruits, supplemented by fishing and hunting. They also wove cotton and made baskets, jewellery

RIGHT *Petroglyphs at the Las Caritas cave, Lake Enriquillo, created by the Taino.*

and woodcarvings, both for their own use and for trade between islands. After about 500 CE, the Taino were organized into chiefdoms of varying sizes, ranging from several thousands to tens of thousands, sometimes with hereditary leaders who had priestly attributes. Taino culture was infused with belief in nature spirits, and ritual and ceremony were central to social life. The island which the Spaniards called Hispaniola (today home to Haiti and the Dominican Republic) had many chiefdoms, under leaders called caciques, some of which combined into confederations of considerable power.

The small islands of the Lesser Antilles in the eastern Caribbean were home to more recent migrants, drawn from the Carib people of northern Amazonia. They differed from the Taino in social organization, living in smaller, more equal societies which chose their chiefs in time of conflict. They were feared for their prowess in war, manifested in their seaborne attacks on Taino villages. The Spanish branded them as 'cannibals', a variant of Caribes, the Spanish word for Carib. This depiction was only partly true: the Carib ate parts of the flesh of enemy warriors, a common Native American custom; they did not treat human flesh as food.

BELOW *Taino bowl and figure.*

SOUTH AMERICA

CHIEFDOMS OF THE NORTHERN ANDES

The lands of northern South America (modern Colombia, western Venezuela and Ecuador) covered a wide environmental range, from temperate basins in the Andes to humid tropical forests on the Pacific and Caribbean coasts. Here, ecological diversity was conducive to population growth, and several regions saw the evolution of chiefdoms of considerable size and power. In Ecuador and Colombia, large chiefdoms emerged from around the 6th century, with central sites composed of temples and elite residences, and foundations in intensive agriculture.

The Tairona chiefdoms of the northeastern highlands, close to the Caribbean, grew into one of the largest polities of South America between the 11th and 16th centuries. Using irrigation canals and terracing, the Tairona developed an agriculture capable of supporting around 300,000 people and drew federations of villages and towns together in large composite settlements. The recent discovery of a 'Lost City', near Santa Marta, shows a very considerable urban area, with long stone causeways linking settlements and many stone foundations.

ABOVE *The 'Lost City' near Santa Marta, Colombia.*

Large polities also appeared deep inland, in the highland basins around Bogotá. When the Spaniards arrived in 1537, they found the Muisca (or Chibcha) people of the region divided into two warring chiefdoms. Both had large populations, ruled from wooden fortress towns which enclosed temples and palaces. Their stone sculptures were few and their timber buildings left scant traces, but Spanish reports tell us that they were rich in gold, which they obtained from the Tairona and others in return for emeralds and used for decoration and ceremonial purposes. Chiefs began their reign by plunging into a lake to wash off gold dusted on their bodies, a propitiatory offering accompanied by throwing gold ornaments into the waters. From this sprang the legend of El Dorado, 'the Golden One', a lure for treasure hunters until late in the 20th century. The Calima and Quimbaya peoples of Colombia's southern highlands are also renowned for exquisite gold work, mostly pendants depicting animals and humans, and small flasks designed to hold the lime that was chewed with coca leaves.

LEFT *A Tairona gold pendant.*

CHIEFDOMS OF THE CENTRAL AND SOUTHERN ANDES

The largest chiefdoms of South America developed further south, in the highlands of the central and southern Andes and along their Pacific coasts. The Inka empire is the most renowned of these, but it had several precedents in chiefdoms and states that arose in Pacific coastal valleys and Andean highland habitats. In regions where cultivable land was scarce and drought a persistent problem, Andean peoples developed a highly efficient agriculture that allowed for the concentration of large populations, the building of cities and the creation of complex religious and political institutions. Their societies also had some unusual features. On the Pacific coast, the abundance of marine resources underpinned early urbanization, while in the high Andes people herded llamas and alpacas, which were used for meat, wool and transport. Another striking feature of the region was the abundance of metals and its peoples' refined skills in working gold, silver, copper and tin. The use of wool was unique in pre-Columbian America and Peruvian weaving was without parallel. Andeans also produced some outstanding works of engineering, in road networks, agricultural terracing and irrigation, and buildings designed to cope with frequent earthquakes.

ABOVE *A Quimbaya gold figurine.*

PERUVIAN PACIFIC CULTURES

The sequence of regional centres that preceded the Inka began around 800–300 BCE, when a series of religious hubs appeared in Peru, with temples and mounds, and priestly groups dedicated to the worship of a feline deity. Chavín de Huantar, in the northern Peruvian highlands, was the first of these religious centres and a powerful influence on those that followed. Its large stone temples attracted people from other regions and its textiles, metalwork and other artefacts were widely disseminated.

After Chavín's decline, other cities and states emerged on the Pacific coasts and in the Andean highlands, together with the construction of large irrigation systems, and the florescence of ceramics, textiles and metalworking. Those in the highlands have left a more lasting mark, largely because they were built in stone rather than the mud bricks used in coastal cities. However, major cultures flourished at several points along the Peruvian coasts in the first millennium CE.

BELOW *Chavín de Huantar.*

An outstanding example was the Mochica culture that flourished between the 3rd and 8th century CE. It extended over several valleys on the north coast but was focused on a large city in the Moche valley, with huge adobe pyramids, a great plaza and a residential zone, all sustained by a canal-based irrigation system that carried water over long distances. At times, the various valleys seem to have been autonomous parts of a confederation. At other times, the city was the headquarters of a centralized elite that subjected neighbouring regions to military conquest. The Mochica are best known for their extraordinary pottery, which vividly depicts many aspects of their social and spiritual life, and for their metalwork in copper, silver and gold, which employed some of the most advanced techniques of the time. Their eventual decline apparently resulted from earthquake damage to irrigation systems and/or extended periods of drought and flooding caused by the recurrent climate pattern known as El Niño.

ABOVE *A wall at Chan Chan, capital of the Chimu.*

ABOVE *An example of Mochica pottery.*

Co-existing with the Mochica, the Nazca people developed their own distinctive culture on Peru's south coast. It was based on chiefdoms at several centres in different valleys, without a single capital. The Nazca wove exceptionally fine textiles but are now best known for the giant geometric and figurative designs which they etched on rocky ground, perhaps for religious or calendrical purposes. Like the Mochica, Nazca culture was undermined by climate events, probably associated with El Niño.

The most powerful coastal state was that of Chimu (or Chimor) founded about 800 CE, once again in the Moche valley. This multi-valley conquest state had its capital at Chan Chan, a city of 15,000–30,000 inhabitants. Like other Pacific coastal states, Chan Chan depended on irrigation, but its hydraulic works were distinguished by their grand scale. One project for bringing river water from the hills was a canal 84 km (52 miles) long, an extraordinary addition to the already large network of canals supplying fresh

LEFT *Nazca lines, seen from the air.*

ABOVE
Tiahuanaco, Gateway of the Sun, Bolivia.

water to the valleys. Chimu was evidently a society of deep inequalities, topped by kings and royal clans who commanded a strong state capable of building large public works and maintaining a wide network of trade that provided goods for leaders to redistribute to their supporters and subjects. Its main products were mass-produced ceramics, a wide variety of textiles, and luxury goods made from gold, silver and other precious materials. Chimu goldsmiths were so highly regarded that the Inka, after conquering Chimu in 1465, forced groups of them to resettle in their capital at Cusco.

The rapid expansion and large scale of the Chimu kingdom was driven by practices of royal succession, reflected in the character of its capital at Chan Chan. Built largely of adobe bricks, the city was an extensive grouping of large residential compounds, each created by the reigning king. On his death, his patrimony passed to junior relatives, which left the heir to build his own fortunes, embodied in a residential palace of his own, plus another for preserving his memory. This practice of splitting the king's wealth at his death goes some way to explaining the dynamism of Chimu's state, as it required successive rulers to find untapped resources, whether by bringing new lands under cultivation, raising new taxes or conquering more territory.

ANDEAN HIGHLAND STATES AND THE INKA EMPIRE

The history of Andean highland empires, of which the Inka was the greatest, begins with Tiahuanaco, from c.400–1000 CE. Here, on a mountain plateau at around 3,840 m (12,600 ft) above sea level, in the southern Andes close to Lake Titicaca, a great city with 20,000–40,000 inhabitants developed on an earlier ceremonial site. The remains of monumental stone architecture show that its centre was formed by avenues lined with temples, some on platforms, together with tombs and elite residences. Food was cultivated on land reclaimed from lakeside marshes, using canals that resembled those of cities in central Mexico. The religious practices of Tiahuanaco drew on the earlier Chavín culture and centred on the worship of a so-called Staff God which stood in the 'Gateway of the Sun'.

At its height, the Tiahuanaco state established four classes of settlement, with residences for administrators and farmers in centres outside the main city. Ruling elites seem to have imposed standard designs for pottery, textiles and wooden and metal ornaments, which were traded over a wide area. Tiahuanaco's reach spread far and wide, both south into Chile and east into the jungles, where economic colonies were set up to provide lowland products such as coca, maize, peppers, tropical fruits and medicinal plants. These were linked to the centre by llama caravans and prefigure Inka efforts to establish a system of vertical control reaching from the high Andes down into tropical forest and coastal lowland areas.

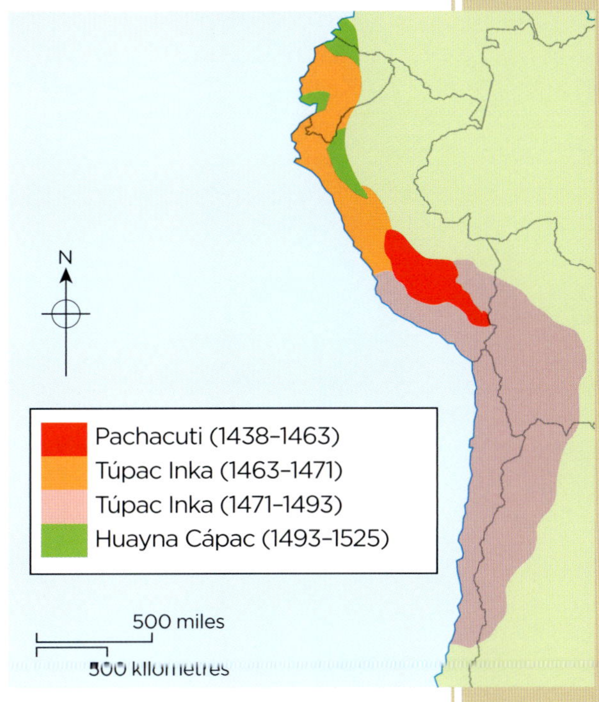

ABOVE *Map of Inka expansion.*

Tiahuanaco was subsequently displaced by the Wari culture, focused on a city in another mountain basin about 800 km (500 miles) to the northwest, near modern Ayacucho. Wari resembled Tiahuanaco in terms of its layout and building styles, and, starting around 700 CE, also created an empire that reached from the highlands to the Pacific coast. Wari might have been an outgrowth of the Tiahuanaco state, perhaps starting as a colony before becoming the northern capital of a dual-centre empire. One of its features was a road network of a kind that was later to be greatly extended by the Inka, to articulate their much larger empire. Its collapse was followed by a period of turmoil in the southern highland region, during which competing chiefdoms with similar cultures fought for territory.

The Inka were one of these chiefdoms. Based in the Cusco Valley, they became a dynamic, dominating force from around the beginning of the 15th century, when in quick succession their kings defeated rival chiefdoms in the Tiahuanaco basin, in Quito, and the Chimu kingdom on the coast. From around 1440, the Inka created the Tawantinsuyu, the 'realm of the four quarters', a vast territorial empire which at its peak extended over 4,000 km (2,500 miles), from southern Colombia to central Chile, and ruled over a hundred ethnic groups comprising a population of perhaps 10–12 million people.

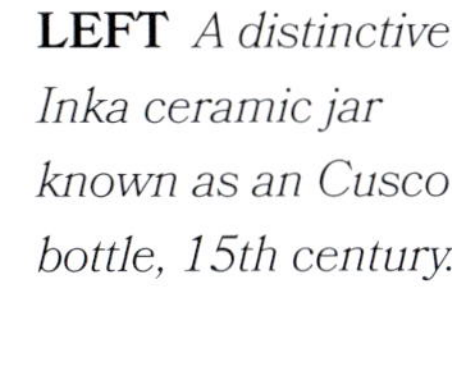

LEFT *A distinctive Inka ceramic jar known as an Cusco bottle, 15th century.*

The Inka realm was ruled by an absolute king, called the Sapa Inka, who claimed descent from the sun god, Inti. The Sapa Inka was supported by an aristocracy, an army, and a priesthood which organized religious rituals in Cusco, the 'navel of the earth'. Unlike the Aztecs, the Inkas established their own governments in the territories they conquered. This was underpinned by force but consolidated by alliances with peoples defeated in war or won over by promises of rewards in return for collaboration. Conquest was easiest in regions where strong central authority and class structures already existed.

ABOVE *A gold Inka figurine, 15th century.*

The empire was divided into four parts, each with an Inka noble as governor in his own capital. Inka nobles held command and imposed their rule and religion. However, they encouraged fealty by allowing local religious practices and co-opting chiefs of subordinate ethnic groups to exercise regional and local authority under the overarching Inka power. Such alliances were reinforced by redistributing part of the tributary goods demanded by the Inka among subject communities. This was a strategic political use of the social principle of reciprocity widely practised in Andean communities, which recognized mutual rights between community members and between communities and their leaders. It has been confused with a 'welfare state', where government officials met the needs of the poor by the redistribution of goods, particularly in times of economic difficulty. In reality, the Inka system was a highly unequal exchange. It was designed to legitimize the power of the Inka ruling elites, who lived in great luxury and enjoyed many privileges denied to commoners. Protection of the poor was left to the communities in which they lived.

The Inka state's combination of coercion and co-optation allowed it to achieve a scale and cohesion unique among Native American civilizations, reinforced by an extraordinary road system which ensured transport and rapid communications over exceptionally long distances. Although they lacked a form of writing comparable to those in use in Eurasia, the Inka had a vital tool for empire in their system of recording and transmitting information by means of knotted strings (quipus). Inka rulers professed a 'civilizing mission' designed to bring peace under a benign autocracy, a shared religion and a common language, Quechua. Rebellions by subject peoples were not uncommon, however, and, in their search for new lands and tributes, Inka kings tended to overstretch their capacities for control. Instability within the Inka empire was, in fact, an important contributor to its collapse. Shortly before the intrusion of the Spaniards in 1532, a dispute between Inka noble clans over royal succession, combined with a provincial rebellion, fuelled a civil war. When the Spanish invaders arrived, these divisions within the Inka state did much to facilitate a Spanish takeover, initially under a puppet Inka king.

BRAZIL AND THE SOUTH

The Inka explored the eastern slopes of the Andes but did not enter the huge tropical plains traversed by the great river systems of the Orinoco and Amazon, nor did they reach into the southern regions of South America. On the Atlantic seaboard of modern Brazil and in the great river basins, most communities were smaller and less complex than those of the Andean world. There is some evidence of large societies sustained by irrigation in the lower Amazon, but society was mostly village-based and had limited potential for growth and development. Food was obtained from riverine and maritime resources, combined with slash and burn agriculture, and villages often moved seasonally. Leadership was provided by shamans and war leaders, and indigenous groups engaged in persistent conflict, focused on the seizure of captives who were used as slaves or for sacrificial cannibalism.

BELOW *A quipu, a collection of knotted strings used to record information.*

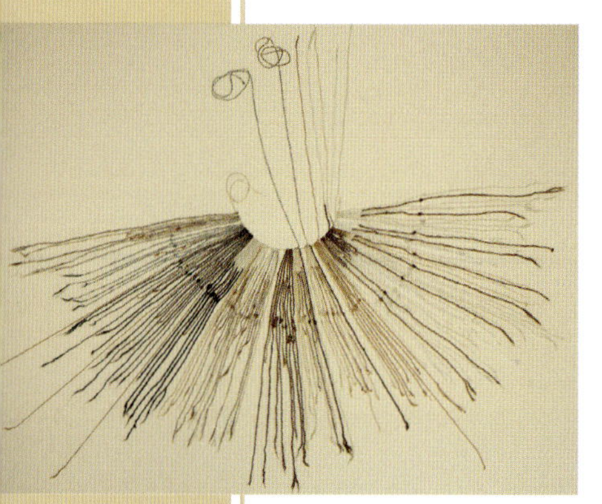

The regions south of Brazil, in modern Paraguay, Uruguay and Argentina, were also devoid of urban development and generally did not form large chiefdoms. Many communities, like those living on the great plains of the Pampas, depended on nomadic hunting and gathering, though some, such as the Araucanians of Chile, were more settled and powerful than others.

NORTH AMERICA

The indigenous societies and cultures of North America differed from those of Mesoamerica and South America in some important respects. First, their agriculture started later. It began in the southwest of the modern United States around 2000 BCE, among the Hohokam, Mogollon and Anasazi peoples, then spread to the lower Mississippi Valley and elsewhere after 1500 BCE.

Second, large urban concentrations in city-states were relatively rare. Third, the development of ceramics, stonework, sculpture, weaving and metallurgy was less sophisticated than in Mesoamerican and South American civilizations, and no North American culture had forms of writing or calendrical systems comparable to those of Mesoamerica. Finally, exceptionally large areas (mostly in modern Canada) were inhabited by small communities of a few hundred people – now called Woodland cultures – who lived by hunting and gathering in boreal forests, while to their north peoples of the Inuit culture dominated the Arctic and subarctic lands from Greenland and Labrador to the northwest Pacific coasts and Alaska.

BELOW *Map of North American cultures.*

CULTURES OF THE SOUTHWEST

In the southwest, maize was introduced from Mexico by around 1600 BCE and three successive cultures created semi-urban societies based on intensive agriculture using irrigation to cultivate maize and other crops. The Anasazi created a rare architecture, with apartment complexes and structures made of stone, adobe mud and other local material, sometimes built into canyon walls. Their buildings were often multi-storied and incorporated communal spaces for the hundreds or even thousands of people who lived in them. They were centres for religious celebrations and for trade across large areas and show influences of the ideas and practices of central Mexico. One Anasazi site, Gran Chaco Canyon in modern New Mexico, comprised a population of around 5,000 in several towns linked by causeways.

EASTERN NORTH AMERICA

In eastern North America, among temperate woodlands, several cultures with common features appeared after around 500 BCE. The earliest was the Adena people of the Ohio Valley. They lived by combining hunting and gathering with horticulture and their settlements included burial mounds associated with ancestor worship. After the Adena, the Hopewell people (100 BCE–400 CE) developed a flourishing culture that extended beyond the Ohio Valley along the neighbouring Illinois and Miami rivers. They built larger structures, with more complex burial mounds and enclosures for housing which suggest growing populations. Maize was incorporated into indigenous crop husbandry around 300 BCE, but for centuries remained as one food in a broader diet, until it was transformed into a staple crop between the 9th and 13th centuries CE.

RIGHT *The cliff palace at Mesa Verde, an Anasazi settlement, built c.12th to 13th centuries.*

ABOVE *Chaco Culture National Historical Park, New Mexico, USA.*

The final phase of North American mound-building cultures came with the emergence of the Mississippian peoples, starting around 600 CE. They were concentrated in the Mississippi Valley and the southeastern river regions of rich alluvial soils and developed an agriculture, mostly of maize and beans, that allowed greater population density. They built mounds on a large scale, and, possibly influenced by links with Mesoamerica, grouped them around a central plaza and ball courts. These sites were also towns, possibly with thousands of inhabitants, which engaged in long-range trading for materials such as obsidian, copper and conch shells from Florida, and had artisans who worked in wood, clay and stone. The largest settlement in North America at this time was Cahokia, near present-day St Louis. It occupied an area of several square kilometres and had a population of 30,000–40,000 at its peak around 1150. Cahokia was abandoned in the 13th century, possibly because of flooding, the invasion of nomadic peoples or internal conflicts. However, large Mississippian chiefdoms survived in the southeast into the 16th and 17th centuries, until undermined by exposure to Old World diseases brought by the Spanish into neighbouring regions.

NORTHEASTERN NORTH AMERICA

The Algonquian, Iroquoian and Soiuan-speaking peoples dominated the vast region from the Atlantic to the Great Lakes, reaching into modern Canada, while Muskogean speakers inhabited modern Georgia and Florida. Their cultures were broadly similar. Most were villagers who subsisted on maize, beans and squashes, supplemented by hunting wild game. Some were more sedentary than others and the size of settlements varied considerably. Though linked by long-distance trade networks, groups were often at war.

One sign of such conflict was the creation of a confederacy of Iroquois chiefdoms around the 12th century, the first of several that appeared in the centuries that followed. Warfare was an important feature of indigenous life but differed from that of Mesoamerica and Andean America in some key respects. War was usually aimed at securing control of hunting territories or dominating trade routes, rather than imposing government on or taking tribute from others, and tended to be on a small scale. Forces were rarely massed in the manner of Aztec and Inka armies, and weapons generally consisted of lances, bows and arrows, and clubs.

When the first waves of European settlement started in the early 16th century, the American indigenous population may have been around 54 million, unevenly distributed over the vast expanses of North America and South America. The greatest densities were in Mesoamerica, especially central Mexico, and in the Andes, particularly Peru and Bolivia. Although these populations were soon to be decimated by Old World diseases, the demographic distribution at the time of the European discoveries left a deep historic mark. Mexico and Peru, with their large peasant populations and precious metals, became the richest regions of the Spanish American world. In Brazil, Portuguese settlement was long confined to cities on the Atlantic coast and African enslaved people were imported to compensate for the scant indigenous population. The British, French and Dutch regions of the Caribbean and the southern agricultural regions of North America were also short of indigenous peasant labour and in time became slave-based societies. This broad structure of wealth and power was, as we shall see, to change during the 19th century. Then, the demographic patterns which colonial America inherited from the pre-Columbian past shifted significantly, when the United States stimulated mass immigration and industrialization, transforming its economy and overshadowing its Latin American neighbours.

BELOW *Cahokia, one of the largest sites of the Mississippian cultures.*

CHAPTER 2

AMERICA DISCOVERED

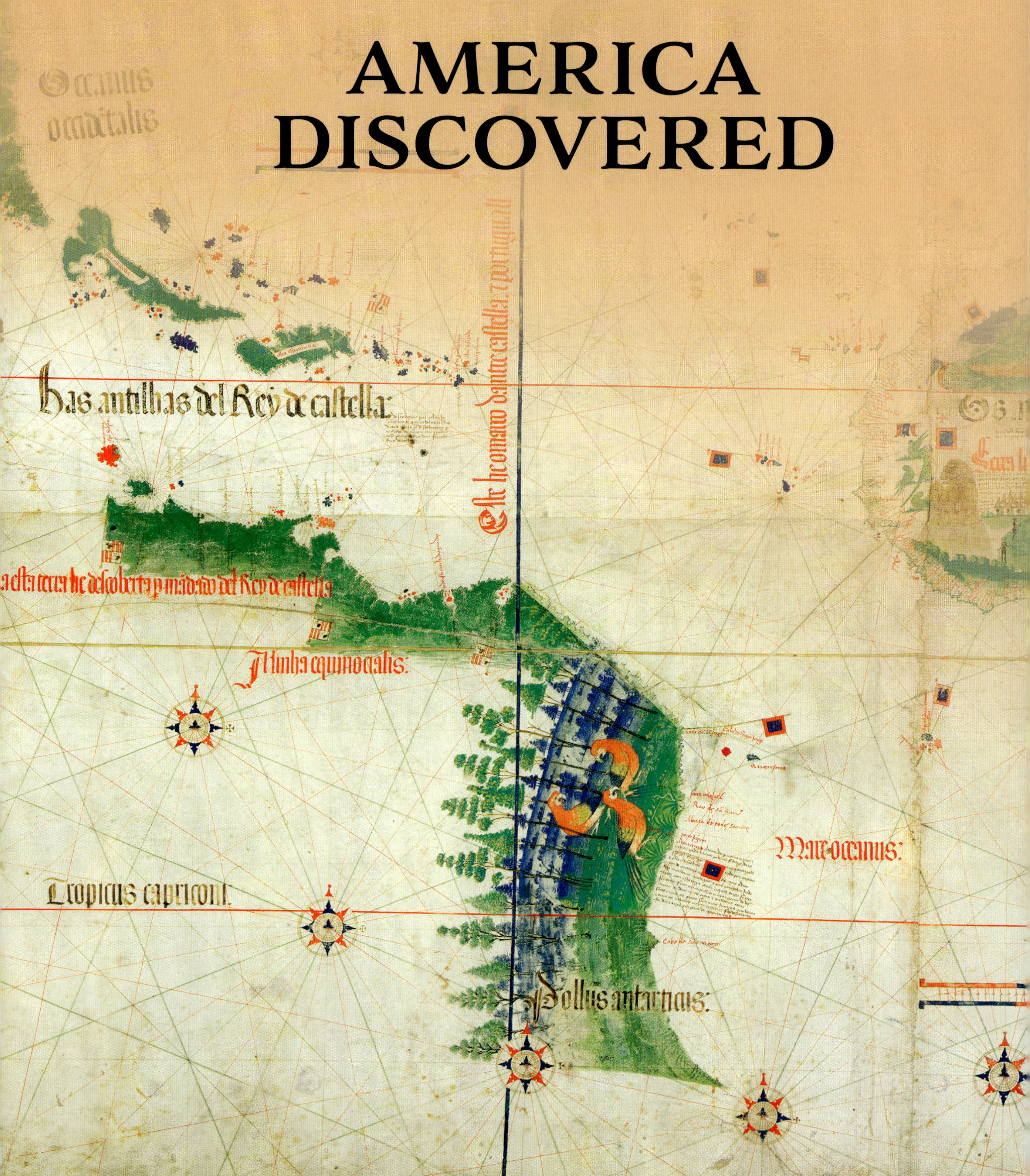

The name 'America' was a European invention, given to the lands that Columbus and other mariners discovered while searching for an all-water route to the 'Indies' of South and East Asia. Sponsored mainly by Portuguese and Spanish monarchs, the quest for the Indies arose from the entangled economic, political and religious ambitions of late medieval European princes, merchants and clerics. An important driving force was the desire to open a direct maritime route to the sources of high-value Eastern porcelain, silks and spices, commodities that promised dazzling profits for the monarchs and merchants who managed to control their flows. Strategic political and cultural considerations also came into play. At a time when the Ottomans were pressing on Europe's eastern flanks, Christian princes and prophets dreamed of outflanking Ottoman power in the Mediterranean and Middle East and finding new allies against Islam in Africa and beyond. Last but not least, the leaders of the Catholic Church saw overseas exploration as a means to fulfil the Biblical imperative of converting the world to Christianity and, in so doing, ushering the world to its providential conclusion.

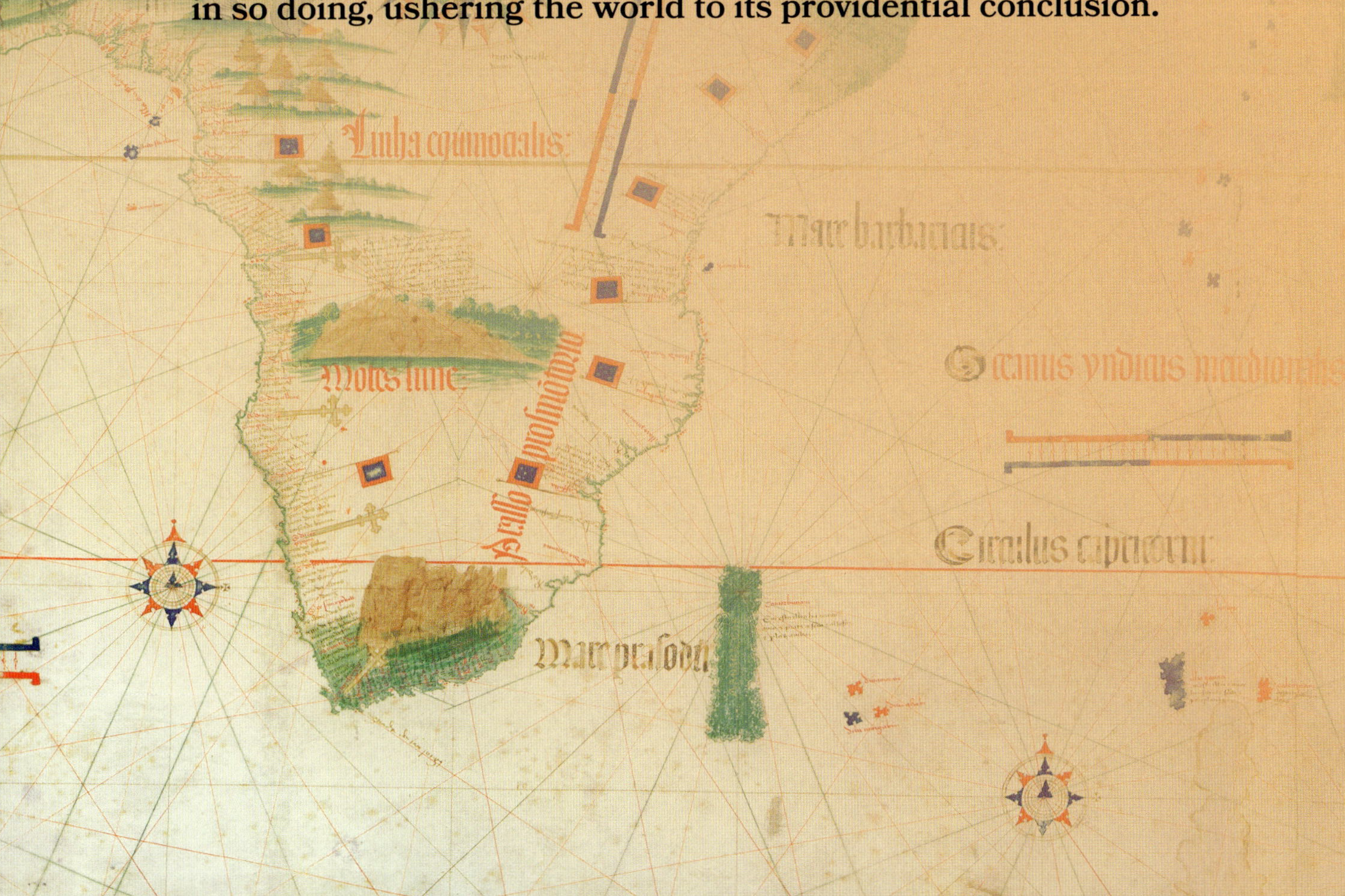

EXPLORATIONS AND DISCOVERIES

ABOVE *Christopher Columbus.*

Throughout the 15th century, these ambitions drove reconnaissance into the Atlantic, the 'Ocean Sea' that extended west from Europe. By mid-century Portugal and Spain had established their first Atlantic colonies in the Azores and Canary Islands, while their subjects gradually pushed southwards along the African coast in search of gold, ivory and a possible passage to the Indies. The Portuguese believed that the most plausible route was by circumnavigation of Africa, a feat that Bartolome Dias achieved when he reached the Cape of Good Hope in 1488, and Vasco da Gama consolidated by taking a fleet to India in 1498. Christopher Columbus, however, that sailing west across the Atlantic would open a shortcut to China. Born in Genoa in 1451, Columbus acquired his seagoing knowledge from trading voyages in the Mediterranean and then in the Atlantic. He settled in Portugal in the mid-1470s and married into a rich merchant family with Atlantic trading connections. While based in Lisbon, Columbus frequently sailed to Madeira and became familiar with Portuguese and Spanish trading and colonizing ventures on the Atlantic islands and African coast. In the mid-1480s, he sought support for a westward voyage of discovery from the monarchs of Portugal, Spain, England and France. He succeeded in 1492, when Spain's monarchs Ferdinand and Isabella granted him the money and political authority he required. His first voyage, in 1492, was followed by three others, in 1493, 1498 and 1502, during which his reputation was gradually eclipsed by his failings as a colonial governor. Columbus died in 1506, still believing that he had found a fast route to China.

When closer reconnaissance revealed land masses to the south and west of the

RIGHT *A 1622 map from the* Descriptio Indiae Occidentale, *a republication of a 1601 work by the Spanish historian Antonio de Herrera y Tordesillas, showing the Tordesillas line.*

First Impressions

When trying to understand those they called 'Indians', Europeans initially viewed them through classical and medieval cultural lenses. Indigenous peoples were accordingly categorized according to myths which portrayed them as either innocents living in a world uncorrupted by civilization or barbarians whose brutal natures reflected their need for civilization.

LEFT *In this 1580 Dutch engraving by Van der Straet, Vespucci encounters America as an innocent naked woman, together with cannibals in the background, reflecting contemporary European perceptions of American natives as either innocents or barbarians.*

Caribbean, European cartographers discarded Columbus's ideas and redrew their world maps, adding a new continent to the traditional tripartite division of Europe, Africa and Asia. The initial step came after the Italian Amerigo Vespucci claimed that his voyage along the South American coast in 1501–2 had revealed a *Mundus Novus*, a 'New World' rather than the eastern edge of Asia. This soon gave rise to the idea of 'America', when in 1507 the German cartographer Martin Waldseemüller placed this new land on a global map for the first time and named it 'America' in Vespucci's honour.

Spain and Portugal quickly asserted exclusive rights to rule over the territory and people of the New World. Soon after Columbus's landing, their monarchs signed the Treaty of Tordesillas (1494), an agreement to bisect the Atlantic with a notional north–south dividing line and to allot new discoveries west of that line to Castile while those to the east went to Portugal. At the time, no one had any idea of the shape or extent of the Americas, and it was only in the following decades that Spain's claims west of the Tordesillas line ensured that it took the lion's share of American territory and resources.

THE CARIBBEAN FRONTIER

Spain's first footholds were fixed by Columbus. After making his earliest landfall in the Bahamas in October 1492, he explored the Caribbean for several months, especially the coasts of Cuba and Hispaniola. On returning to Spain in 1493, his reports persuaded Spain's Catholic monarchs to support further voyages, intended to create permanent settlements. Columbus informed Queen Isabella I of Castile and King Ferdinand II of

ABOVE *Nicolás de Ovando.*

Aragon that the native people were, 'fearful and timid . . . guileless and honest'. He also told his royal patrons that they were easy to conquer, suitable for subjugation and open to Christianization. He presented Ferdinand and Isabella with a few captured Tainos, but his plan for enslaving the native peoples was rejected by the queen, who declared that they should be treated as free subjects of the Castilian crown. Indeed, when Nicolás de Ovando replaced Columbus as Governor of Hispaniola in 1502, he was explicitly ordered to ensure that 'the Indians were well treated, that they might go safely through the land, and that no one should use force against them or rob them or do any other harm or evil to them'. But these benign intentions were soon shrugged off. Ovando decided that, to fulfil his primary responsibilities for establishing royal authority and stabilizing settlement, he was justified in imposing harsh measures on native peoples and destroying any resistance from them.

This set a pattern throughout the Caribbean and beyond. Spaniards had no interest in tilling the soil alongside indigenous farmers. They wanted native peoples to provide forced labour for Spanish enterprises, whether in mining alluvial gold or building Spanish settlements and cultivating food supplies. So, although officially banned, the enslavement of indigenous people was impossible to eradicate in practice and continued for decades. Moreover, to satisfy settlers' demands for labour, the crown sanctioned the coercion of indigenous workers by granting trusteeships called *encomiendas*. These allowed the trustee (*encomendero*) to collect the tribute that the indigenous people owed to the monarch, in either goods or labour, in return for good governance and Christianization. In reality, this delegation of royal authority sanctioned the exploitation of indigenous people as a subjugated workforce and made them vulnerable to brutal treatment.

The Caribbean islands were the first frontier of Europe's America. As Spanish adventurers moved through the Greater Antilles, from Hispaniola to Puerto Rico (1507), Jamaica (1509) and Cuba (1511), the lethal impact of their violent invasions was sharpened by the effects of Old World epidemic diseases, to which native peoples had no resistance. The arrival of smallpox in 1518 accelerated rapid demographic decline in the larger islands and, to fill the vacuum left by the virtual elimination of Taino peoples, the Spaniards raided other, smaller islands for slaves. In an ominous portent, they also began to import enslaved Africans, starting a transatlantic trade that expanded over the course of the 16th century.

BELOW *An* encomienda *in a 1595 engraving by Theodor de Bry.*

The devastation of indigenous communities provoked horrified responses among missionaries. In 1511, the Dominican friar Antonio de Montesinos condemned the Spaniards of Hispaniola for the 'cruel tyranny' they inflicted on native people who, he said, were humans with 'rational souls' and had every right to live peacefully in their own lands. This denunciation of Spanish settler behaviour as immoral and illegal reverberated in Spanish governing circles, and the crown responded by asking theologians to define the circumstances in which a 'just war' against indigenous people was possible. Clerical deliberations provided scant protection, however. War was declared to be 'just' when indigenous people resisted papal and royal authority, even if their ignorance of Spanish meant that they were unable to understand the terms which Spaniards offered. Nor did churchmen resolve the wider problem of how to reconcile the rights of native peoples with the demands of settlers. Indeed, these early protests were the start of a profound polemic about the rights of indigenous peoples, led by the Dominican friar Bartolomé de las Casas. His tract, *A Short Account of the Destruction of the Indies*, was an extraordinarily graphic account of the brutality he had witnessed in the Caribbean islands, and his passionate criticisms persuaded Spanish monarchs to mandate that all indigenous people be treated as free subjects, with rights under Castilian law. By the 1540s, his appeals to the royal conscience led to curbs on wars of conquest and restraints on the exploitation of indigenous peoples, notably by abolishing the *encomienda*.

LEFT *Bartolomé de las Casas.*

Qualms about the morality of war and conquest were, however, no obstacle to extending exploration and conquest beyond the Caribbean islands. During the early 1500s, Cuba was a key base for reconnaissance towards and into the Gulf of Mexico, and Spanish adventurers also set up bases on the shores of Venezuela, Colombia and Panama, where they attacked indigenous communities and helped themselves to pearls, gold and slaves. In 1513, the conquistador Vasco Núñez de Balboa's traversal of the Isthmus of Panama and his sighting of the Pacific Ocean opened additional channels for exploration in South America, by sailing southwards down the Pacific coast. Taken together, these movements were a prelude to momentous discoveries. In the 1520s and 1530s, two major arenas for conquest and colonization emerged, first in Mexico then in Peru, leading to the wider extension of Spanish dominion throughout the American continents.

LEFT *Vasco Núñez de Balboa.*

THE CONQUEST OF AZTEC MEXICO

The conquest of Mexico stemmed from Spanish settlers in Cuba, whose expeditions along the coasts of the Yucatán Peninsula alerted them to the presence of rich societies inland. One expedition proved crucial. In 1519, Hernán Cortés set out from Cuba with 11 ships, more than 500 men, 16 horses, firearms and crossbows, and packs of the aggressive dogs that were used to terrorize Indians on the islands. His sponsor, the Governor of Cuba, wanted an information-gathering expedition but Cortés had his own plans. After landings along the Yucatán coast, he moved north into the Gulf of Mexico, where he founded the town now known as Veracruz and, on this eastern fringe of the Aztec empire, learned of a great kingdom in the interior. Confident that there were riches inland, Cortés demolished his ships and, with this gesture, persuaded his men to follow him on a mission to conquer or die.

RIGHT *A map of Cuba from Girolamo Ruscelli's atlas, published in 1562.*

By now, the Spaniards had an asset that was vital for their progress. In the Yucatán, they had found two translators who enabled them to communicate with both Maya speakers and the Nahuatl people of central Mexico. One was particularly valuable: Malintzin, a Maya woman who became Cortés's mistress, proved to be an indispensable interpreter and ally during the long journey inland. Cortés and his party left the coast in mid-August 1519 without a clear sense of direction but with the intention of finding and negotiating with the Aztec king, Moctezuma. This was far from easy, given that Moctezuma refused to receive the intruders and made several attempts to stop their advance. However, after fighting off the warriors of the city-state of Tlaxcallan (modern Tlaxcala), Cortés created an alliance which allowed him to push on towards Tenochtitlan, the Aztec capital. In early November, a few hundred Spaniards, accompanied by thousands of indigenous porters and warriors, reached the causeway that led into Tenochtitlan, where they were greeted by the splendidly dressed and bejewelled Aztec emperor, Moctezuma, borne in a litter by his noble entourage. After an exchange of greetings and gifts, the Spaniards and their allies entered the centre of the city, watched by countless spectators.

BELOW *Hernán Cortés with Malintzin (far right) in an image from the* Codex Azcatitlan.

Cortés's meeting with the Aztec emperor came

ABOVE *A 17th-century representation of the meeting of Moctezuma and Cortés.*

at a price. Once installed in Tenochtitlan, the Spaniards were locked into a water-bound fortress city where they were vastly outnumbered. While Moctezuma's guest, Cortés managed to paralyze Aztec opposition by making the emperor his hostage, but this tactic had only a temporary effect. When the Governor of Cuba sent an expedition to arrest Cortés for rebellion, he was forced to return to the coast, while the news of discord among the Spaniards encouraged Aztec nobles to plot their downfall. Cortés's deputy, Pedro de Alvarado, responded with a pre-emptive strike. He ordered the massacre of unarmed Aztec nobles at a religious festival, an act of unbridled aggression which worsened an already deteriorating situation. When Cortés returned from the coast, he faced growing hostility from the Aztec leadership and, fearing that the city was a death trap, he ordered an evacuation under cover of night. The retreat brought the Spaniards to the brink of total defeat. More than 800 Spaniards were killed, and, of the remaining 500 or so, many were wounded. Thousands of Tlaxcalteca auxiliaries also died, but the Spaniards escaped annihilation thanks largely to their allies, for Cortés was able to take shelter in Tlaxcala and regroup his forces.

Despite his defeat, Cortés's determination was undimmed. He responded by taking the offensive with a sustained military campaign against the Aztecs and their allies. This attracted Spanish recruits from the Caribbean but, more importantly, marshalled thousands of native allies, mostly from Tlaxcallan.

ABOVE *Two macuahuitls, wooden swords embedded with obsidian blades, a weapon commonly used by Aztec warriors.*

The Tlaxcalteca were indispensable. They made and carried supplies for war, including crossbow bolts, arrows and the timbers for boats needed to besiege Tenochtitlan; they were also enthusiastic and experienced fighters, seasoned in war and eager to wreak vengeance on their old enemy. In December 1520, Cortés led more than 500 Spaniards and 10,000 Tlaxcalteca to confront Tenochtitlan's allied city-states around Lake Texcoco, with the aim of proving his military superiority and persuading them to switch sides.

This was an intense and bloody war, keenly contested. However, Cortés's victories outnumbered his defeats and opened the way to a final assault on Tenochtitlan in May 1521. Cortés now commanded large forces. His 700 Spanish foot soldiers, with arquebuses, artillery, boats to breach the lake, and 86 armed horsemen, were supported by an army of around 75,000 native warriors, eager to plunder Tenochtitlan. The Aztecs, under a new leader, refused to surrender, but after months of warfare, starvation and a deadly smallpox epidemic, their resistance finally broke in late August 1521. The siege of Tenochtitlan ended in a bloodbath; the city which had dazzled the Spaniards was reduced to rubble. Even Cortés expressed sorrow for its people, whose suffering he found 'so great that it was beyond our understanding that they could endure it'.

BELOW *A 17th-century depiction of the fall of Tenochtitlan.*

How and why were Cortés and his men able to achieve this extraordinary feat? Cortés himself contributed a great deal. He combined high ambition with ruthless determination and was a talented leader of men, able to command support in the face of danger and defeat. He also had the education and political acuity to win support at court and to play on the imperial ambitions of the newly crowned Spanish king, the Hapsburg Charles I (also Charles V, Emperor of the Holy Roman Empire). The conquistadors who went with Cortes were vital to victory, too, for the valour and resources they brought to the fight. Indeed, several later complained that Cortés had taken too much glory, wealth and power from a collective endeavour in which many sacrificed their lives.

Broken Spears

This Mexica poem written by an anonymous author soon after the fall of Tenochtitlan captures the suffering and sense of disaster felt by its people:

Broken spears lie in the roads;
we have torn our hair in our grief.
The houses are roofless now, and their walls
are red with blood.
Worms are swarming in the streets and plazas,
and the walls are splattered with gore.
The water has turned red, as if it were dyed,
and when we drink it,
it has the taste of brine.
We have pounded our hands in despair
against the adobe walls,
for our inheritance, our city, is lost and dead.
The shields of our warriors were its defence,
but they could not save it.

The Spanish did not achieve their conquest alone. Indigenous allies were essential, especially the Tlaxcalteca, who took were quick to see that the Spaniards' military skills would serve them in war against their Aztec enemies. Weapons were of course important. Firearms, crossbows, steel swords, armour and war horses gave advantages over warriors with obsidian-tipped spears, clubs and bows and arrows, for they acted as a force multiplier against numerically greater indigenous forces, rather like European repeating rifles and machine guns in 19th-century African wars. But this technological superiority was not enough to overcome far more numerous enemies. Here, the Spaniards were helped by ingrained elements of Aztec culture, by their military practices and by their underlying political weaknesses.

Cultural factors complicated Aztec responses from the outset. Spaniards later circulated the idea that the Mexica saw them as gods, possibly by association with the legendary deity Quetzalcoatl, whose return was prophesied for precisely the year that Cortés arrived. Moctezuma and his people were undoubtedly bewildered by the strange beings who entered their land, with their terrifying weapons, their horses which were like 'deer... as tall as roof terraces' and their huge, voracious dogs. Moreover, they aggravated their anxiety by interpreting this new phenomenon through the lens of past prophecies. Unlike the Spaniards' readiness to make and adapt their plans by gathering timely information about their enemy, the Aztecs responded to events in the light of past, often doom-laden predictions. Small wonder, then, that when the Spaniards entered Tenochtitlan, witnesses recalled that, 'there was

BELOW *Spanish conquistadors attack a Mexican temple with assistance from Tlaxcallan allies.*

terror, there was astonishment, there was apprehension, there was a stunning of the people'.

On the military side, the Mexica and their allies had the advantage of overwhelming numbers and much experience of warfare. They were, however, hindered by their custom of fighting wars of a ritualistic kind, timed in accord with a religious calendar and governed by inflexible rules. Warriors sought honour and reward by single combat with prestigious opponents, in which they aimed to seize stunned captives for human sacrifice. This put them at a serious disadvantage when facing tactics and methods common to European warfare, such as night attacks, tactical retreats, the use of artillery and armed horsemen, and a focus on killing rather than capturing the enemy. The Aztecs learned to adapt, of course, and put up an impressive resistance at Tenochtitlan. But this was after they had suffered defeats that undermined their reputation for military invincibility and thereby opened underlying divisions.

ABOVE *Aztec human sacrifice.*

Although Aztec kings exercised absolute power within Tenochtitlan, their so-called empire had never been a unified polity under centralized political control. Instead, it rested on a shifting set of alliances between autonomous city-states, among rivals who manoeuvred for advantage. So long as they could demonstrate ferocious military might and overawe their enemies (as well as their own people) with the terrors of mass human sacrifice, the Mexica elites could dominate. But when the Spaniards showed that Tenochtitlan could be defeated, its neighbouring cities became less fearful of Aztec revenge and more prepared to pursue their own interests. In this changing environment, several cities undertook their own campaigns against Tenochtitlan and played a key part in besieging and overrunning the city. Without their support and that of Tlaxcallan, the conquest of the Aztecs by Cortés might have taken longer or even been stopped.

RIGHT *The capture of Cuahtemoc, the last Aztec emperor, on 13 August 1521.*

Indigenous peoples were, in short, indispensable partners in overthrowing the greatest power in pre-Hispanic Mesoamerica.

The fall of Tenochtitlan did not mark the conquest of Mexico or even of the entire Aztec empire. It was nonetheless a historical turning point. Cortés triumphed over armed resistance far greater than any encountered in the Caribbean and showed that Spaniards could win against overwhelming odds, overcome great kingdoms and win great wealth. His feats also acted as a magnet for other adventurers and provided a platform for launching fresh expeditions across Mexico and into Central America.

The pace of expansion was fast but not always immediately rewarding. In northern Mexico, Spaniards came up against peoples who resisted conquest for years; those who went south and fought the Maya in western Guatemala also ran into stiff resistance; so too did expeditions into the Yucatán Peninsula and parts of Central America. Spaniards succeeded eventually in establishing themselves in these regions, invariably with the aid of indigenous allies. The Spanish invaders' rewards came in land and labour rather than the great plunder of moveable wealth taken by Cortés and his fellow conquistadors, and some, notably Cortés's friend Pedro de Alvarado, moved to Peru in the 1530s in pursuit of fresh windfalls of gold and silver.

ABOVE *Pedro de Alvarado.*

THE CONQUEST OF PERU

After the conquest of Mexico, the next great bonanza was in South America, where Francisco Pizarro sought to emulate the extraordinary achievement of Cortés and his followers. In 1532–5, Pizarro and a small group of Spaniards overthrew an Inka emperor, seized control of his centralized state and created the second great hub for Spanish colonization in the Americas.

The discovery and conquest of Peru originated in years of exploration along the Caribbean coasts of Venezuela, Colombia and Panama, where Spaniards first heard rumours of a great, gold-rich civilization deep inland. Exploration into the interior was slowed by indigenous resistance and hostile terrain, until Balboa's discovery of the Pacific opened a route by sea. In 1523, Pizarro joined forces with the Catholic priest Hernando de Luque and the conquistador Diego de Almagro to form the Empresa del Levante (the Levant Company), whereby they agreed to fund and lead explorations of the Pacific coast and share whatever spoils they accrued. Based on this understanding, Pizarro led two expeditions along the Pacific coast between 1524 and 1528, accumulating valuable knowledge and experience – but hardly any of the gold, silver and other riches he expected to find. Yet despite this lack of material success, Pizarro and his backers were able to persuade the king back in Spain that the region was worthy of further investigation, particularly a great kingdom inland called 'Peru'. In late 1530, Francisco Pizarro, armed with a royal warrant, launched his third and final expedition.

Francisco Pizarro

Francisco Pizarro was born in Trujillo, Spain, *c.*1475, the illegitimate son of a soldier and a poor woman. With no education or prospects for advancement in Spain, he set his sights on a military career in the New World. In 1509, Pizarro joined an expedition to create a colony at Urabá, in Colombia, and after its failure accompanied Vasco Núñez de Balboa in crossing the Isthmus of Panama and discovering the Pacific in 1513. He later executed Balboa for treason and became a prominent figure in the newly established town of Panama. The military skills and business contacts he acquired during the years of warfare against indigenous people underpinned his efforts to raise money and secure royal recognition for expeditions in search of Peru. As a reward for his leading role in the conquest of Peru, he was ennobled as the Marqués de la Conquista and made Governor of New Castile, a great swathe of South America stretching from Lima, Peru, in the west to Belém, Brazil, in the east. But Pizarro's success and power won him several enemies, not least his old business partner, Diego de Almagro. He had been appointed governor of neighbouring New Toledo and the two men soon found themselves at odds over their precise areas of jurisdiction in the two territories. This turned violent and, by the late 1530s, had morphed into a personal feud that saw Diego de Almagro defeated in battle and executed by Pizarro-led forces in 1538. Almagro's son, Diego – popularly known as 'El Mozo' – swore revenge, which he duly received three years later when he briefly seized power in New Castile and had Francisco Pizarro assassinated.

LEFT *Francisco Pizarro.*

While Pizarro's first two voyages had been viewed as failures, this one would result in a stunning success. He landed on the coast of modern Ecuador in January 1531 and, over the next 18 months, trekked overland into northern Peru. As he progressed, Pizarro's hope of riches began to materialize. He seized gold, silver and emeralds, and, strengthened by new recruits from Panama and Nicaragua, organized a push into Inka territory. After founding the first Spanish town in Peru at Piura, to serve as a point of communications with Panama, Pizarro led 106 foot soldiers and 62 horsemen into the Andes, in the hope of meeting the Inka king.

This was a dangerous mission, given that the journey into a mountainous interior reduced the chances of retreat to the sea. The risks were multiplied when they approached the Inka emperor Atawallpa at his camp near the Andean town of Cajamarca, in November 1531. The Spaniards knew by this time that the Inka realm was emerging from a destructive civil war between competing royal clans, and they hoped to take advantage of the divisions it had caused. They had no warning, however, of the overwhelming odds against them until they were invited to meet Atawallpa, who was marching south from Quito with a huge victorious army, en route to his coronation in Cusco. On receiving reports of the small band of strangers in his vicinity, Atawallpa was curious to see them and confident that they and their horses would soon become his captives. Pizarro and his men, on the other hand, were unnerved by the Inka ruler's display of power and decided that their only hope was to kidnap Atawallpa and hold him hostage. This desperate stratagem, learned from other indigenous wars, worked perfectly. When Atawallpa went out to meet Pizarro on 16 February 1533 at the town of Cajamarca, the Spaniards launched a surprise attack which not only captured the king but created a panic that allowed Spanish horsemen to slaughter thousands of fleeing soldiers without suffering a single casualty.

ABOVE *Atawallpa.*

The capture of Atawallpa and the decimation of his army had momentous consequences. By seizing the Inka leader, the Spaniards temporarily neutralized armed opposition, as Atawallpa's generals only took their orders from their king. To save himself, Atawallpa offered a legendary ransom: a room filled with gold and silver, carried from Cusco under the command of his generals. This bought him time but did not save his life, for the Spaniards decided to execute Atawallpa when they learned that they could find a puppet king from rivals among his kin. Pizarro duly chose another royal brother, Thupa

Atawallpa's Ransom

It took many months to fulfil Atawallpa's promise, given the stupendous quantity of bullion carried to Cajamarca by hundreds of porters. The artefacts piled up in the so-called Ransom Room that Atawallpa decreed should be filled with gold and silver were said to have weighed more than 11 tonnes. The Spaniards smelted down 6,087 kg (13,420 lb) of 22½-carat gold ingots and 11,793 kg (26,000 lb) of silver. Francisco Pizarro and a small committee decided on the distribution of this enormous booty among the Spaniards who had fought at Cajamarca, in amounts proportionate to their rank, and their material and military contribution to the expedition. Pizarro, however, excluded his business partner Diego de Almagro and his men from sharing in these spoils of war, as they had arrived in Cajamarca after the battle had been won. This decision would contribute to the breakdown in relations between Pizarro and Almagro that would ultimately lead to the violent deaths of both men.

ABOVE *Manco Inka Yupanki.*

Wallpa, to sustain the pretence that the Spaniards ruled with Inka consent and, after a formal coronation, they resumed their march to Cusco.

The Spaniards' alliance with Thupa Wallpa did not prevent continuing warfare. The Spaniards' advance was opposed by Atawallpa's former general Quisquis, who repeatedly attacked them with thousands of soldiers. The Spaniards were, however, saved by their superior weapons and speed on the battlefield. Like the Aztecs, Andean warriors found that lances, arrows and stone and wooden clubs were no match for Spanish steel and cavalry. Their methods of war were also inadequate for opposing external invaders. The Inka had expanded their empire more by diplomacy and the threat of force than by superiority in warfare, and while they could deploy large armies, these were mostly composed of peasants from many ethnic and linguistic groups who fought under their own lords with their own weapons. Coordinating large armies of this kind was very difficult, especially when battle was under way, as its many components lacked a central command. Emphasis on ritual was another impediment, designed as it was to intimidate rather than overcome an enemy. This made for magnificent spectacle but did nothing to deflect Spanish fighters who gave no quarter.

In mid-November 1533, Pizarro entered Cusco and, following the death of Thupa Wallpa, he installed Manco Inka Yupanki, another scion of the Inka royal family, as his puppet. With Manco's cooperation, the Spaniards looted Cusco, adding tonnes of gold and silver to the already massive hoard acquired from Atawallpa's ransom. Although they were impressed by the orderly beauty of the city, they nevertheless ransacked its cultural riches. The first chronicler of the conquest of Peru, Cieza de Leon, recalled that, 'when the Spaniards opened and entered the doors of the houses, in some they found heaps of very heavy and splendid gold pieces, in others large silver vessels ... the city was full of treasures. In the fortress, the royal house of the Sun, they found grandeur unseen and untold, because the kings had there all things imaginable'.

While the conquistadors melted down their massive plunder for return to Spain (including a 20 per cent share for Charles V), Pizarro sought to consolidate his conquest by eradicating any remaining Inka resistance. He combined his men with thousands of indigenous fighters raised by Manco Inka and returned to the offensive against Quisquis. By June 1534, this Spanish–Inka army had forced Quisquis to retreat to his native Quito, more than a thousand miles to the north, and the Spaniards' position was further strengthened by the arrival of a stream of men from Panama and the Caribbean, all drawn by news from the Peruvian front. These included Pedro de Alvarado, Cortes's friend and fellow conquistador, who sailed from Central America to

RIGHT *Sebastián de Benalcázar.*

Peru's north coast with an army of 500 Spaniards, 100 horses and over 4,000 Guatemalans. Quito and Tumipampa, cities rumoured to be richer than Cusco, were the targets for conquest.

In 1534–5, three contingents of Spanish forces headed for the Quito region. Alvarado, however, managed to take a wrong turn while negotiating the mountainous terrain and this severely delayed his progress. Pizarro, meanwhile, pressed on, as did his fellow conquistador Sebastián de Benalcázar, who arrived in the region before his compatriots and was the first Spaniard to attack the Inka forces, which were led by Rumiñawi, Atawallpa's northern commander. Diego de Almagro, Pizarro's erstwhile business partner, also brought reinforcements and, more importantly, deflected Alvarado from the area by buying his ships and supplies on condition that he return to Guatemala – thereby ensuring a greater share of any captured loot for those that remained. Spanish military success owed much to support from the Cañari people, who had been cruelly treated by the Inka, and divisions among the Inka forces themselves. After military defeats in December 1534 and January 1535, Inka resistance in Quito crumbled. When Quisquis returned, he was killed by his own men, who wanted to negotiate peace; Rumiñawi also faced mutiny and was soon caught and executed by the Spaniards.

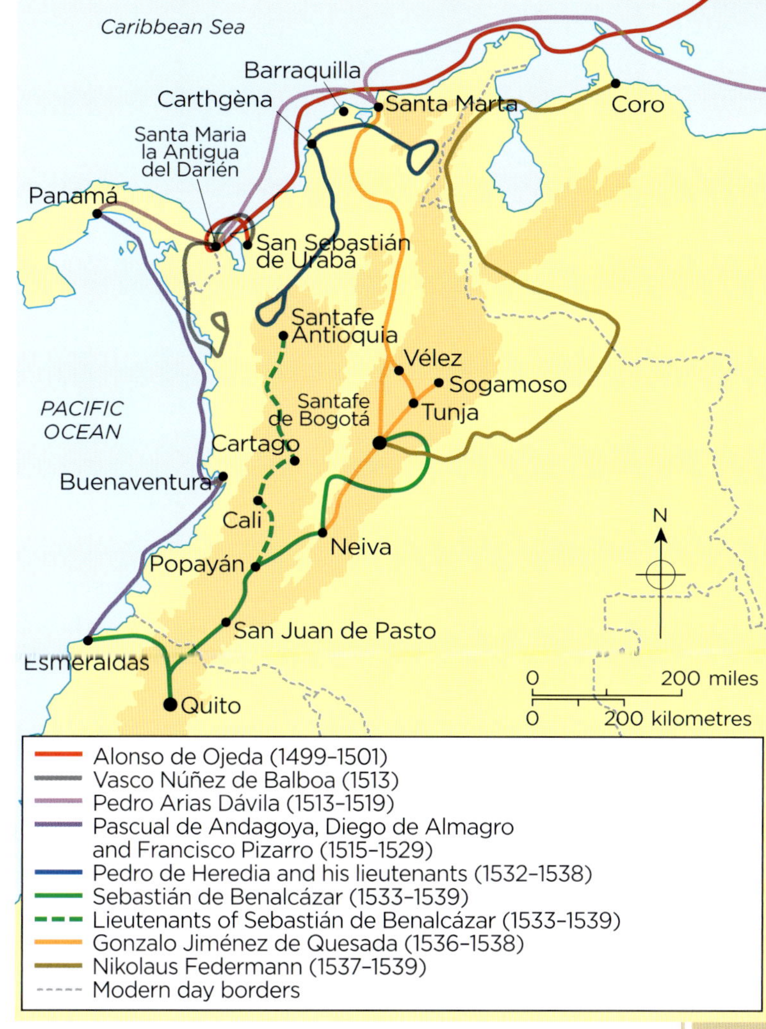

ABOVE *The Spanish conquest of Colombia.*

The conquest of lands north of Quito was the next main phase of conquest in South America. Sebastián de Benalcázar moved into Colombia, where he founded towns at Pasto, Popayán and Cali, and then headed northwards into the eastern cordillera of the Colombian Andes. This region, rumoured to be extraordinarily rich in gold, also attracted other Spaniards, who came southwards from their bases on the Caribbean coast, especially from the town of Santa Marta. Lured by rumours of El Dorado, Gonzalo Jiménez de Quesada left Santa Marta in early 1536 and, despite suffering heavy losses from hunger and disease, entered Muisca territory near Bogotá in 1537. He found what the Spaniards wanted: emerald mines, gold artefacts and a fertile, well-populated area, ruled by competing chiefdoms. Jiménez de Quesada claimed the region for Charles V and called it the New Kingdom of Granada, to evoke the rich Andalusian region taken from Muslim rulers in 1492. Shortly afterwards, his conquest was compounded by other Spanish explorers. Nikolaus Federmann – a German backed by Charles V's bankers, the Welsers of Augsburg – reached Bogotá in 1538 after a lengthy expedition through Venezuela. Sebastián de Benalcázar, the conqueror of Quito, arrived in the same year. The three captains agreed to cooperate and, after setting up Spanish towns in the Muisca heartlands – at Bogotá, Tunja and Vélez – they returned to Spain together, to seek reward for their achievements.

ABOVE *Diego de Almagro.*

The conquerors of Peru also went south from Cusco, into lands known to their Inka allies. In mid-1535, Diego de Almagro, accompanied by Inka nobles and soldiers, led a large expeditionary force through Bolivia and the Atacama Desert into Chile. He took the land in the king's name but, disappointed by its failure to yield treasures, abandoned the idea of settlement and returned to Cusco in 1537. The conquest of Chile was left to Pedro de Valdivia, who in 1540 began a successful campaign to overcome native resistance and created a small Spanish colony in Chile.

The South American conquests took time to stabilize, particularly in the Peruvian heartlands. After they had seized the heights of Inka power in Peru, the followers of Francisco Pizarro and Diego de Almagro quarrelled over the distribution of the spoils. Pizarro sought to strengthen his hold on Peru by establishing a new capital on the coast, controlling the entry of the Spanish fortune-seekers who flocked to Peru. In January 1535, he founded Lima, the 'City of Kings', but in so doing nearly lost Peru. In his absence, his brothers treated Manco and his retinue so badly that the Sapa Inka raised a massive rebellion. It started with a siege of Cusco in May 1536 and continued with attempts to take Lima. The Spaniards narrowly survived these assaults, which challenged their hold on Peru, but factional discord soon led to war between them. In April 1537, Diego de Almagro returned from Chile with his forces and, finding Cusco in disarray, arrested Pizarro's brothers and took control, initiating a full-scale civil war among the Spanish. During these troubles, Manco Inka had retreated to the jungles of southern Peru, where he founded a breakaway neo-Inka state. In his absence, Diego de Almagro crowned Manco's half-brother Paullu as the new Inka king and prepared to defend Cusco against Francisco Pizarro's forces. The Pizarros and their faction won the ensuing struggle for Cusco, at the Battle of Las Salinas in April 1538. After Almagro was executed and Paullu changed sides, the Spanish factions briefly co-existed in an uneasy peace, until the assassination of Francisco Pizarro in June 1541. This opened another phase of conflict, triggered by the attempts of the Spanish crown to impose its authority on conquistador Peru.

It was at this point that, under the influence of the theologian Bartolomé de las Casas, Charles V introduced laws designed to curb the abuses of the conquistadors and provide the indigenous people with protection from injustice. In Peru, his 'New Laws' of 1542 were strongly opposed by a Spanish faction led by Gonzalo Pizarro, Francisco's brother, who among other things objected to the creation of a new administrative structure, the Viceroyalty of Peru, that was designed to be under greater control of the Spanish crown. With the support of fellow *encomenderos*, he raised an armed rebellion against the new regime and killed Peru's first viceroy in battle. But Peru did not become an independent kingdom under conquistador control. Gonzalo Pizarro was soon defeated and executed, and the crown gradually extended its authority over Spanish Peru. The Inka rebellion also dissipated. Manco's neo-Inka kingdom in the jungle survived until 1571 but exercised little or no power in the rest of the country. Back in Cusco, meanwhile, the heirs of the

LEFT *Túpac Amaru I (1540–72), heir to Manco Inka, last Inka ruler of the breakway neo-Inka state, 1570–2.*

Inka royal clans compromised with the conquerors. The Spanish crown respected their aristocratic rank and allowed them property and authority in return for fealty. Inka culture was preserved, but any hopes for the restoration of the Inka empire quickly became a distant dream, restricted to occasional messianic movements that prophesied a future in which a dead Inka king would be resurrected and overthrow the Spaniards.

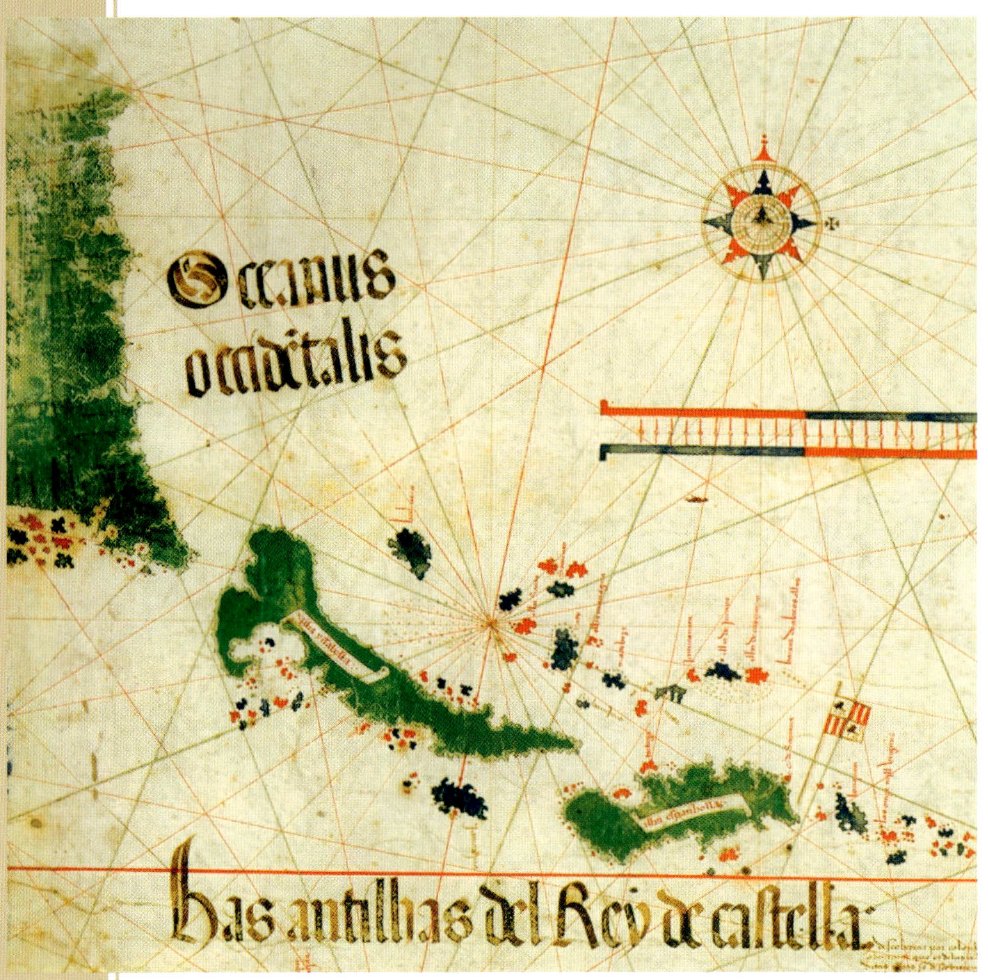

The construction of royal government – signalled by the appointments of viceroys in New Spain (1535) and Peru (1544) – took time. Conquests and early settlements were not directed from the centre but were the work of private enterprise, with minimal royal input. The crown claimed sovereignty over conquered lands and a share of profits, but exploration and conquest were organized by bands of adventurers in search of plunder. Typically, expeditions were mounted by leaders who obtained royal licences which gave them rights to material rewards and political authority in conquered lands and found the means to pay for an expedition, often through partnerships with other investors. In addition to plunder, successful conquistadors received *encomiendas* which enabled them to collect tributes from indigenous peoples, in labour or goods. Most of these freelancers were young men from the towns and middle ranks of society, with leaders drawn from the Spanish gentry. Few were from the top and bottom of society, since aristocrats had better prospects at home and peasants lacked the means to emigrate. Those who went provided their own weapons, horses and supplies and coalesced under leaders who promised them rewards proportionate to each individual's contribution. Bernal Díaz del Castillo, who fought with Cortés against the Aztecs, summed up their motives: he and his companions were inspired by desires, 'to serve God and His Majesty, to give light to those who were in darkness, and to grow rich, as all men desire to do'. Some became enormously rich. Most did not and many died in the Indies, often in poverty.

ABOVE *Florida, Cuba, Hispaniola and other Caribbean islands from the 1502 Cantino map.*

On these foundations Spain gradually built an empire of vast proportions. On first arriving in the Caribbean, Columbus had aimed to set up a trading colony, exchanging goods with native peoples en route to China. However, his vision of a maritime network based on coastal trading bases was irrevocably altered by the conquests of Mexico and Peru. The great windfalls of wealth which they provided were a magnet to migrants and a stimulus to ambitions for territorial empire, akin to that of ancient Rome. Two hubs stand out. First, Mexico, from which Spaniards entered Central America, taking control of the lands between Guatemala and Panama. Second, Peru, the hub for expeditions of conquest along routes that went south to Chile and Bolivia, north into Ecuador and Colombia, and eastwards into Argentina. Spaniards also established a presence along the Atlantic-facing coasts of South America, in Venezuela and in the River Plate region, inland from Buenos Aires. The latter had sparse indigenous populations and lacked precious metals, but their strategic importance as gateways to the interior ensured that Spain defended them closely. One offshoot was the settler colony in Paraguay, where explorers along the Paraná River system created an unusual agrarian colony of small farmers who intermarried with local Guarani women.

The attenuation of conquest was even more obvious in North America. During the 1530s, Álvar Núñez Cabeza de Vaca and Hernando de Soto launched expeditions into Florida in hopes of finding unknown civilizations but their speculative travels in search of fabled cities ended in suffering and death, without revealing anything remotely comparable to the riches of Mexico and Peru. Francisco Vásquez de Coronado's expedition to northern Mexico, which aimed to find Cíbola, a city supposedly richer than Tenochtitlan, did no better. He returned empty handed, his reputation sullied by reports of extreme violence towards native people. Indeed, the main effect of these expeditions was to sow disease and destruction. In De Soto's wake, the well-populated chiefdoms and towns in the Mississippi watershed were destroyed by pandemics, while Coronado's cruelty raised rebellion among the Pueblo towns in southwestern North America, forcing him to return to Mexico City no better off than when he had left.

ABOVE *Hernando de Soto.*

Nor did Spain succeed in strengthening its claims to possession of other parts of North America. Small bases were established in Florida to forestall foreign intrusion and protect Spanish shipping sailing back to Europe, but they were difficult to settle and sustain. And, although Spaniards explored and charted the lands north of Florida, the northeastern coasts raised no serious interest as places for colonization and left openings for later occupation by foreigners. Expansion north from Mexico into North America was also blocked. Attempts to create a 'New Mexico' around 1600 attracted few colonists and the area around the Rio Grande remained a distant military frontier, described a century later as 'the ends of the earth ... remote beyond compare'. In any case, the dense indigenous populations and potential for silver and gold mining found in Mexico and South America were far greater attractions, and those regions became the keystones of Spain's overseas empire.

PORTUGAL'S DISCOVERY OF BRAZIL

The first Portuguese discovery in America came shortly after Spain's. In 1500, Pedro Álvares Cabral was sailing to India when, swinging far to the west en route to the Indian Ocean, his fleet landed on what he took to be a previously unknown Atlantic Island, akin to those that Columbus had found in the Caribbean. Cabral immediately claimed it for Portugal, seeing a potentially useful station for outward fleets to India and another trading post in Portugal's expanding system of overseas trade. In fact, Cabral's discovery foreshadowed the emergence of 'Brazil', a land in which Portuguese language and culture gradually took root in a large and prosperous colony.

BELOW *Pedro Álvares Cabral.*

Here, however, there were no conquests of the Spanish kind. Following Cabral's landing in 1500, Brazil attracted little attention. Until the 1560s, Portuguese overseas expansion focused on South and East Asia, the sources of spices and other luxury goods which sold at great profit in Europe, and West Africa, with its burgeoning trade in gold and enslaved people. This expansion was built on a string of fortified trading posts and a few coastal strongholds, from which Portuguese merchants imposed themselves on valuable commercial networks in the Indian Ocean and beyond. Portugal did not, however, build a land empire comparable to Spain's. Its territorial expansion in Asia and Africa was constrained by the presence of powerful, well-armed states who presented formidable opposition to colonization. In Brazil, early Portuguese settlers entered an environment that was also unconducive to large-scale territorial expansion, albeit in other ways. The native peoples of the coast were easy to defeat when engaged in battle because they had only primitive weapons and small forces. However, as they were divided among small uncoordinated groups organized in village communities, they were more difficult to control than large, centrally administered chiefdoms and were unaccustomed to supply tribute and forced labour in the manner of the Mexican and Peruvian peasantries. Nor did the Portuguese find precious metals of the kind which energized migration and settlement in Spanish America. So, while Spanish colonization advanced rapidly after taking control of states with large, disciplined indigenous peasantries, Portuguese colonization was much slower to begin and developed along different lines.

Portugal's initial interest in Brazil was linked to trade in 'brazilwood', a tree which produced such a vivid red dye that it was likened to *brasa* (burning coals). Portugal's monarchy claimed the territory under the terms of the Treaty of Tordesillas and drew an income from it by licensing private traders to obtain and export the timber. This was, however, a minor interest compared to the riches generated by Asian trade. So, for several decades, Brazil was left on the edges of Portuguese expansion. Its few settlers were from the lowest levels of Portuguese society: deserters, sailors and convicts, all poor men who made a life in Brazil by mixing with local Indians and their women, learning their languages and customs, and acting as intermediaries with Portuguese traders.

BELOW
Brazilwood.

Otherwise, Brazil did little to distract Portugal's kings and their subjects from the much richer returns found in Africa and Asia. In fact, the crown did nothing to encourage colonization until forced to defend its claim to Brazilian territory from foreign intruders. In 1531, the king fended off French ambitions to create an 'Antarctic France' on Brazil's southern coast, by sending Martim Afonso de Sousa to settle the region. Sousa founded a town at São Vicente, distributed land among several hundred settlers, and built the first sugar mill. The intention was to follow the example of Portugal's Atlantic islands of Madeira and São Tomé by cultivating sugar for export to Europe, using enslaved labour, and, by 'showing the flag', to assure Portugal's territorial claim against foreign competitors.

This was the prelude to a more grandiose plan. In 1534, João II divided Brazil into 14 hereditary

ABOVE *A 16th-century map of Brazil.*

'captaincies', which he granted to 12 proprietary lords who were given feudal powers over huge tracts of unexplored lands in return for developing and governing them. This scheme had limited success, however. Some proprietors neglected their new lands, others abandoned them. And, while the crown concentrated on expanding its maritime empire in Africa and Asia, Portugal's small home population was unable to supply significant numbers of emigrants to Brazil. By the 1540s, Brazil had only about 2,000 colonists in 15 settlements along 5,000 km (3,100 miles) of coastline, and it was only when threatened by foreign intrusion that the crown paid serious attention to colonizing and governing the territory.

Early Portuguese activity in the Americas pales into insignificance when Brazil is compared to Spanish America. In the first half of the 16th century, Spaniards ranged over the vast and varied lands that lay between Mexico and Chile and traversed the continents from east to west. Crossing mountains, deserts and forests, Spanish explorers opened frontiers for settlement across a wide compass of distinctive physical and climatic environments, and, most important, took control of dense indigenous populations and rich mineral deposits. During the same half-century, the Portuguese accomplished little. While Spanish America became a constellation of extensive territories, some with large indigenous societies and abundant resources, Portuguese settlements in Brazil were small and scattered and looked to the sea. Rather than seeking to colonize inland, settlers clustered 'like crabs' on Atlantic shores, in a few widely separated towns that depended on trade with Portugal.

CHAPTER 3

THE AMERICAS TRANSFORMED

The arrival of Europeans in the Americas from 1492 could not but have a transformative effect. There was no single change but rather a series of transformations that played out as successive waves of settlers – the Spanish, Portuguese, British, French and Dutch in particular – made their mark on the New World's life and landscape. In many locations, indigenous populations were, in time, almost extinguished by disease and conflict, with those that survived marginalized as the Americas became a great colonial resource to be both exploited and settled by its new rulers. The introduction of enforced labour in the early 17th century, almost exclusively from Africa, further shaped and reshaped the new society that was developing.

SPAIN IN AMERICA

Spain's role in reshaping the Americas was manifold. Spaniards created the first regular connections between the New World and the Old, via transatlantic convoys which carried people and goods in both directions. From Spain came flows of immigrants, small at first but growing over time, including merchants, artisans, farmers, miners, priests and government officials. Spaniards also introduced enslaved Africans, initially as personal servants, then as workers for mining and agriculture. Spaniards brought new goods, too. These included manufactures such as textiles, iron and steel tools and weapons, plus foods unavailable in America, like olives and wine, and cultural artefacts such as books, paintings and music, which also helped sustain a Spanish way of life in American environments. In return, the Americas yielded a remarkable array of commodities, some known and some new. Precious metals and jewels were the most immediately valuable, but in the long term new foods, especially staples such as maize and potatoes, had a huge impact on the European diet and on agriculture.

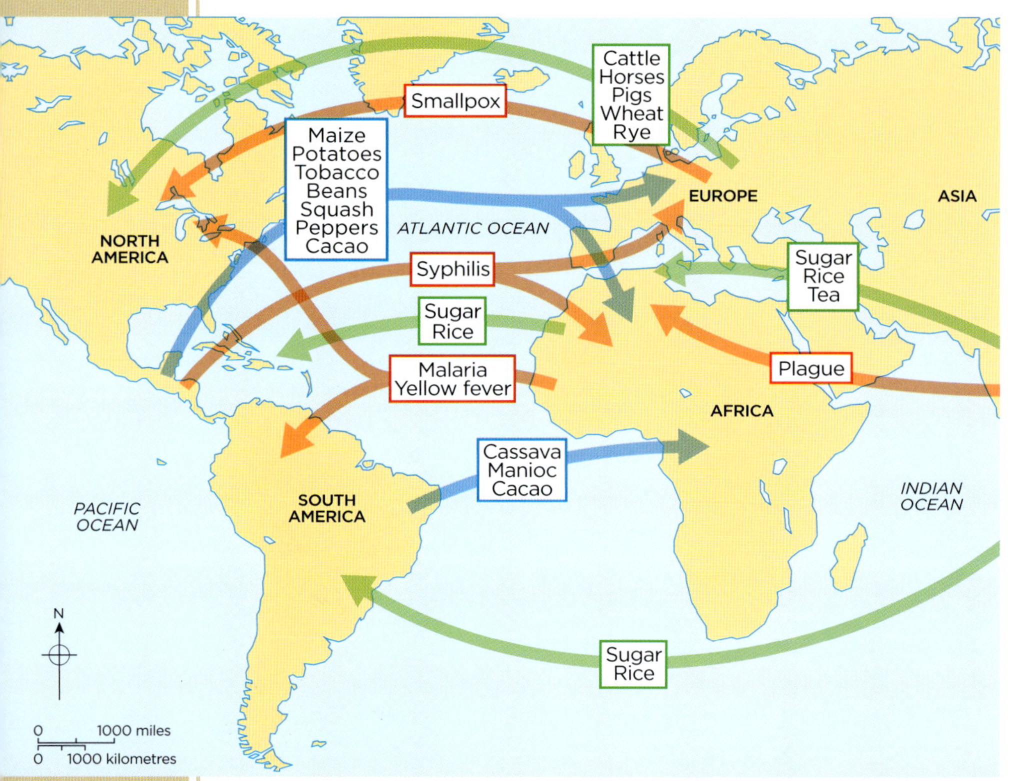

ABOVE *The Columbian exchange.*

This 'Columbian exchange' had a dark side too, for it brought the extinction of some native communities and the decimation of many others. The collapse started in areas colonized by Spain, where large indigenous societies were deeply disrupted by the settlers' appropriation of their land and the coercion of their labour. But the greatest destruction was caused by the impact of Old World diseases, disseminated by Europeans wherever they went. Pandemics of smallpox, influenza, measles, typhus and other imported diseases had horrifying short-term effects. A Spanish missionary recalled how the indigenous people 'died in heaps like bed bugs' in one of Mexico's early pandemics. Epidemics and pandemics also inflicted long-term damage by undermining the social cohesion, economic productivity and reproductive capacity of the communities exposed to them. This made recovery difficult, sometimes impossible. The number of losses is still debated, but historians agree that they were on a huge scale. The native population of Mexico may have fallen from around 25 million in 1519 to fewer than a million in 1630, while the population of Peru probably fell from 10–12 million to around a million over a comparable period.

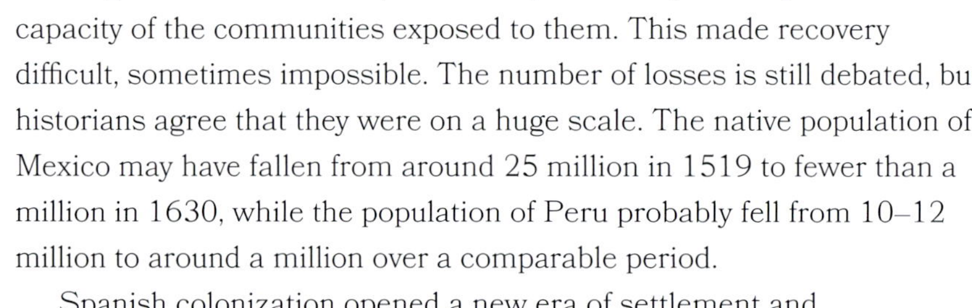

BELOW *Aztec smallpox victims from the 16th-century* Florentine Codex.

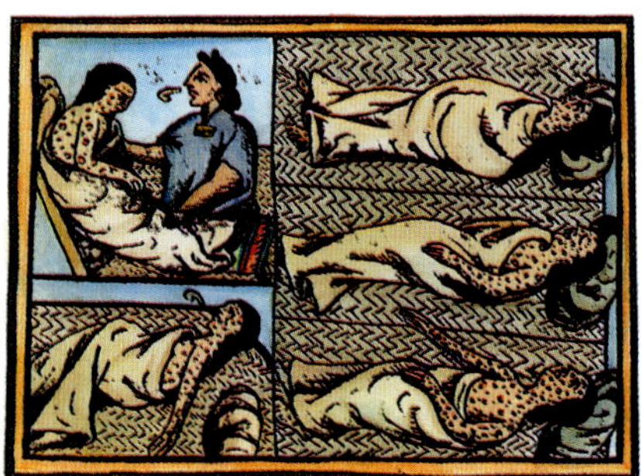

Spanish colonization opened a new era of settlement and urbanization in the Americas. Streams of migrants – mostly men at first, then growing numbers of women – brought life to the many towns

ABOVE *Spanish America trade routes.*

and cities which became the building blocks of Spanish American societies. By around 1570, between 125,000 and 150,000 Spaniards were distributed among 225 towns and cities, mostly in New Spain, which attracted the largest number of migrants. Some Spanish towns, such as Mexico City and Cusco, were superimposed on indigenous sites. Others, especially on the Atlantic and Pacific coasts and in the Caribbean, were new sites designed for new purposes, usually as ports for transoceanic and inter-regional trades which had not previously existed. Veracruz, Havana, Cartagena, Lima and Panama are prime examples, as the hinge points for Spanish transatlantic trade. A new Pacific trade also appeared, routed through New Spain: Acapulco became the transit point for imports of Chinese goods, carried from the Philippines by ships from Manila and subsequently redistributed through Mexico, to Europe, and by Pacific coastal trade to Peru.

ABOVE *View of Acapulco, c.1700.*

Spanish American cities differed from pre-Columbian cities in function and appearance. Like their predecessors, they ruled the rural hinterland and channelled flows of tribute and trade. But they also introduced a new civic culture based on the Iberian understanding of cities as the essential setting for civilization. The precepts for city building were laid down by royal decree. Philip II's *Ordinance for New Discovery and Settlement* (1573), with its many rules for layout and architecture, reflected the vision of the civilized order which the Spaniards believed that they were bringing to America. Towns were built on a grid pattern, with streets radiating from a central square. On the square were buildings that housed civil and religious authorities, on a scale which reflected local wealth and power. These included a church or a cathedral, a town council house, and sometimes the residences of leading officials, such as viceroys, governors, judges and bishops. Prominent families lived in houses around the plaza, while lesser citizens lived in the

blocks beyond it. On the outer margins of the grid were more informal dwellings, shacks where indigenous commoners and people of mixed race gathered, close to their workplaces.

Other innovations underpinned the transplantation of European ways of life. Before Europeans arrived, the concept of private landownership was largely unknown. In some Mexican and Peruvian city-states, a few lords had their own lands worked by slaves or other landless labourers, but this kind of property was rare. Land was invariably held communally by indigenous communities, whose leaders distributed it among individuals and families according to need. Spaniards, on the other hand, wanted land as an exclusive possession and they created individual landholdings on the European model, ranging from small farms to large estates (haciendas). They reorganized the use of labour, too, partly by adapting pre-existing systems of draft labour used by native states – such as the Inka mita, where citizens were required to work for the state for a set number of days each year – to meet their new demands for agricultural and mining workers. Later, Spaniards also introduced money wages.

ABOVE *The building of Mexico City, 16th century.*

Major changes in land use and diet followed the introduction of new crops, such as wheat, barley and sugar, together with a new range of fruits and vegetables (e.g., citrus fruits, apples, pears, peaches, grapes, melons, bananas, onions, radishes). As bread was a staple of the Spanish diet, wheat was particularly important and soon became a commercial crop for sale in urban markets. And, with European crops came European tools, mainly iron and steel digging implements, especially ploughshares. These made it possible to extend the area of cultivation, especially when combined with the new sources of animal power that crossed the Atlantic.

The import of cattle, horses, pigs, sheep, goats and chickens revolutionized American agriculture. Grazing animals proliferated on wild pastures where they had no natural predators, and their presence altered pre-Columbian patterns of consumption and production. Some effects were beneficial. Domestic animals provided new sources of protein and materials in the form of meat, leather, dairy products and wool for weaving, and were gradually incorporated into indigenous peasant farming. On the other hand, the unchecked growth of large herds caused environmental degradation and damaged indigenous community farming. In some regions, cattle and sheep pushed peasants off the land and allowed the Spanish to appropriate village holdings. In other places, ranching brought uncultivated lands into use and opened new frontiers for settlement. The introduction of Old World quadrupeds also had radical

BELOW *Plaza Mayor, Lima, 1680.*

LEFT *Hacienda Jaral de Berrios, Guanajuato, Mexico.*

social effects that spread beyond the range of European settlement. In the South American grasslands (especially Argentina, Uruguay and Chile), in northern Mexico, and on the great plains of North America, some indigenous societies shifted from farming to a nomadic life based on hunting from horseback.

Another facet of the ecological and economic revolutions that transformed the Americas was the introduction of mining. Spaniards had initially been attracted by the presence of gold and, after plundering existing supplies, they turned to the systematic exploitation of gold and silver deposits. European miners brought a new technology to the Americas which, when combined with the use of enslaved and indigenous forced labour, pushed production of precious metals to unprecedented levels. From the mid-1500s, the gold mines of New Granada and the silver mines of Mexico and Peru entered a century-long cycle of growth that did much to reshape American life. Mining stimulated urbanization, agriculture and commerce, and by financing trade with Europe underpinned an Atlantic economy which bound the Americas to Europe. The wealth generated by mining and its related activities also provided the Spanish crown with immense tax revenues that allowed it to consolidate its position as a great power.

BELOW *Painting of the silver mines at Potosí, 1585.*

Spain was the first to bring European monarchical government to the Americas, with institutions adapted from its traditional framework of governance. At first, the newly discovered 'Indies' were treated as an extension of the Kingdom of Castile, governed by its ruler and subject to Castilian laws and institutions. Then, as Spain's possessions expanded, the Reinos de las Indias (Kingdoms of the Indies) became parts of the vast 'composite monarchy' ruled by the Spanish Habsburgs (1516–1700). This was not a colonial empire in the modern sense; it was a collection of many kingdoms and provinces, each of which owed allegiance

to a single king while retaining its own identity, laws and institutions. Spanish America was, however, more subordinate to central power than other parts of the monarchy. At the time of the conquests, Spain's monarchs were intent on strengthening their authority in Spain and did so by reducing the powers of the aristocracy and the medieval Parliaments (the Cortes). Unsurprisingly, they were equally determined to avoid constraints on royal power in America and so prevented the emergence of an American feudal aristocracy or American representation in a Cortes.

The institutions of government in the Americas were essentially those of Habsburg Spain. The supreme task of the monarch was to provide justice, through institutions which blended judicial, legislative and executive authority. At the highest level, the king's authority over these kingdoms was exercised through state councils – the Councils of Castile, Aragon and so on – and a similar institution, known as the Supreme Council of the Indies (1524), was used to oversee government in America. This Council stood at the apex of an expanding 'government by paper'. It screened all official correspondence from America, made decisions on the king's behalf and became the central law-making and executive body for the whole of Spanish America.

ABOVE *Pedro Moya de Contreras, Archbishop of Mexico and president of the Council of the Indies.*

Within the Americas, the basic element of government was the town council (*cabildo*), which had responsibilities for keeping order and delivering justice at the local level. A *cabildo* was composed of a town's leading citizens but was not representative of its population. In fact, *cabildos* tended to become self-perpetuating oligarchies, in which offices were bought and sold and passed through generations of the same families. The key powers and responsibilities of government were held by royal officials, appointed by the crown. At the top were the viceroys, who embodied the person of the king and had overall responsibility for the administration and defence of large regions. They shared some of their powers with the judges of *audiencias* (high courts), and with the regional governors, the *corregidores* (district officers) and treasury officials who enforced the king's laws and collected his revenues. A third arm of authority was the Catholic Church. In return for a commitment to propagate Christianity, the Papacy gave the Iberian monarchies powers to choose bishops and other clergy. Throne and altar were thus joined in a close partnership and founded on mutual support.

RIGHT *The* cabildo *of Buenos Aires, Argentina.*

The 'Kingdoms of the Indies' differed from the European realms of Spain's composite monarchy. In the first place, the Spanish colonies had very few aristocrats and came under closer royal control. In the mid-16th century, the crown blocked the emergence of a landed nobility by stopping the *encomenderos* from taking control of indigenous communities and their lands. Instead, it appointed royal officials to supervise Spanish relations with indigenous communities, to prevent excessive exploitation by landowners and traders. Another difference was the special kind of government allowed to indigenous peoples. The crown decreed that they were free subjects whose communities were able to govern themselves under the overarching authority of Castilian law, but without making them equal to Spaniards and creoles. They had to pay tribute to the crown as recompense for their evangelization, and they were treated as legal minors. Nonetheless, indigenous people enjoyed some essential freedoms, such as the right to retain their corporate landholdings and to govern themselves under their own leaders, in 'Indian republics' (repúblicas de indios) subject to supervision by crown officials.

ABOVE *The monastery of La Asunción in Cuernacava, Mexico, a 16th-century Franciscan monastery.*

One of the greatest changes pioneered by Spain was the introduction of Christianity and the installation of the Catholic Church. The institution of the Church was present throughout society, made visible in the multitude of churches, convents and monasteries, and the rituals they practised.

Missionaries underpinned Spanish rule by converting indigenous people to Christianity and persuading them to accept rule by the Spanish monarchy. Churches, not fortresses, proclaimed Spanish dominance. The crowded calendar of religious observance was not just a source of spiritual guidance and discipline: it also permeated community life via the frequent religious celebrations that were public affirmations of religious unity. The Church penetrated society in other ways too. Parishes, monasteries and convents provided charitable works for the poor and were the main providers of education. Schools and universities were mainly for the elites, however, and rates of literacy were very low.

BELOW *A scene from the* Mixtec Codex *– Mixtecs come to worship at a cross set up by Spanish missionaries, early 16th century.*

RIGHT *A criollo family from Mexico City, c.1735.*

Together with their religion, Spaniards imported their concepts and forms of social organization. They brought the medieval European belief that society should be organized in a hierarchy, in groups (or 'estates') which played complementary roles in securing the common good. The basic social division was between nobles, who enjoyed social and political privileges, and plebeians, who provided manual labour and paid taxes. When transferred across the Atlantic, these concepts were altered to fit American societies in which white immigrants and their descendants arrogated pride of place. All whites tended to see themselves as 'noble' in relation to indigenous and other non-European peoples, but among themselves they varied in wealth and status, ranging from the 'well-born' and wealthy who held key positions in society and government, to poorer groups such as artisans, small farmers and traders. Those born in Europe were a small minority, mostly royal officials, priests and visiting merchants. Most whites were American-born Spaniards (criollos or creoles). In towns and cities, leading creole families formed a local ruling class, usually supported by mining and landed wealth.

BELOW *Mexican 18th-century casta paintings.*

In Spanish America, the place of plebeians was assigned to non-Spaniards, which included Africans, those of mixed descent and indigenous people. A few indigenous subjects, such as the descendants of Inka and Aztec lords, were recognized as nobles and given the corresponding privileges. But the majority were compressed into a class of commoners, known simply as indios, who mostly lived in their own communities, spoke their own languages and paid a head tax to the crown.

Other plebeian groups arose from one of the great changes caused by Iberian colonization: the emergence of a mixed-race society. This stemmed from the 'sexual conquest' that went with Spanish invasion and migration. Most of the early Spanish incomers were young men who took indigenous and African women as sexual partners, albeit rarely in marriage. European-indigenous mixing produced mestizos; European-African offspring were called mulatos. To these new groups, other, more complex intermixtures arose over time, from parents who were already of mixed origins. All were lumped under the generic title of castas, an artificial grouping which categorized people according to the ethnic origins of their parents.

Taken together, people of mixed race made an important contribution to the growth of the population and the development of a multi-layered Hispanic society. Although they lacked the privileges of whites, the castas were free of the constraints imposed on native peoples and slaves and tended to identify with Spanish-speaking criollos. Occasional mobility across the boundaries of ethnicity and colour did not promote racial equality, however. On the contrary, old prejudices remained intact. In Spain and Portugal, medieval kings and nobles had stirred animosity towards Jews and Muslims as a means of promoting political and religious unity among Catholics, and this strain of intolerance took on new forms in the Americas. Iberian American whites regarded indigenous people, Blacks and people of colour as inferior because they lacked 'pure' Christian ancestry and were tainted by their servile status or enslavement. Here were the germs of racist attitudes that permeated Iberian American cultures long after they broke with Spanish rule and became politically independent.

PORTUGUESE AMERICA

During the half-century after Pedro Álvares Cabral's discovery of Brazil in 1500, Portugal was slow to follow Spain's colonizing example. It made no plans to develop Brazil until French intrusion prompted intervention during the 1530s, with the creation of hereditary

BELOW *Olinda, Brazil, 1662.*

captaincies, run by absentee lords chosen by the Portuguese king. Of these, the most successful were São Vicente in the south and Pernambuco in the north, where settlers found ideal conditions for cultivating sugar. These were exceptional, however, and fuller exploitation of Brazilian resources awaited direct royal participation and investment in the sugar trade. This began in 1549, when King João II took the captaincy of Bahia into royal ownership and sent an expedition of 1,000 people (mostly men) under Tomé de Sousa to people a new royal colony. Sousa founded a town at Bahia, which became the capital of the first royal government in Brazil. His expedition also carried six Jesuits, a sign that Portugal aimed to follow Spain in Christianizing native peoples.

ABOVE *A 17th-century painting of an* engenho.

The foundation of Bahia heralded a lasting change. It strengthened Portugal's grip on Brazil, assured that the crown would take a more active role in its development and imposed a system of colonial domination on indigenous peoples. The Jesuits played a key role in bringing indigenous people under Portuguese rule by forcing them into new villages (*aldeias*) where they could be socialized under Christian management. Those who refused to comply were violently subjugated and used as enslaved labour by Portuguese settlers.

The impact on indigenous peoples was disastrous. Missionaries were unable to protect them from being forced to toil on sugar plantations and, as they were unaccustomed to heavy agricultural labour, indigenous enslaved workers had short lives and required constant replacement. The depletion of the indigenous population was worsened by Old World bacteria and viruses, the swift and silent killers of the 'Columbian Exchange'. Around 1560, influenza and haemorrhagic dysentery cut the first swathes through coastal regions, followed by pandemics of smallpox and plague. Brazilian sugar planters accordingly turned to Africa to provide a supplementary source of labour, by enslaving people who had more relevant agricultural and artisanal skills than the indigenous people of the Americas. With the growing demand for sugar in Europe, Brazil became the first American economy based on the exploitation of enslaved Africans working on large sugar plantations. From around 1650, this combination was to spread to other parts of the Americas, especially the Caribbean islands.

ABOVE *Map of Brazil in 1750.*

Like Spain, Portugal transferred the ideas and institutions of its traditional monarchical government to its colonies. The king's responsibility to deliver justice meant that courts and magistrates played a key role in making and implementing law, while treasury officers collected taxes, and town councils managed local affairs. Between 1580 and 1640, a royal succession crisis in Portugal meant that the country fell under the control of the Spanish crown. In this period, colonial rule from Iberia was actually strengthened by reforms such as the introduction of a high court (the *relacão*) at Bahia similar to the *audiencia* that had legal jurisdiction in Spanish realms. In keeping with Brazil's smaller territory and population, the system of royal government did not operate on as large a scale as in Spanish America, where, in addition to the *audiencias*, the king's presence was represented by viceroys and a range of royal officials who reached down to city and provincial level. Brazil, however, had closer connections to its parent power because of the relative ease of transatlantic communications between Lisbon and the coastal towns of South America. This advantage had a downside, however. From the 1620s, Brazil suffered repeated Dutch attacks on its trade and territory, culminating in the occupation of Recife and the region of Pernambuco, the leading sugar producer, between 1630 and 1654.

Sugar was to Brazil as silver was to Mexico and Peru: a valuable product that generated trade with Europe, stimulated economic growth and underpinned a society of a distinctive kind. By 1600, Brazil was the largest sugar-producing area in the Western world. On the coast, social and economic life revolved around the *engenho*, a complex of land, enslaved labour and mills for grinding cane and manufacturing sugar, all of which were owned and organized by a rich and powerful *senhor de engenho*. These landed patriarchs imposed Portugal's seigneurial landed gentry system on Brazil, creating powerful families who came to dominate the territory's economy and society. The central role of the *engenho* also ensured that Brazil differed from Spanish America by having the rural plantation rather than the city as its defining institution.

With Brazil's burgeoning sugar industry came the emergence of a new society, in which Europeans and Africans replaced indigenous peoples. By the end of the 16th century, Brazil's white population had risen to around 40,000–50,000, mostly males, clustered in towns and plantations, while its Black population grew ever larger. Enslaved Africans were arriving in Brazil at a rate of 10,000–15,000 a year in the 1580s, the prelude to growing numbers in the 17th and, especially, the 18th centuries.

LEFT *Diamond mining in Brazil.*

Portuguese America long remained an archipelago of coastal settlements, with its main centres in Pernambuco, Bahia and Rio de Janeiro, all based on plantation economies. From the later 17th century, new developments appeared. The town of São Paulo became a spearhead for movement into the interior, launched by locals – or 'Paulistas' – of Portuguese descent and by frontiersmen known as *bandeirantes* ('flag bearers'), who were mostly mamelucos, as white-indigenous mixtures were called. In their search for indigenous slaves and precious metals, they uncovered deposits of alluvial gold and diamonds, which in turn attracted an inrush of Portuguese immigrants with their slaves.

The region of Minas Gerais (named for its prolific mines) rapidly added a new dimension to colonial Brazil. Although the gold boom passed its peak around 1755, mining injected a new vitality into the Brazilian economy and tightened its connections to Portugal. New regions of settlement were created in south-central Brazil, based on mining and ranching, while Rio de Janeiro, the closest port, became Brazil's capital in 1763. Transatlantic trade then reached new heights. By the end of the 18th century, Brazil had become one of Europe's richest American colonies, overshadowing smaller, poorer Portugal.

Brazil was also a very distinctive society, due to its heavy reliance on enslaved labour. Between 1550 and 1800, some 2.5 million Africans were carried into slavery in Brazil. Most worked on plantations where life was hard and short; many were also employed in skilled artisanal work, domestic service and a host of other tasks. Combined with Portuguese immigration, the forced migration of enslaved people produced a complex multiracial society, divided by deep inequalities associated with ethnic origin and skin colour. At the top of the social hierarchy were wealthy whites; at the bottom were enslaved Blacks. Between these extremes were poor whites, freed slaves, and increasing numbers of free people of mixed white, Black and Indian heritage. Thus, while the Portuguese culture of its white society was similar to that of Spanish America, Brazil had a strong Afro-Brazilian element which set it apart from its Spanish American neighbours.

EUROPEAN CHALLENGES IN AMERICA

The question of who should share in the riches of the Americas was increasingly contested during the 17th century. By 1600, the Iberian powers had taken the lion's share of American territory and had embedded their languages and cultures, together with Christianity and rule by Catholic monarchies. They had also blocked attempts by others to colonize the territory. From the 1520s, the English, French and Dutch preyed on Spanish trade by piracy and smuggling, but none succeeded in planting permanent settlements. This began to change in the 1620s, when people from these nations succeeded in setting up colonies on the northeastern seaboard of North America, in the Gulf of Saint Lawrence, and among the smaller Caribbean islands.

Initially small and insignificant, these colonial enclaves became increasingly important arenas of American life. Although none had resources comparable to those of the densely populated and precious metal-rich regions of Spanish America, their growth inaugurated another era of transformation in the American world, enlarging the spaces occupied by Europeans, bringing new immigrants, and adding new patterns of social and economic development which differed from Iberian America.

The new American colonies were founded on the voluntary migration of growing numbers of northern Europeans in search of work, cheap land and a better life. Those situated in temperate regions of North America were generally colonies of white settlement, based on migrant communities engaged in family farming for subsistence and local markets. Colonies in tropical regions, notably in the Eastern Caribbean, started as colonies of white settlement but soon turned into societies in which small minorities of whites dominated large numbers of Black enslaved workers, who were forced to labour in plantations growing produce for export to Europe. The English, French and the Dutch had colonies of both kinds, which they imprinted to differing degrees with the languages and cultures of the societies of their mother country. The largest and most dynamic were the English colonies, which grew at an increasingly rapid pace in the 18th century and in North America became the site of the first of the American republics of the modern era.

BRITISH AMERICA

European and Euro-American Populations in the Americas, 1600–1800

Region	1600–50	1750–1800
Spanish America	450,000	3,200,000
Brazil	50,000	1,010,000
British North America	25,000	2,150,000
New France and Canada	3,000	75,000
Non-Spanish Caribbean	75,000	400,000
Totals	603,000	6,835,000

England's interactions with the Americas began in the 1560s, with raids on Spain's territories, trade and abortive attempts at colonization. The politician and explorer Humphrey Gilbert planted a short-lived colony in Newfoundland in 1583, with plans to make it a sanctuary for English Catholics; Walter Raleigh tried twice to create a small colony in North America named Virginia (in honour of Elizabeth I), in 1585 and 1587.

The first attempt disappeared without trace, as did the second effort at Roanoke, led by Raleigh's proxy, John White.

Raleigh later attempted to revive his reputation by leading an expedition to the land he called Guayana, where he hoped to find El Dorado and create an entry into Spanish Peru. These ventures came to nothing. Conceived in a spirit of adventure, they were all ill-resourced, badly planned and lacked support at home. Indeed, they were overshadowed by English colonization in Ireland, whose 'plantations' of Protestant settlers offered better opportunities than untried lands on the other side of the Atlantic. But the failure of English ambitions was temporary. Colonizing ventures revived during the opening decades of the 17th century, driven by the hope of finding space and resources in regions untouched by Spain.

The English method of colonization differed from Spain's. Instead of giving powers to individual commanders and colonizers to distribute land and resources, the English crown issued royal charters which gave exclusive rights to companies that were formed with the explicit purpose of establishing colonies in designated areas. The Virginia Company, founded in 1606, and the Massachusetts Company, founded in 1629, played key roles in early English settlement in North America, while other chartered companies were involved elsewhere. The key feature of these companies was their autonomy. The British crown did not seek close control over the lands claimed in its name but left the settlers of new colonies to govern themselves within the framework of their royal charters. This allowed for the emergence of autonomous and representative governments in the colonies, where free males with the right qualifications were able to elect deputies to colonial 'assemblies' which had rights to make laws on their behalf.

BELOW *John White's drawing of a Secotan Indian, 1585.*

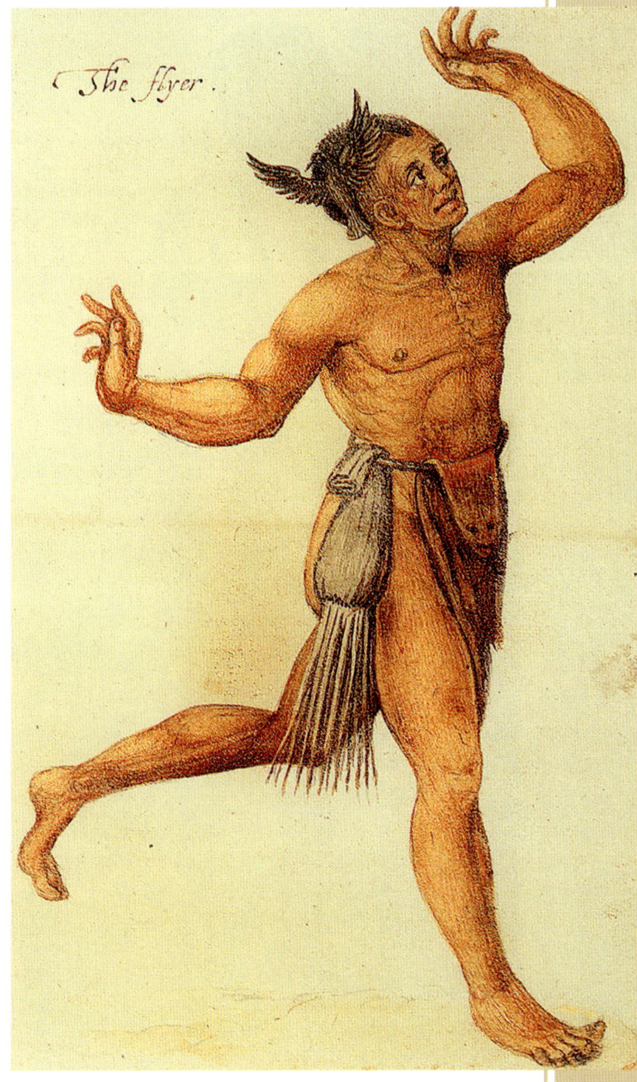

The first settlements were at Jamestown in Virginia (1607), New Plymouth in New England (1620) and Bermuda (1612–16). Other colonies sprang up in Saint Christopher (1623), Barbados (1625) and other small islands in the Lesser Antilles in the decade that followed. These were reinforced during the 1630s by many migrants who left the British Isles to resettle in various colonies in the Americas. This 'Great Migration' saw about 30,000 leave for North America and about 20,000 head to the Caribbean, giving substance, permanence and a platform for future growth for an emergent Anglo-America.

One stream went to the sparsely populated regions of New England (mostly Massachusetts), where Protestants who dissented from Church of England doctrines created self-governing congregations where they could follow their own beliefs. These migrants were mostly people of the 'middling sort' who could pay their own passage and migrated in families, sometimes entire village communities. The first emigrants, called the Pilgrims, founded a village community at New Plymouth in 1620, but the main Puritan colonization began in 1630, under the leadership of John Winthrop, a wealthy Suffolk-born lawyer.

ABOVE *A map resulting from Walter Raleigh's failed expedition to Guyana.*

Another stream went to Virginia and Maryland, where early settlers hoped to profit by producing 'Spanish tobacco' for English consumers. A third stream headed into the Caribbean, where English colonizers in Barbados and other islands of the Lesser Antilles also pursued commercial goals by cultivating and exporting tropical crops, chiefly tobacco and sugar. Both the Chesapeake and Caribbean islands relied on attracting British emigrants who differed from those who went to New England. They were mainly poor, single males who hoped to escape poverty by contracting to work as 'indentured' labourers for fixed periods (usually several years), in return for wages or the promise of land.

British colonies evolved along different lines. In the New England colonies, settlers worked the land with family labour and were united by religious purposes – a pattern which later extended to the Middle Colonies of New York, New Jersey and Pennsylvania. Chartered companies gave grants of land to men who came together to found towns and these men distributed land among households. Given that farming relied on family labour, these grants were relatively small and evenly distributed. The Chesapeake and Caribbean colonies, on the other hand, had a different social base. Landownership was concentrated in the hands of a few planters and merchants who invested in plantations and tools, while the majority of the population were indentured workers controlled by their employers. This in turn led to a gradually deepening divergence between Britain's American colonies. While the New England colonies developed from a base of

BELOW *Reconstruction of the original settlement at Jamestown, Virginia.*

small rural towns peopled by independent, landowning family farmers, the Chesapeake and Caribbean colonies developed an economy of large plantations where a landed oligarchy presided over poor and landless labourers. This pattern of deep social inequality hardened when indentured workers were replaced by enslaved Africans, for this accentuated the differences between Anglo-American colonies based on free whites transplanted from Britain and those based on African slavery.

This change, which began in the sugar plantations of the Caribbean colonies and was later followed by tobacco and rice planters in Virginia, Maryland and the Carolinas, had historic consequences. The rapid growth of sugar economies was strengthened by the seizure of Jamaica from Spain in 1655 and the Caribbean islands became the dynamic centre of Britain's nascent empire. The British 'West Indies' (Jamaica, Barbados and the Leeward Islands) produced sugar, which they exported to Britain, and molasses (used to produce rum) which they sold to Britain's North American colonies. In return, they bought enslaved people from Africa, manufactured goods from Britain, and timber and other commodities from North America. These trades generated considerable wealth on both sides of the Atlantic and bound the colonies closer to Britain. The West Indies became a major market for British goods and the considerable wealth of the West India planters, sugar merchants and slave traders also ensured them a powerful presence in British society and politics. Caribbean markets also helped the farms and fisheries of New England and the Middle Colonies, which prospered by supplying them with commodities

John Winthrop, Governor of Massachusetts

John Winthrop represented a group of affluent Puritans who obtained a royal charter for the Massachusetts Bay Company and used it to create a self-governing colony. Winthrop and his associates mobilized England's Puritan gentry and clergy to recruit migrants from their communities, calling on them to join a Christian exodus and set up a colony conceived as a new Zion. Winthrop aimed to create a 'Bible Commonwealth' that would be a model to the world, 'as a City upon a Hill'. It was the most radical government in the contemporary European world, running as a republic with elective offices and a legislature. Winthrop served repeated periods in office as its governor before his death in 1649.

LEFT *John Winthrop.*

ABOVE *Sugar cane plantation in the West Indies.*

such as timber, codfish and other products.

Britain's North American colonies differed from those of Iberian America in several respects. They were founded by chartered commercial companies rather than by armed conquerors and missionaries, and from the outset they depended on the labour of immigrants rather than native peoples. Unlike Spain and Portugal, Britain allowed a wide range of European immigration into its North American colonies, especially during the 18th century. Increasing numbers of Scots-Irish, German, Huguenot and Swiss immigrants were drawn to the Middle American colonies of New York, New Jersey and Pennsylvania by the prospect of cheap land, relatively high wages and freedom of worship. Pennsylvania was a striking example. Founded by William Penn as a refuge for English Quakers, its reputation as 'the best poor man's country' attracted large numbers of migrants seeking cheap land, including many German-speaking family farmers in search of both economic and religious autonomy.

On these foundations, New England and the Middle Colonies developed distinctive societies. They were composed mainly of white immigrants, mostly small farmers and artisans, who found in America a place where they could acquire cheap land and wages higher than those at home. Their government also differed from the Iberian American pattern. British colonials enjoyed greater political autonomy through their participation in elected assemblies which, like parliaments, could restrain the powers of royal officials and shape local legislation. These assemblies were not democratic institutions. Their members were chosen by a narrow franchise and ingrained habits of social

RIGHT *William Penn meets with the Lenape Indians to obtain land to establish the colony of Pennsylvania.*

of
Treaty with the
INDIAN'S

deference ensured that politics was dominated by wealthy landowners and merchants. However, they embodied a degree of political participation by a voting public of a kind found nowhere else in the Americas.

Another distinctive characteristic of British America was its diversity of religious belief and practice. Unlike Iberian America, where the Catholic Church controlled religious life, British America enjoyed religious pluralism. At its outset, colonial settlement had a strong element of religious dissent. In New England, Puritan exiles aspired to create 'godly' communities, founded on a covenant to live by religious ideals and to set an example to others. The Church of England was the official church, sanctioned by the monarch who was its head, but it remained weak until the 18th century. Even then, its influence was curbed by the growth of immigration rooted in European religious communities of several kinds (such as English Quakers, Baptists and Methodists; French Huguenots; German Lutherans, Moravians and Mennonites). By the time of the American Revolution, most religious practice took part among Protestant congregations of many kinds, of which the Church of England was only one. Here, then, was an enduring religious diversity that was entirely absent in colonial Iberian America.

THE FRENCH IN AMERICA

French colonization was preceded, like the English, by raiding and trading in the Spanish Caribbean, quests for a northwestern route to China through North American waters, and searches for precious metals and Indian civilizations in lands which Spain had not occupied. In the 1530s and 1540s, Jacques Cartier and Jean-François Roberval advanced French claims to American territory when they explored the Gulf of Saint Lawrence. Their reconnaissance yielded nothing of material value but advanced geographical knowledge of North America and allowed the French king to claim possession of the land later called 'Canada' or 'New France'.

The absence of obvious wealth and bitter northern winters initially discouraged colonization. Instead, France turned south, to Brazil and Florida. Admiral Gaspard II de Coligny, Henri II's Huguenot minister, aimed to challenge Iberian Catholicism by creating Huguenot colonies on Portuguese and Spanish territories. The projects began with Vice-Admiral Nicolas Durand de Villegaignon's effort to settle on the coast near Rio de Janeiro in 1555, followed by attempts by Jean Ribault and René de Laudonnière to set up fortified settlements in Florida. Both were quickly erased by military action. French colonial enterprise then faded while France descended deeper into religious and civil wars, and did not reappear until the first half of the 17th century, with renewed exploration in North America and attempts at colonization in the Caribbean.

Ideas for colonial settlement revived when Samuel de Champlain's pioneering exploration of the Great Lakes led to the foundation of Quebec in 1608, followed by the revival of settlement at Acadia (present day Nova Scotia) on the Atlantic coast in 1610. From these precarious foundations, a new structure gradually appeared. Influenced by Cardinal Richelieu's desire to create Catholic colonies, the French crown granted a monopoly for trade and settlement in Canada to the Company of New France in 1628.

ABOVE *La Salle claims Louisiana for France.*

This generated a new, more serious attempt at American empire building, sparked by the state. Unlike contemporary English and Dutch companies, the Company of New France was primed by the crown, which sold a third of its shares to government officials. It received a monopoly of the North American fur trade, the right to grant seigneurial lands to wealthy proprietors and a commitment to transport 4,000 French Catholic settlers, mostly indentured servants (*engagés*), to Canada. Conversion of native peoples to Catholicism also became an explicit goal for New France, as a justification to colonize comparable to that of Spain and Portugal.

The Company dissolved in 1663 and was replaced by a military colony under direct royal rule. Influenced by Jean-Baptiste Colbert, his controller general of state finances, Louis XIV installed a royal government in New France, under a governor, an intendant responsible for finance and internal administration, and a force of more than 1,000 soldiers. The colony grew to around 10,000 settlers by 1685, and became a base from which explorers, including Jesuit missionaries, expanded French frontiers. They reached into the Great Lakes region in the 1670s and 1680s and, in an expedition led by René-Robert Cavalier, sieur de la Salle, moved southwest along the Illinois and Mississippi rivers towards the Gulf of Mexico. La Salle believed that France could create an empire in the middle of North America by controlling trade through the great river systems and occupying lands outside Spanish and British

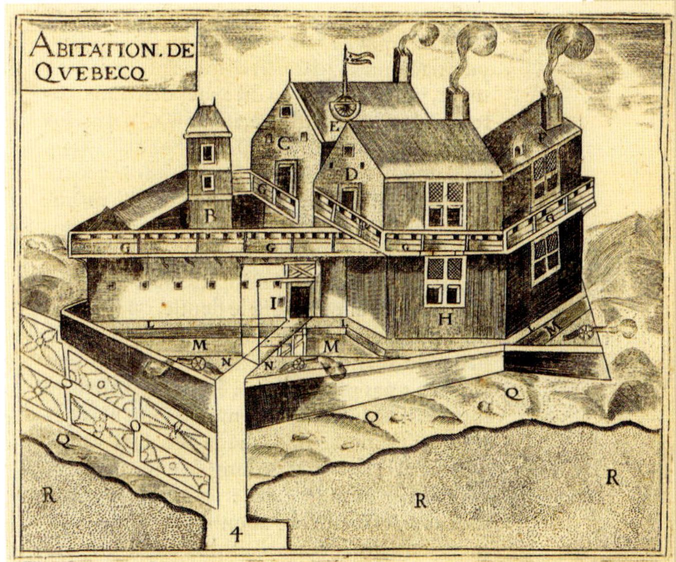

BELOW *The Quebec settlement, 1608.*

control, and he claimed the vast Mississippi Valley for France, naming it La Louisiane in honour of Louis XIV.

La Salle's dreams of a North American empire comparable to those of Britain and Spain were never realized. Although France had a large population, capable of peopling new lands, New France attracted few immigrants from the mother country. The habitants in the east were small populations, tied to their farms and fisheries. Exploration of the interior was left to fur trappers and evangelization of the Indians to Jesuit missionaries. This allowed France to exercise loose control over large areas of the interior and to attack British frontier settlements inland from the Atlantic colonies. France could not, however, build a land empire comparable to Britain's. By the mid-18th century the French population of Canada was only around 70,000 people, compared to about 1.5 million in the British North American colonies. And, while the British colonies were concentrated on the Atlantic seaboard, the French colonial population was dispersed over a huge area from the Saint Lawrence to the Mississippi rivers. Plans to convert indigenous American peoples to Christianity and to unite them with French settlers also made little headway. Jesuit missionaries reached far into the interior, but had relatively little impact on native cultures, particularly when compared to the Spanish. To defend Canada against the British, the French had to treat indigenous people as allies rather than subjects, especially the Six Nation Iroquois, whose domination of the forests hindered British incursions on to French territory.

The wealth of France's American empire was in the Caribbean, where, by the 1640s, France had created colonies on Martinique, Guadeloupe, Dominica and some smaller islands. At first, the islands' landed proprietors produced sugar using indentured workers from France but, because Europeans suffered very high rates of mortality from hard labour, poor

LEFT *Agostino Brunias, dancing scene on Dominica, c.1780.*

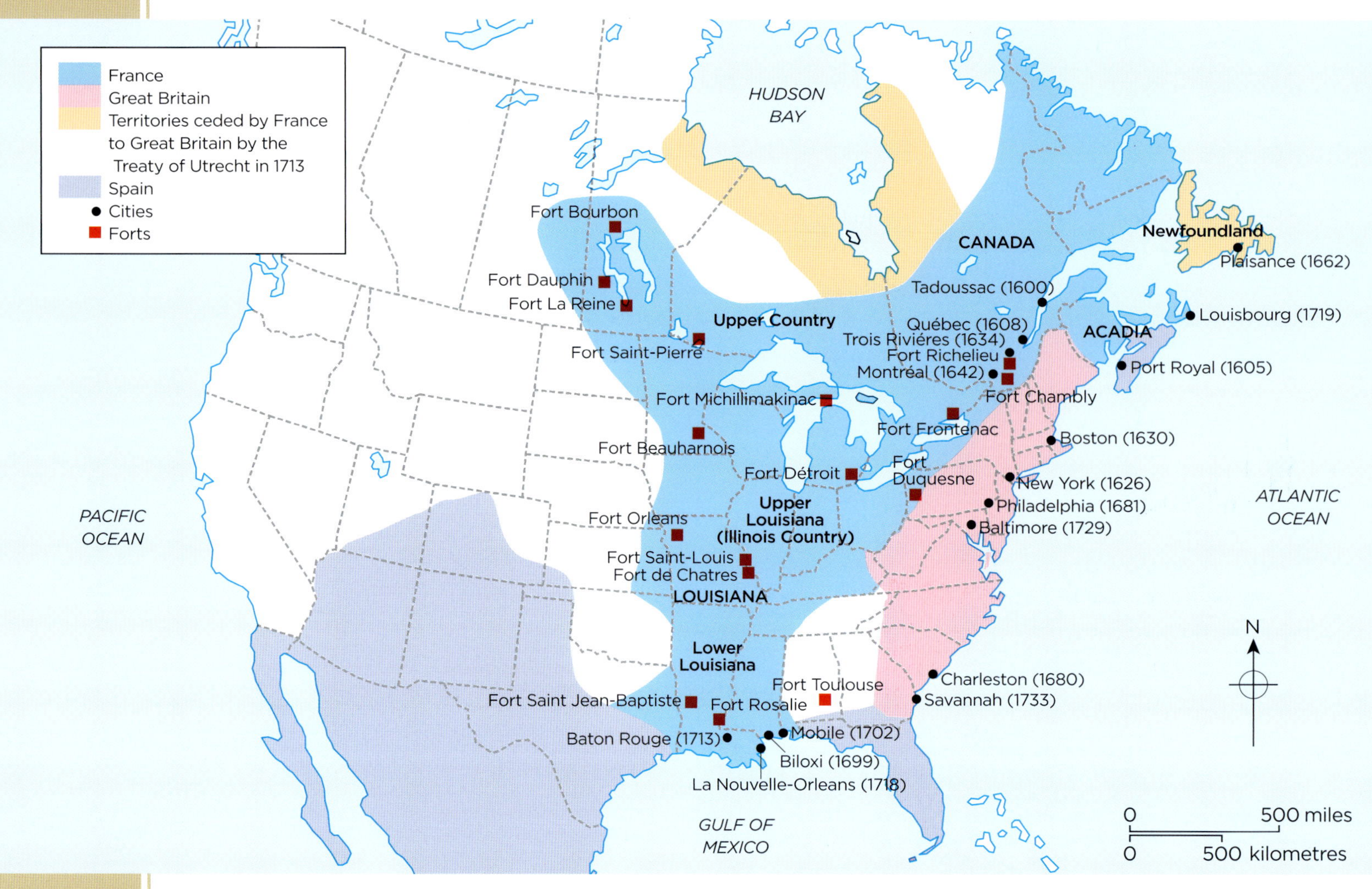

ABOVE *Map of New France.*

food and tropical conditions, they were an unreliable and unsustainable workforce. So, like the English, French planters turned to enslaved Africans to provide the labour needed to grow and process sugar and, in so doing, created dynamic export economies which attracted many more immigrants than Canada.

The growth of the French Caribbean accelerated during the 18th century, after Spain ceded the western third of the island of Santo Domingo in 1697. The new French colony of Saint-Domingue quickly became a plantation powerhouse where the cultivation of tropical crops reached new heights. Saint-Domingue was particularly important for its exports of sugar and coffee, and to a lesser extent cacao, indigo and cotton, and after the Seven Years' War of 1756–63 it became a crucial source of commerce and revenue for France. Indeed, by the late 18th century, Saint-Domingue was the richest colony in the world, producing about 40 per cent of the world's sugar and half of its coffee. It was also the most voracious consumer of African enslaved labour, supplied by French slave traders. By the 1780s, Saint-Domingue was importing about 30,000 slaves a year, and of its total population of around half a million between 80 and 90 per cent were enslaved. So, together with the British and Dutch, the French were instrumental in entrenching plantation slavery, that peculiarly American institution which extended from the Chesapeake region and the Carolinas, through the Caribbean and into Brazil.

THE DUTCH

Following rebellion against Spanish rule in the Habsburg Netherlands, the merchants and shippers of the Dutch Republic (which declared independence in 1588) began to extend their trades towards Africa, the Indian Ocean and Brazil, where they preyed on Portuguese commerce. Imitating the English example, they created private joint-stock companies which invested in the spice trade and, after the success of some early ventures, the Republic's government granted a charter to the Vereenigde Oostindische Compagnie (Dutch East India Company) in 1602, with exclusive rights to trade east of the Cape of Good Hope and west of the Straits of Magellan.

The Company focused on trade rather than settlement. It did not organize large-scale overseas migration, nor seek to create a land empire. Emigrants to Asian outposts were mostly company employees, single men who intended to return home and were reluctant to intermarry into Asian societies. The few who stayed were mostly absorbed into the Indo-Portuguese culture of their womenfolk and did not create a tropical 'New Netherland' in the East. Dutch expansion in the West differed. It was also organized by a private joint-stock company, the West-Indische Compagnie (1621), aimed at conquest and permanent colonization. In 1630, this Dutch West India Company succeeded in occupying the rich sugar-producing region of Pernambuco, which it intended to turn into a Dutch possession, renamed 'New Holland'.

BELOW *Painting of a Black woman and child by Albert Eckhout.*

The Dutch held the territory for nearly a quarter of a century but failed to turn New Holland into a solid base of Dutch settlers and Dutch Protestant culture. Schemes for colonization by Dutch, German and Scandinavian Protestants failed, missionary activity among native peoples was virtually non-existent, and Portuguese Brazil remained firmly Catholic. Memories of Dutch rule in Brazil are inscribed on paper rather than places or people, most vividly in the extraordinary collection of images and information about Brazilian people, flora and fauna gathered under the auspices of Governor General Johan Maurits.

The Dutch settlement of New Netherland, established in 1624 on the Hudson River and shores of Manhattan, seemed a better prospect for colonization. Here was a temperate environment in which colonists might work and worship in ways familiar from home, without having to contend with the Portuguese Catholic milieu found in Pernambuco. But New Netherland in North America had no greater staying power than New Holland in South America. It never attracted more than a small population (fewer than 8,000 people at its height), scattered across isolated farming villages and vulnerable to incursions from the expanding settlements of New England. English aggression was unstoppable, and, shortly after an English expedition took the fortified town of New Amsterdam in 1664, renaming it New York, the Dutch Republic turned away from North America. New Netherland was exchanged for the English sugar plantation territory in Suriname, where Dutch planters built a slave society dedicated to sugar cultivation, echoing their experience in Brazil.

New Netherland left some cultural marks. Non-Dutch settlers took up the Dutch language, joined the Dutch Reformed Church, and, through intermarriage, helped to keep Dutch manners and customs alive in New York well into the 18th century. On the whole, however, the Dutch were no more significant in territorial and cultural terms in America than they were in Asia or Brazil. Merchants aimed to take over existing trades and their governments devoted few resources to securing permanent territorial dominion. And, although their leaders were officially committed to converting native peoples to the Calvinist version of Christianity, the Dutch had no effect in the missionary field.

The most enduring Dutch influence was in the Caribbean. Here, the Dutch established a lasting presence in small colonies at Curaçao and in the Lesser Antilles, and the Windward and Virgin Islands, which they used for illegal trading with the possessions of other powers. The Dutch were, however, most important for the part they played in spreading the sugar-slavery complex. After their expulsion from Brazil in 1654, Dutch entrepreneurs took their capital and expertise to the Caribbean, where they joined with

BELOW *New Amsterdam.*

British and French settlers in developing crops for export, as well as starting their own sugar-based colony in Suriname. In this, they made an essential contribution to turning the Caribbean Basin into the platform for a new phase of American colonial development, based on the expansion of plantation economies and the forced migration of captive Africans. Without slaves to work plantations of sugar, tobacco and coffee, these lands would have been poor and isolated outposts. With slaves, islands such as Barbados, Jamaica and Saint-Domingue became some of the richest colonies in the Americas and, during the 18th century, an arena for warfare between European powers that competed for their riches.

ABOVE *Slave camp on a Suriname plantation, c.1860.*

RIGHT *Self-portrait of slave-catcher John Stedman in Suriname.*

NATIVE AMERICA AFTER COLUMBUS

ABOVE *Baroque facade of the Church of San Lorenzo, Potosí, Bolivia, designed by the Indian architect José Kondorí in the early 18th century.*

For indigenous Americans, the arrival of Europeans marked a momentous change. Throughout the Americas, pandemics and epidemics of Old World diseases wreaked havoc. Europeans had long experience of such diseases, which had been carried across continents by trade and war and were nurtured among people who lived close to domesticated animals or in filthy medieval cities. Indigenous Americans, who had few domestic animals, relatively few cities and no trade with the Old World, had no comparable exposure or immunity. Historians generally agree that contact with Europeans carried a phenomenal human cost everywhere in the Americas, described by the historian Alfred Crosby as 'the greatest tragedy in the history of the human species'. There were possibly 54 million American natives in 1492, or about 7 per cent of the world's population. By 1800, it was less than 1 per cent.

The great demographic decline caused by Old World pathogens was accompanied by an 'ecological revolution', driven by the invasion of outsiders along with their plants and animals, including weeds and vermin such as rats. Indigenous American responses to this challenge varied, mainly because their societies had different capacities to react to new settlers and their intentions.

In Mesoamerica and the Andes, the large hierarchical societies organized in states and chiefdoms retained some of their character, as Spaniards were primarily interested in collaborating with local elites and taking control of tribute-paying peasantries. In areas where social organization was limited to small, village-based communities, on the other hand, such as the Atlantic coasts of North and South America, indigenous societies gave way to European settlers who drove them out of their lands. It was only in areas where indigenous people had commodities which Europeans could only obtain by trade, such as furs, and where they were needed as allies in conflicts between Europeans, that local inhabitants retained a relatively strong position, using commercial and diplomatic relations to slow or even stop the advance of European settlement.

In many parts of Spanish America, indigenous communities adopted European economic and political practices. In Mexico and Peru, for example, indigenous farmers added European crops and livestock to their agriculture and participated in the commercial economy by buying and selling goods in local markets. They also adapted existing institutions for providing tributary labour, such as the Inka mita, to meet Spanish demands for forced labour in agriculture and mining. Indigenous people engaged with the new institutions of government introduced by Spain, too, by creating town councils which were run by their own ethnic leaders. And many integrated into Hispanic culture by

ABOVE *An auto-da-fé in San Bartolomé Otzolotepec, Mexico, 18th century.*

living in Spanish towns, where they worked as manual labourers, artisans and domestic servants. Indigenous people also worked with Spaniards to design churches and produce the works of art that adorned many of them.

Adaptations to European innovation also appeared in indigenous religious belief and practice. Willingly or not, indigenous people were assimilated into a monotheistic Christian world which demanded that they abandon beliefs and practices that were incompatible with Catholic doctrine. Native temples and objects of worship were replaced by Christian churches and images, native priests were persecuted, and native elites subjected to heavy pressures to convert, so that commoners would follow their leaders' example. Whole communities were resettled in villages with a parish church, where they could be taught Europeanized, Christianized ways, by practising Catholic rituals and forming religious confraternities (*cofradías*) dedicated to patron saints.

This 'spiritual conquest' was rarely complete, however. The Catholic clergy could not eradicate indigenous cultures and identities, nor did they always seek to. Some missionaries admired indigenous cultures and, by seeking to isolate their converts from corrupting influences, they helped to conserve elements of indigenous America within the shell of Christianity. Indigenous people also preserved their own beliefs by blending them with Christian teachings, and sometimes they appealed to Christian teachings for self-defence against exploitation or, more rarely, as justification for rebellions against injustice. Indigenous languages were another means of preserving cultural identities. In Peru and Bolivia, large numbers of people continued to speak Quechua and Aymara; in southern Mexico, Mayan languages were widely spoken; in Paraguay, most of the population spoke Guaraní. Indeed, throughout Latin America, including Brazil, many native languages

ABOVE
The Virgin of Guadalupe, 1700.

survived, together with other key cultural markers such as dress and diet.

Broadly speaking, most indigenous populations were part of two general categories. The most numerous were peasant societies that were integrated into colonial states; less numerous but more territorially widespread were indigenous peoples who remained outside European control.

The effects of Portuguese, English and French colonialism on indigenous peoples differed from those in the Hispanic world for several reasons. In the first place, settlers in Brazil, North America and the Caribbean entered quite different social and economic environments. Nowhere did they find native societies comparable to the populous and centralized tributary states of the Aztecs or the Inkas and they generally failed to find ways of permanently exploiting indigenous labour in the Spanish manner. Contacts were more commonly mediated through trade, as indigenous peoples wanted European goods, especially metal tools and weapons. Throughout North America, indigenous people responded to the French, Dutch and English presence by building new trading relationships. Where Europeans sought furs and hides, local inhabitants exchanged them for European cloth and metal tools that improved on their traditional bone, stone, wood and copper tools. Iron axes, hatchets, knives, fishhooks, hoes, brass and copper kettles, as well as guns, mirrors and alcohol were popular trade goods, especially guns, which could be used for both hunting and war.

Where Europeans wanted to possess land, their peaceful relations with indigenous trading partners invariably broke down. In New England and the Chesapeake, for example, encroachment on indigenous lands escalated into warfare and, on occasion, genocide. Weakened by warfare and disease, the native peoples were pushed out of their territories and few of those who survived were integrated into the colonizers' society. A similar fate awaited indigenous people in areas of early French settlement on the Saint Lawrence, where their attacks were gradually worn down by disease and military countermeasures. When French fur traders and missionaries penetrated deeper into the Canadian interior, relationships improved. Individual trappers and traders did business the indigenous way, took local women as wives and were sometimes absorbed into tribal life, producing mixed-race children (métis) who became important cultural intermediaries. French officials also cultivated good relations with indigenous peoples whom they wished to use as allies in wars with the English, and they strengthened groups such as the Iroquois Confederation by providing them with trade and arms. Most indigenous people were, however, unaffected by Catholic evangelization. When French rule ended in the 1760s, outside a few mission towns close to Montreal and Quebec the great majority rejected European beliefs and customs.

The same was true of indigenous peoples in or bordering Protestant English America. There were some missionary endeavours in New England – notably the 'praying towns' of indigenous converts established in Massachusetts (1646–75) – but they were paltry in comparison with the evangelizing enterprises of the Catholic religious orders in Spanish America, or even the modest efforts of Jesuit missionaries in French territories. Indigenous people were spared the imposition of Christian culture, partly because English Protestant communities focused more intently on their own salvation than with that of 'barbarian' outsiders. English settlers regarded themselves as the superior ethnic caste and saw indigenous populations as ignorant, brutish people who might be used for trade and war but had no place in white society. So, rather than incorporating indigenous people into the framework of neo-European society, as the Spanish and to a lesser extent the French did in their American dominions, most English settlers regarded them as an obstacle to colonization, fit only to be separated or removed.

Broadly speaking, most indigenous populations fell into one or other of two general categories. The most numerous were peasant societies that were integrated into colonial states, largely in Spanish America. The other general category consisted of the many (and highly varied) indigenous peoples who remained outside European control. Throughout the centuries of European colonial rule, many indigenous groups preserved complete independence and, although they were often willing to deal with Europeans, they did so on their own terms. This was the case in very large areas of the Americas. Throughout northern and southern Mexico, northern Colombia, the tropical forests east of the Peruvian Andes, southern Chile, the plains of Argentina, and the Orinoco and Amazon river systems, many indigenous peoples lived beyond the reach of colonial governments, as did the many who lived in the vast North American lands that stretched west of Appalachia and the Great Lakes.

BELOW *Indian leader in ceremonial dress by Vicente Alban, painter of the 'Quito School', 1783.*

ABOVE *A fur trader and his indigenous wife.*

This situation began to change in the 18th century, when colonial governments sought to extend control on the frontiers and settlers sought new spaces to move into. Nonetheless, many escaped full exposure to colonialism until later in the 19th century. In Spanish America, indigenous groups saw some alleviation of pressure after independence, when new states were too weak to confront them, but this was short-lived. Settlers renewed their push into indigenous territories across the 19th century and some states, especially the United States, Argentina and Brazil, saw the replacement of indigenous 'savages' as an explicit goal, necessary for the progress of 'civilization'. In both North and South America, the replacement of the European empires with modern states meant that many parts of 'Indian America' were exposed to new waves of disease, war and dispossession, emanating from mass immigration and expansive 19th-century industrial capitalism.

AFRICAN AMERICA

Africans and their descendants made an important contribution to the evolution of American societies. In fact, European exploitation of American resources depended to a considerable degree on the forced migration of Africans, who made up for the lack of European and indigenous labour in gold mining and tropical agriculture. In the early years of exploration, Africans arrived as enslaved people, carried by a transatlantic traffic started by Portuguese merchants who took captives from West Africa to sell in Spanish America and Brazil. During the later 17th century, the French, British and Dutch (and later Swedes and Danes) set up their own slaving companies and drove a huge increase in the trade over the course of the 18th century. About 12.5 million Africans were carried into American enslavement after 1500 (about half of them in 1701–1800, when the trade reached its peak). Their importance can be gauged from the fact that until around 1800 more Africans arrived in the Americas than European immigrants.

Enslaved Africans were widely but unevenly distributed. Most enslaved people went to Brazil, where they laboured on sugar plantations; later, they were also employed in cultivating coffee, which became Brazil's principal export after independence. The other major destination was the Caribbean, where the development of sugar plantations in the English and French islands (and Spanish Cuba in the 18th century) transformed 'colonies of settlement' into 'colonies of exploitation' based on slave labour.

At first, Africans were incorporated into 'societies with slaves', where enslaved workers co-existed with other forms of free and unfree labour, and the enslaved were a minority

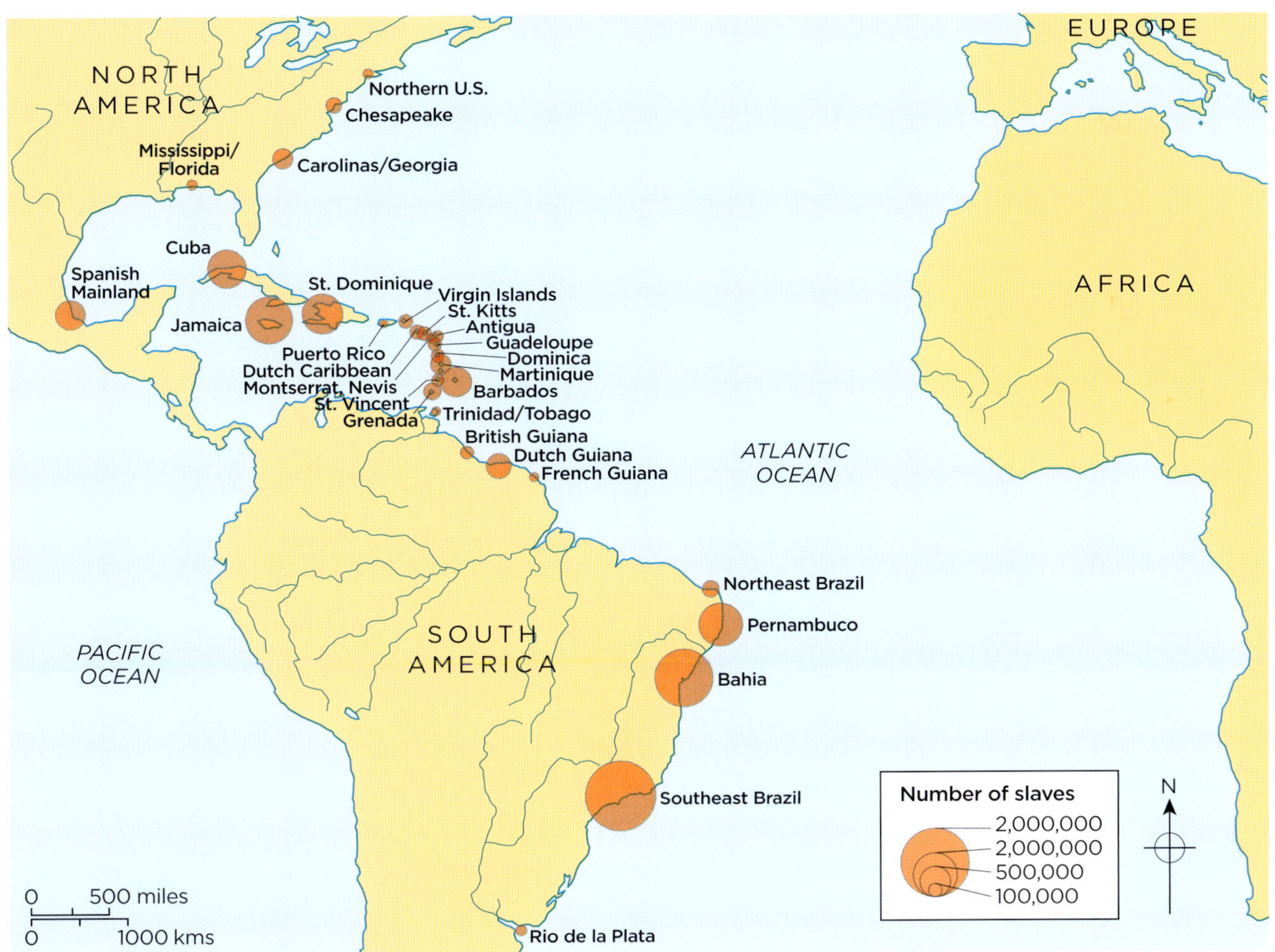

ABOVE *Major regions where slaves disembarked.*

of the population. Slave-owning societies of this kind were common in Spanish America, where the enslaved were sometimes clustered in agricultural work, such as cacao and coffee plantations in Venezuela or gold mining and tropical agriculture in Colombia, or employed in household, agricultural and artisanal activities in towns and countryside. Enslaved people were similarly used in most English North American colonies, except in the south where the development of tobacco, rice and indigo production from Maryland and Virginia southwards changed them into 'slave societies', in which enslaved labour was essential to the economy and unfree workers were either a very large component or a majority of the population. British Jamaica and French Saint-Domingue were extreme examples, where close to 90 per cent of the total population were enslaved Black people,

Destinations of the Transatlantic Slave Trade

Region	1501–1600	1601–1700	1701–1800	1801–1900	Total
North America	0	19,956	358,845	93,581	472,382
British Caribbean	0	405,117	2,139,819	218,475	2,763,411
French Caribbean	0	50,356	1,178,518	99,549	1,328,423
Dutch Americas	0	145,980	339,559	28,654	514,193
Danish West Indies	0	22,610	81,801	25,455	129,866
Spanish Americas	241,917	313,301	175,438	860,589	1,591,245
Brazil	34,686	910,361	2,210,931	2,376,141	5,532,119
Total	277,506	1,875,632	6,494,618	3,873,581	12,521,337

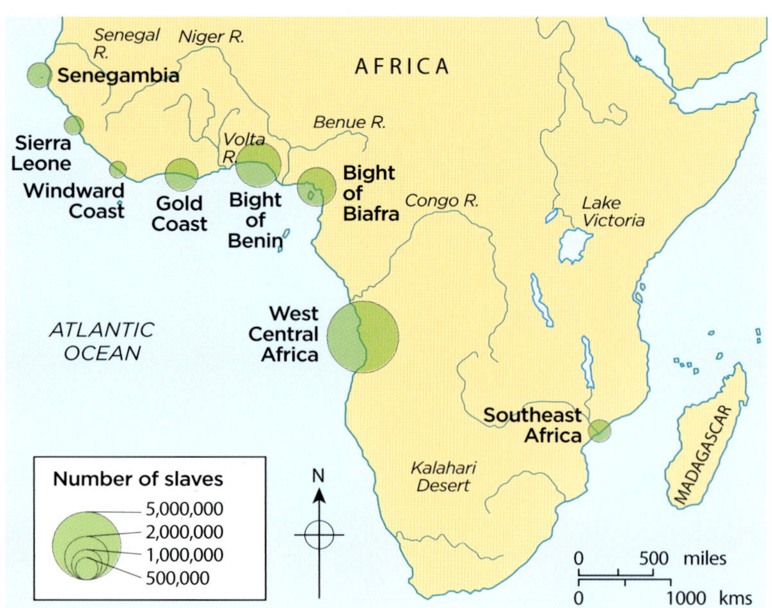

ABOVE *Major slave export points from Africa.*

ruled by a tiny minority of slave-owning planters who controlled local government and exerted almost absolute power. Slavery in the Americas was, then, unlike the slavery of the ancient world. It became identified with Africans and people of colour and, to defend this uniquely oppressive system, slave owners invented a racist discourse designed to justify enslavement in terms of African inferiority.

Africans enslaved in the Americas had diverse origins and different cultures. They came from many parts of West Africa – Guinea, Benin, the Gold Coast (modern Ghana) and Sierra Leone – as well as the Kingdom of Kongo (comprising areas of present-day Angola, the Democratic Republic of the Congo, Gabon and the Republic of the Congo), and later Mozambique and parts of East Africa. In some places, the enslaved population might share linguistic and cultural roots. The dominant group in Jamaica, for example, came from the Gold Coast, while in Haiti the majority were from Benin and Western Nigeria.

Often slavery forced together people from forests and savannas, from matrilineal and patrilineal societies, from

RIGHT *Slaves cutting sugar cane on Antigua.*

ABOVE *Trelawney Town, a maroon community in Jamaica.*

simple kindred organizations and from hierarchical kingdoms. Uprooted from their homelands, thrust into new environments dominated by whites, and without a common language, enslaved Africans found it much more difficult to reproduce their own societies than did free European immigrants. In plantation economies, they did not have a normal rate of population growth, because of high ratios of males to females, together with heavy mortality from disease and overwork, and the tendency of Caribbean and Brazil planters to import continuous replacements from Africa. North America was an exception. There, higher birth rates and lower mortality rates increased the number of American-born enslaved people, possibly because tobacco cultivation was less demanding than sugar or because a better diet improved female fertility. Whatever the reason, towards the end of the 18th century the North American enslaved population was almost as large as Brazil's, despite a much lower level of importation from Africa.

The experience of enslaved Africans and their descendants was shaped by the legal regimes and socio-economic environments in which they lived. In principle, legal codes laid down rules that defined and to some extent curbed the power of slave owners. Spain and Portugal were familiar with the institution of slavery long before they colonized the New World and had developed laws that recognized slavery as an acquired rather than a natural condition. According to Spanish law, the enslaved were human beings with certain basic rights: they had to be converted to Christianity and encouraged to worship; they were allowed to marry, to seek legal protection against maltreatment, and to negotiate and pay for their freedom. These rules and customs did not prevent violence and cruelty but at least allowed the enslaved to assert some minimal rights and even to become free persons. In the English, French and Dutch Caribbean, by contrast, access to the law was more limited and the violent suppression of the enslaved more common. Conditions on the plantations of Jamaica, Suriname and Saint-Domingue were notoriously bad, especially on large sugar plantations owned by absentees and managed by overseers. Work gangs in fields and sugar mills suffered particularly brutal discipline at harvest times and when sugar prices were high, when the lives of the enslaved were routinely sacrificed to the pursuit of profit.

Africans and their descendants were to some extent able to shape their own cultures within the institution of slavery. After the trauma of capture, forced transportation and the loss of family and community ties, this was far from easy. Torn from different African cultures and thrust together in an alien environment, the enslaved – who were mainly young males – could not simply reproduce their own societies in American settings. However, in places where the enslaved were concentrated in large numbers, they challenged the dehumanization inherent in their status by creating localized Afro-American cultures. For example, the enslaved defended communication among themselves by using and adapting African languages. Over time, slaves created 'creole' languages which blended English, French and Dutch vocabularies with African grammatical structures and rhythms of speech. African influences were strong in religious beliefs and practices, too. Distinctive religious cults appeared in Brazil and the Caribbean, sometimes fusing with Christian rites. Obeah in Jamaica, for example, or Vodou in Haiti and Candomblé, Xangó and Macumba in Brazil: all had a strong African basis that included European and sometimes indigenous American elements in syncretic (i.e., blended) belief systems that were peculiar to the Americas.

The enslaved also defended their autonomy in other ways. Where possible, they struggled to sustain forms of family life outside the European norms of marriage, based on the parcels of land they were given for growing food. They took more direct action, too, such as sabotaging their work and damaging the owner's property, or by escaping, or even by taking their own lives. Some runaways formed free communities, known as maroons in Jamaica, palenques in Spanish America and quilombos in Brazil, which were effectively independent of colonial governments. Rebellions by plantation workers were common in Iberian America and the Caribbean but were invariably on a small scale and aimed at improving local conditions rather than overthrowing the institution of enslavement. Only in Saint-Domingue did rebellion turn into a revolutionary movement in which freed enslaved people and people of colour destroyed slave society and created the independent state of Haiti.

Familial Relationships

In his 1774 study of Jamaica, the British judge and historian Edward Long observed of the island's enslaved population that, 'They are all married (in their way) to a husband or wife, pro tempore, or have other family connections in almost every parish throughout the island; so that one of them, perhaps, has six or more husbands, or wives, in several different places; by this means they find support when their lands fail them; and houses of call and refreshment, whenever they are upon their travels.'

Africans and their descendants were not always slaves. Another element of African America was composed of free Blacks and free people of colour, derived from slave manumissions and sexual relations, often forced on Black women by their enslavers. In several Spanish American coastal regions, in Brazil and the French Caribbean, these were large groups which played an important role in social and economic life. They tended to identify with the dominant society and sought autonomy by owning land and making money through trade. They spoke Spanish or Portuguese, were recognized as Christians and were often members of *cofradías*, religious brotherhoods which also acted as mutual aid societies.

Throughout the Americas, African cultural practices continued to be transmitted through generations both during colonial rule and after. African and African-influenced languages, religious beliefs, music and dance were present wherever substantial numbers of enslaved people and free Blacks were concentrated, and they continue to influence national cultures in the USA and Latin America today.

THE CONSEQUENCES OF COLONIALISM

ABOVE *A mulatto woman and her slave, Martinique, 1805.*

European occupation had immense effects on the Americas. The states and peoples of Iberia and northwestern Europe changed the course of American history by transplanting their cultures and creating new sites for the development of European civilization overseas. By implanting Old World animals and plants and applying European tools and technologies, they revolutionized the exploitation of American resources. By establishing transatlantic trade with Europe and Africa, they brought the Americas into a developing world economy, ending their millennia-long isolation. And, despite their differences, Europeans brought a greater degree of cultural and political uniformity. In place of innumerable native languages and cultures, they disseminated the languages of Iberia, Britain and France, together with a common system of writing and recording, similar concepts of marriage, family and kin, and broadly related forms of governance. And, most strikingly, Europeans introduced a common religion. Christianity, whether Catholic or Protestant, imposed a similar set of beliefs in place of the myriad practices of the pre-Columbian world.

The birth of a neo-European world was accompanied by considerable trauma, as Europeans inaugurated a 'swarming' of intruders who tended to relegate or obliterate indigenous populations. Meanwhile, the transatlantic slave trade forced captive Africans into the world's first racially based enslaved societies. Indeed, where Amerigo Vespucci had seen the New World as the site of an earthly paradise, Europeans built an arena for oppression and war. Their rivalry started as soon as Spain and Portugal revealed

America's resources during the 16th century, then intensified when the English, French and Dutch created colonies during the 17th century. This set a pattern which hardened during the 18th century, when rivalry between Britain, France and Spain produced an epic struggle that shifted the balance of power in both Europe and the Americas.

At the start of the 18th century, Spain was the leading power in the Americas, with a territorial and cultural reach that far exceeded its rivals. The Spanish language, Spanish Catholicism and Spanish high culture extended far and wide, exemplified in great cathedrals, universities and the literature and poetry associated with viceregal courts and capital cities. On a smaller scale, Brazil had become a powerhouse of empire, without the cultural polish of New Spain or Peru but with great wealth from sugar plantations and bonanzas from gold and diamond mining. The British and French presence was growing, too. In the Caribbean, planters grew rich from Europeans' taste for tobacco, sugar and coffee. In North America, settlers opened new land frontiers. French explorers moved westwards and southwards from the Saint Lawrence River and Seaway towards Louisiana and French statesmen dreamed of a great land empire at the core of North America. Britain's Atlantic colonies were also a platform for movement into the continental interior, and growing populations competed with the French and their indigenous allies on western frontiers. With these developments, American colonies became more important to their parent powers and more exposed to conflict between them.

BELOW *The Cathedral of Mexico City.*

CHAPTER 4

WARS AND REVOLUTIONS

During the half-century between 1776 and 1826, a great political transformation swept through the Americas. It began in 1776, when 13 of Britain's colonies declared their independence and created the United States of America. Between 1791 and 1804, war and revolution hit the heart of France's American empire, when the French Revolution changed the colony of Saint-Domingue into independent Haiti (1804). In the next decade, Spanish and Portuguese America were also battered by protracted political storms after Napoleon invaded Portugal and Spain, and tried to turn them into satellite states subordinate to France. This generated great turbulence on both sides of the Iberian Atlantic. In 1807, Portugal's royal dynasty fled to Brazil, where it set up a court in Rio de Janeiro and made Brazil a kingdom equal to Portugal. This allowed Portugal to retain control but opened a pathway to independence, which came in 1822, when Brazil turned itself into an independent constitutional monarchy, headed by a prince from Portugal's ruling dynasty. In 1808, Spain's Bourbon King, Fernando VII, was forced to abdicate, while Napoleon passed the throne to his brother Joseph Bonaparte. The ensuing wars in Spain and its American dominions shattered the old Spanish empire. By the early 1820s, most of Spanish America's regions had opted for independence, achieved after prolonged warfare.

These American revolutions had their own unique features, moulded by the societies, political systems and times in which they occurred. Nonetheless, they shared a basic characteristic. All arose, directly or indirectly, from the prolonged struggle between France, Spain and Britain to defend or extend their overseas empires.

COLONIAL CONFLICTS

The context for conflict was shaped by the realignment of the European powers at the beginning of the 18th century, following the death of Charles II, last of the Spanish Habsburgs. In 1700, the Spanish throne passed to the Bourbon prince Philip of Anjou, whose grandfather Louis XIV sought to strengthen France by dynastic alliance with Spain. The Bourbon succession was strongly opposed by the rising maritime powers of Britain and the Dutch Republic, which were determined to prevent France from controlling Spain and its empire. After the War of the Spanish Succession (1701–13), they agreed to the accession of Philip V of Spain on condition that he renounce any future claim to the throne of France. Although this frustrated Louis XIV's ambition to create a super state in which France and Spain were united under one king, it did not prevent further conflict. For another century, the alliance of France and Spain against Britain generated wars which were to transform the political geography of the Americas.

The first major colonial conflict was the War of Jenkins' Ear (1739–48), in which Britain attacked Spanish cities in the Caribbean and Pacific, while also using colonials to attack the French in Canada. The results fell short of expectations. Vice Admiral Edward Vernon captured Portobelo in Panama but failed to take the more important port of Cartagena de Indias in Colombia, where his besieging forces died in droves from tropical diseases. Commodore George Anson's plans to seize Spanish American ports along the Pacific coast

BELOW *The battle of Portobelo, 1739.*

LEFT *The Death of General Wolfe during the battle of the Plains of Abraham, 1759.*

failed too, though he redeemed himself by crossing the Pacific and capturing Spain's fleet of ships known as the Manila galleon off the Philippines, laden with Mexican silver en route to China. This war had, however, prepared the ground for the next. British traders continued to covet Spanish American markets and British settlers continued to press westwards against the barriers formed by French forts and indigenous protectorates. This led to a resumption of war with France in 1756 and with Spain in 1762.

The Seven Years' War (1756–63) marked a new stage in the struggle for empire. Britain and France engaged in global conflict in Europe, the Caribbean, North America, West Africa and India, and Spain joined in to protect its American colonies. This 'Great War for Empire' ended in a treaty that redrew the map of European colonial dominion in the Americas. France and Spain suffered crushing military defeats, which forced them to cede territories to Britain at the Treaty of Paris (1763). Spain gave up Florida in return for Havana, its vital stronghold in the Caribbean. France recovered the valuable sugar islands of Guadeloupe and Martinique but ceded Canada to the British, while also transferring Louisiana to Spain. According to Voltaire, the British capture of Canada was just the loss of 'a few acres of snow', but in fact it marked a significant change. Britain now became the major power in North America, with new responsibilities for defending and governing Canada, and the prospect of further expansion. Meanwhile, France's empire was reduced to its Caribbean islands (plus a couple of tiny islands in the Gulf of Saint Lawrence), in a highly compressed empire populated mainly by enslaved people.

The Seven Years' War had other repercussions, affecting relations inside empires. To meet the demands of war, British and Spanish governments aimed to make their colonies contribute more. This meant political change. The traditional light touch of government was replaced by a heavier hand and higher taxation, which soon provoked resentment. And, during the latter half of the 18th century, American dissatisfactions were reinforced by the diffusion of new ideas. American elites were exposed to the radical changes in philosophy, science and political economy that emanated from the European

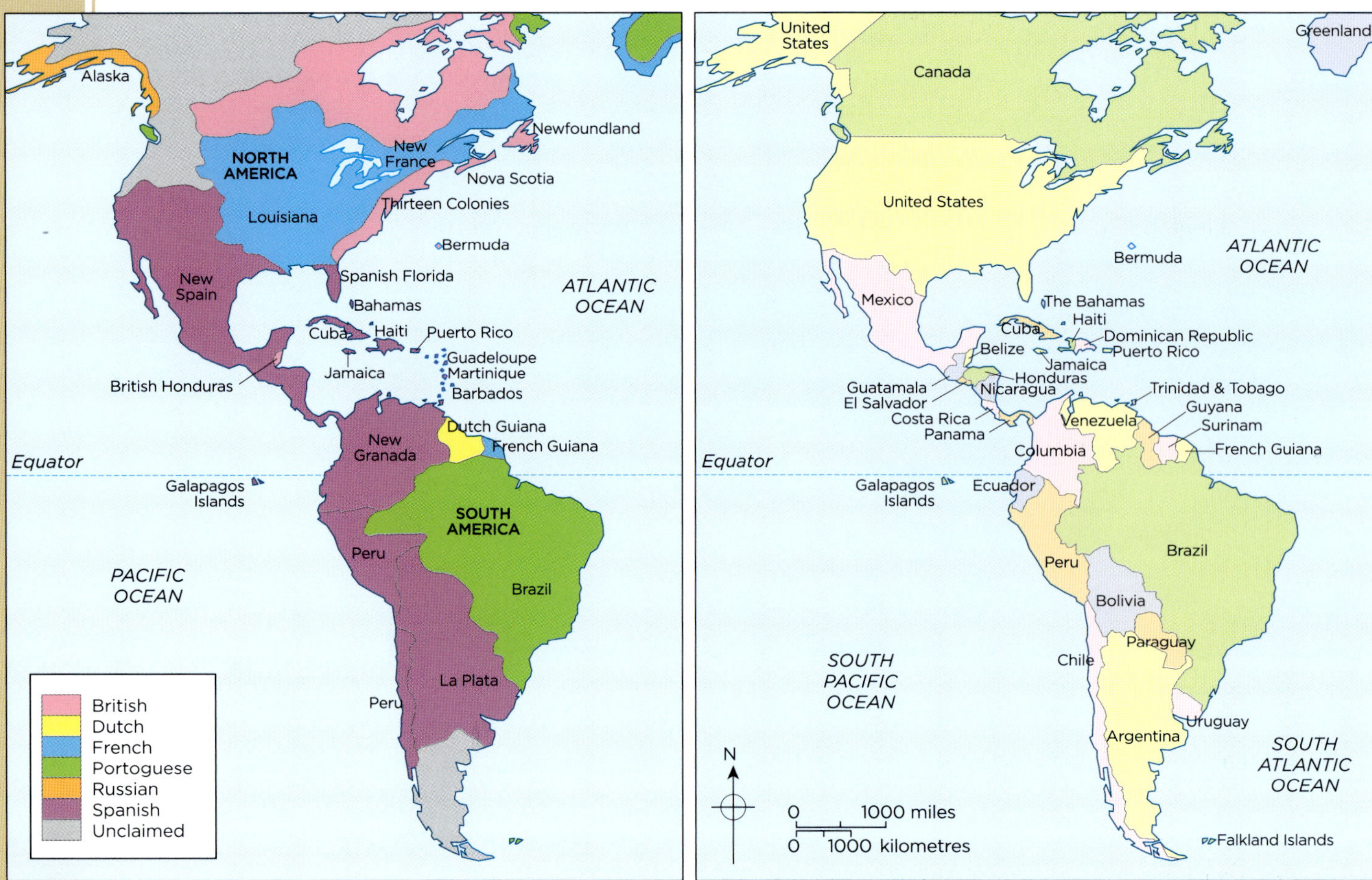

ABOVE *American colonies before 1763 and independent states in 1828.*

Enlightenment. Disseminated by books, intellectual salons and an incipient press, these ideas helped colonial elites to forge new ways of understanding their societies and seeing their futures. This blended with the cultivation of a new identity among Americans, a 'creole consciousness' that questioned ties with Europe and the future of empire. These developments did not immediately generate ambitions for independence, but they helped to form opinions that shaped American responses to the political crises that affected their empires from 1776 through to the mid-1820s.

THE AMERICAN REVOLUTION

The first sign of the effects of imperial rivalry on colonial loyalty came in North America, where Britain's territorial expansion after the Seven Years' War brought changes in colonial attitudes towards government from London. The deterioration of relations began during the 1760s, when London demanded that colonials accept closer regulation of their maritime commerce, curb their westward expansion and pay more taxes. Restrictions on westward movement, which London introduced in order to stabilize relations with indigenous peoples, was particularly irksome. Colonials who believed that victory over the French had opened limitless possibilities for internal expansion now faced curbs on their movement westwards, while also having to pay more taxes.

The Stamp Act of 1765 provoked the first protests. Starting in Virginia, several colonies combined to oppose the new tax, which was levied on publications and official papers produced in the territory. They did this on the grounds that it violated the rights of Englishmen to freedom from taxation not voted by their own representatives. Rioting crowds attacked tax-collectors, and a network of protest groups called the Sons of Liberty joined together to ensure that the tax was unworkable. The British government tried conciliation, but did not resolve the deeper problem. For colonials, the Stamp Act raised a fundamental issue of principle, crystallized in the doctrine of 'no taxation without representation', on which they were unwilling to compromise. Parliament was equally unready to concede on a point of principle and insisted on its sovereign right to legislate all colonial matters. Radicals spread the view that British government had become a despotism intent on destroying American liberty, and popular participation brought new, often poorer men into politics. So, when British ministers continued to impose laws aimed at forcing compliance, they faced growing opposition.

Resistance centred on Boston. In the 'Boston Tea Party' of 16 December 1773, protesters boarded East India Company tea ships and destroyed their cargoes, amidst public celebration. The British prime minister, Lord North, reacted by punishing Boston and the colony of Massachusetts. Issued in 1774, the Coercive Acts closed the port, transferred the seat of provincial government to Salem and amended the charter of Massachusetts to give the royal governor greater powers. Parliament also passed the Quebec Act, which gave Canada a nominated rather than an elected assembly. Taken together, these measures deepened Americans' suspicions that the crown was attempting to undermine their 'ancient liberties' as 'freeborn Englishmen'.

Lord North's strategy of isolating and intimidating Massachusetts did not blunt American resistance. Colonial assemblies in the Thirteen Colonies saw the threat, then convened a Continental Congress at Philadelphia, to devise a common policy for confronting British government. Proposals for conciliation were discussed in London in early 1775, but the response from Lord North and King George III was uncompromising. Parliament's right to tax the colonies was firmly restated and preparations were made

BELOW *The Boston Tea Party.*

Declaration of Independence, 4 July 1776

'We hold these truths to be self-evident that all men are created equal, that they are endowed by their Creator with certain unalienable rights, that among these are life, liberty, and the pursuit of happiness.'

LEFT The Declaration of Independence *by John Trumbull.*

to send soldiers to impose British sovereignty, by force if necessary.

British military mobilization triggered rapid responses, starting with armed skirmishes at Lexington and Concord, near Boston, in April 1775. Thus the colonies were already effectively at war with Britain when delegates from the colonial assemblies reconvened for the Second Continental Congress in May. In June, they considered resolutions declaring the independence of the united colonies, with a plan for their confederation and a decision to seek allies for war against Britain. They also voted to create and finance a Continental army, with George Washington as its commander-in-chief. On 4 July 1776, the delegates agreed on the Declaration of Independence, a statement of principle that confirmed the rejection of British rule that was already under way. War followed, to decide whether the colonies would capitulate to British authority or overthrow it.

Not all Americans joined the cause. From a population of some three million, about half a million loyalists supported British rule. The revolution was therefore a civil war as much as a war of independence and brought bloody confrontations between neighbours. The American patriots had some advantages. They held a defensive position some 4,800 km (3,000 miles) from Britain and could fight in a terrain ill-suited to European methods of warfare. They also had a rural population who were accustomed to using firearms, and who in some areas had experience of warfare. The Continental army was small and ill-trained, however, and it was not long before American military weaknesses were exposed. After an American force tried and failed to take Canada, the United States faced formidable threats: the full weight of Britain's military and naval supremacy, its far greater economic and financial resources and its extensive experience in war.

Britain's plan of action hinged on taking control of the eastern seaboard at three strategic points, then reaching inland to divide and crush the rebels. The first move was to take New England and isolate it from the Middle Atlantic colonies. The second was to take New York and dominate the Hudson Valley, so that British forces could be reinforced from Canada. The third was to establish a stronghold in the South by taking its major ports and controlling South Carolina, Georgia and East Florida.

These objectives were never fully secured. The northern approaches to the continent were taken without difficulty, and a key naval and military base established at Halifax in Nova Scotia. In late 1776, the British also took New York and defeated General Washington's army. But, having forced Washington into retreat, the British failed to finish him off. A year later, he

ABOVE *Map of the American War of Independence.*

scored a major victory by defeating General Burgoyne's attempt to take control of the Hudson Valley and isolate New England from the southern colonies. In October 1777, Washington surrounded Burgoyne's army at Saratoga and forced his surrender.

Washington's victory was important mainly because it persuaded France to join the war against Britain in the summer of 1778, in an alliance which provided money, arms, supplies and naval support. France's entry into the war also turned a local conflict into a global war. Britain now had to deploy its naval and military forces over a much broader front, including India and the West Indies. And, when Spain declared war against Britain in June 1779, the rebels acquired fresh financial and military aid. Henceforth, Britain's chances of reconquering its rebellious colonies were overshadowed by war with France, especially the presence of the French fleet.

As its enemies multiplied, Britain's military strategy came under increasing strain. British forces could not break American resistance by controlling a few cities along the

ABOVE The Surrender of General Cornwallis at Yorktown, 1781 *by John Trumbull.*

coast, since most of the colonial population lived outside them. It proved impossible to provide aid for loyalists or to conquer and hold the interior against American rebels who were at home in their environment and expert in guerrilla tactics. But most important was the difficulty of dealing with the French navy, which impeded the movement of British forces. In 1780, when Britain tried to shift its main army to Virginia, so that it might combine with the British army in New York, Washington countered by marching into Virginia, where he confronted General Cornwallis's army at Yorktown. He then called on the French navy to cut Cornwallis off from the sea, while his army blocked retreat by land. Besieged by Washington's superior forces and unable to escape by sea, Cornwallis capitulated in October 1781.

This reversal marked the beginning of the end for the British. British troops remained in the colonies but, over-extended by its global conflict, a war-weary Britain entered negotiations to end the conflict. In September 1783, the two sides concluded a formal treaty that separated the Thirteen Colonies from Britain and acknowledged their transformation into the United States of America. For the first time in the history of the Euro-American world, colonial peoples had permanently overthrown rule by a European government and created an independent state based on the sovereignty of the people. Colonials now had an independent state, delimited by borders on the Great Lakes and the Mississippi in the north and west, but with boundless possibilities for future expansion into the vast interior.

RIGHT *Portrait of George Washington.*

This extraordinary event reverberated around the Euro-Atlantic world. Its clearest consequences were in the Americas, where the nascent United States set itself apart from Europe and envisaged a future as a hemispheric power. Its ambitions were soon mirrored in westward expansion. In 1803, the US made the largest land purchase of all time, buying Louisiana from France at a bargain price and doubling the size of the United States at the stroke of a pen. The Louisiana Purchase changed American history. It opened the West beyond the Mississippi to settlers, fed visions of an 'Empire of Liberty' that crossed the continent, and launched a rise to international power. Florida was added in 1819, in a deal with Spain which extended the republic's southern reach and furthered its hold on the continent and saw the nation's emergence as the most important state in the Americas.

ABOVE *The handover ceremony of Louisiana from France.*

The repercussions of the American revolution were also acutely felt beyond the Americas, in a chain reaction which undermined the French and, later, Iberian empires. The first effects were in France, where the American Revolution did much to destabilize the old regime. Not only did the new republic provide a model for political change, but the war with Britain imposed such huge financial strains on the state that the king opened a path to reform. Bankrupted by war, Louis XVI was forced in 1788 to call the Estates General, the body for representing the nation which had been dormant since 1614. The ensuing process for electing representatives transformed French politics, by raising expectations of reform across social classes. In 1789, the deputies of the Estates General moved on to a revolutionary path. They reconstituted the Estates General as a National Assembly, with powers to make laws and direct government, and issued the Declaration of the Rights of Man, which announced the freedom and equality of citizens in a constitutional monarchy. More radical reform followed. After Louis XVI tried and failed to enlist foreign aid for a counter-revolution in 1791, he was arrested and the monarchy abolished. In 1792, the National Assembly (renamed the Convention), created the first Republic of France and in 1793 executed Louis XVI and his queen. France now entered a prolonged period of war with other European powers, mixed with rebellion and insurgency in its Caribbean colonies, especially Saint-Domingue.

THE HAITIAN REVOLUTION

Haiti rose from the ruins of Saint-Domingue, the epitome of an 18th-century slave society. Situated at the western end of Hispaniola and bordering with Spanish Santo Domingo, its mountainous lands were separated by fertile plains dedicated to cultivating sugar, coffee, cotton and indigo, using African enslaved labour. The northern plain was home to one of richest towns in the Caribbean, in the regional capital of Cap Français (modern Cap Haitien), while the south and west had several port towns, of which the most important was Port-au-Prince. This was the centre of royal government, which was dominated by royal appointees sent from France – although in practice a small minority

of rich planters imposed their own systems of control over the majority population of enslaved Africans.

As its population grew to more than half a million people in the 1780s, Saint-Domingue became a more volatile society, riven by antagonisms between racial groups. Its economic growth rested heavily on imports of enslaved Africans, financed by a booming plantation agriculture, and the enslaved formed by far the largest element of the total population, at around 450,000 people. The white population was also growing rapidly. Following an influx of poorer whites (*petits blancs*) after France lost Canada in the Seven Years' War, it stood at around 30,000 by 1789. The *petits blancs* were, however, facing growing competition from the rapidly rising population of *gens de couleur*, free people of colour, who almost equalled whites in number. In the south and west, they composed nearly half of the free population, employed in a broad range of trading, artisanal and farming activities. Some of them were landowners, with slaves of their own.

White dominance over the enslaved population relied heavily on cooperation from free people of colour, who identified more closely with whites than with Black enslaved people. In a potentially combustible slave society, the planter class were always vigilant for signs of rebellion from below, especially on rural plantations. Fearful of poisoning by enslaved workers and anxious to prevent uprisings and escapes, planters employed a regime of extreme repression, from floggings to outright murder. They used the instruments of local government, too, in militias and rural constabulary, to invigilate and intimidate. Usually composed of free men of colour led by white officers, the militias reflect the cooperation of free non-whites in sustaining the colonial regime.

LEFT A Fête on a Plantation in Saint-Domingue, *by François-Jules Bourgoin, c.1800.*

That balance of power started to shift in 1789, when the upheaval in Paris acted as a catalyst for change in the French Caribbean. Political destabilization sprang from the decision of the National Assembly in Paris to allow the colonies to send representatives to join its deliberations. This gesture of inclusion was designed to preserve French rule and was limited to electors and deputies chosen from the white ruling group. This was soon exposed as a mistake, as it stirred dissent among free people of colour, who demanded equal rights of representation.

The emergence of free people of colour on to the political stage stemmed from demands for social respect which had grown louder during the later 1700s, when, as they grew more numerous and prosperous, they became more resentful of white privileges. The onset of the French Revolution encouraged their aspirations. In France, the 'Society of Friends of the Blacks', founded in 1788, became a voice for free men of colour who resided in Paris. They demanded representation in the new politics and sparked direct action in Saint-Domingue, under the banner of the Rights of Man. In 1790, Vincent Ogé, a wealthy mulatto planter who resided in Paris, returned to Saint-Domingue with a plan to seize power in the north. His rebellion was quickly quashed and followed by a wave of executions, in which Ogé was himself put to death by being broken on the wheel.

Repression solved nothing, however, and the *gens de couleur* continued their confrontations with whites. The French National Assembly attempted to calm the situation by prescribing legal equality for propertied free men of colour, but this diluted version of civil rights was still anathema to whites. Even the *petits blancs* who embraced the revolutionary idea of universal male suffrage balked at including non-whites, who might outvote them. This division over who should have citizenship rights had momentous consequences. It not only generated armed conflict between whites and free people of colour but also provided opportunities for enslaved people to raise rebellions of their own.

BELOW
Vincent Ogé.

Although the enslaved were totally excluded from participation in politics, news of revolution in France was quickly disseminated among them. Enslaved people on plantations came from different parts of Africa but had long been able to develop a wider sense of community through a common language (Kreyòl) and shared religious practices, particularly vodou. This helped to develop a sense of solidarity and provided valuable networks for gathering information about the world. In fact, the social gatherings of plantation slaves on Sundays were an important medium for discussing

ABOVE *The Battle of Crête-à-Pierrot, 4 March 1802, during the Haitian Revolution.*

and spreading news of the revolution in France, as well as a base for organizing and coordinating rebellion in August 1791.

The first slave rebellions erupted on many of the large sugar plantations on the northern plain, fuelled by rumours that whites were concealing orders from the king to improve their lives. Slaves rose against their owners and administrators, burned their crops, seized and sacked their buildings, killed many whites, and even launched an attack on the city of Cap Français. Smaller rebellions broke out in southern Saint-Domingue near Port-au-Prince, but it was on the northern plain that whites faced their greatest threat, mainly from slave forces led by Jean-François Papillon and Georges Biassou, and later by Toussaint Louverture. They were skilled leaders who, helped by recently enslaved Africans with military experience from Kongolese wars, gradually succeeded in creating disciplined insurgent armies.

The rebels' strength was insurgent rather than positional warfare and, after failing to take the ports, they had to confront a counterattack from France. In 1792, the National

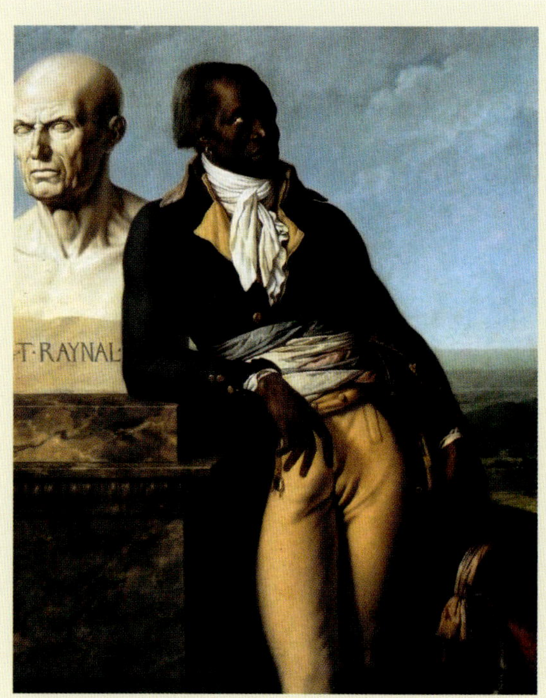

Jean-Baptiste Belley

Jean-Baptiste Belley, who fought with enslaved rebels, was one of three deputies elected to the Convention in Paris by the northern region of Saint-Domingue in 1793. He spoke in favour of the abolition of slavery in the 1794 Convention.

LEFT *Jean-Baptiste Belley.*

Assembly in Paris sent Civil Commissioners to take command of government, backed by a new Governor General with 6,000 troops. Commissioner Léger-Félicité Sonthonax took responsibility for the north, Commissioner Étienne Polverel for the south, and they aimed to reimpose French authority by using free people of colour as an ally against rebellious whites and Blacks.

Rebuilding French government was hindered by foreign invaders, who allied with France's enemies. When Britain and Spain went to war with France in 1793, their attacks on Saint-Domingue prolonged the internal war which France was trying to end. In the north, Spanish forces supported rebels led by Biassou, Papillon and Louverture against the French republic and its local allies. In the south and west, the British allied with royalists against the French republicans, who included a considerable cohort of free people of colour led by the French-educated mulatto, André Rigaud. These wars changed French policy fundamentally, for they persuaded the republican commissioners that the best way to restore French sovereignty was to abolish slavery. This was ratified by the French Convention in February 1794, which proclaimed the unity of France and the colonies under one set of universal laws and ended racial hierarchy and slavery.

This unprecedented decision brought rebellious slaves back to the French side, guided by Toussaint Louverture. Though sceptical about French intentions, Louverture decided that the best chance for freedom was to make terms with the French. He therefore turned against the Spanish, consolidated control of the north, and backed the French authorities in the city of Cap Français. Meanwhile, André Rigaud extended French authority over the south, where the British alienated potential Black allies by showing their intention to restore slavery. Harassed by Rigaud and Louverture, British military strength was also depleted by the effects of yellow fever, 'the black vomit', which cut swathes through their ranks. Unable to secure reinforcements from Jamaica, Britain negotiated with Louverture to allow a peaceful withdrawal in 1798. They signed a secret treaty, in which Louverture

secured his key aims. The British affirmed that they would cease to interfere in Saint-Domingue, while Louverture promised that he would not export his revolution to Jamaica. He also secured the freedom of the enslaved people who had fought with the British by allowing them to remain in Haiti rather than returning to Jamaica.

Toussaint Louverture's success against the British was an important step towards stabilizing Saint-Domingue under his authority. But domestic conflict continued. The old colony was now divided between a Black-controlled north under Louverture and a mulatto-dominated south led by Rigaud, both with ambitions for supreme leadership. They clashed in the 'War of the Knives' (1799–1800), which left Louverture as the effective leader of the whole of Saint-Domingue. In this new setting, Louverture, backed by officers such as the ex-slave Jean-Jacques Dessalines and the free mulatto Henri Christophe, tried to achieve a stable power base by proclaiming loyalty to France and rebuilding the plantation system under new ownership, using forced labour to replace slavery. He promulgated Haiti's first constitution in 1801, in the hope of entrenching his own authority as Governor General under the umbrella of the French republic. He ended slavery and called for equal civil rights for all, while taking strong, centralized powers for himself, with a view to reviving the trading economy and restoring social order.

Although Louverture stopped short of independence, his relations with Napoleon were soured by Louverture's ambition for political autonomy and concentrated power.

ABOVE, LEFT
Toussaint Louverture meets the British general Thomas Maitland in 1798.

ABOVE, RIGHT
General Leclerc's campaigns in Haiti, 1802–3.

Toussaint Louverture

Toussaint Louverture was born in 1743 of enslaved African parents on the Bréda sugar plantation, on the northern plain of Saint-Domingue. Called Toussaint Bréda, he learned to read and write, became a plantation supervisor and, thanks to his personal talents, was freed aged about 30. He continued to live on the estate, where he had relatives among the enslaved community, acquired property and rented enslaved workers. He joined the slave rebellion led by Jean-François Papillon and Georges Biassou shortly after it broke out in August 1791 and rose to military and political leadership. He took – or won – the name Louverture (the 'opening') from his ability to seize political advantage from fast-moving military campaigns and for his role in exploiting the conflicts between France, Britain and Spain. He became an almost absolute ruler of Saint-Domingue until he was deported to France in June 1802, where he died in prison the following year. Toussaint was one of the most celebrated leaders of independence in the Americas, rightly regarded as the New World's greatest leader in the fight against enslavement.

LEFT *Toussaint Louverture from an 1802 French print.*

Angered by 'this gilded African', Napoleon despatched General Charles Leclerc to Saint-Domingue with an army of 30,000 men, later reinforced by thousands more, to reimpose colonial rule.

When he first arrived in February 1802, Leclerc sought a political solution by endorsing the freeing of the enslaved and promising Louverture's leading officers that they would retain their ranks in the French army. In return, Louverture stepped aside – and was promptly arrested and sent to France. Dessalines and Christophe were integrated into Leclerc's army and many freemen of colour and freed enslaved people welcomed the chance to enjoy freedom and the plunder of war. But rumours that France intended to reinstate slavery soon undermined the pact with Leclerc. An insurgency broke out in the north, under Dessalines' direction, and Leclerc responded with a bloody war of reprisals. A French soldier recounted mass executions of Blacks and mulattos by burning, hanging and drowning, in a brutal war of annihilation that killed thousands.

Leclerc's ferocity did not save his army. About two-thirds of his soldiers, including the general himself, died from tropical diseases. His successor the Vicomte de Rochambeau lacked the resources to fight on and, when the mulatto leader Alexandre Pétion defeated the French in the south and allied with Dessalines, French plans to recolonize collapsed. In November 1803, Rochambeau evacuated the remnants of his army, leaving Haiti finally free. On 1 January 1804, Jean-Jacques Dessalines declared the independence of Haiti, the indigenous name for the island, before crowning himself as Emperor Jean-Jacques I in September 1804.

Haitian independence was an extraordinary revolution, more like the French Revolution than the American uprising of 1776. For, with dramatic political change came a fundamental social change, based on the abolition of slavery and an ensuing inversion of colonial white supremacy. In 1805, Dessalines introduced a constitution with eminently liberal principles. He abolished slavery, made all citizens equal before the law and ended distinctions based on colour. At the same time, he banned Europeans from holding property and sought to expel them from the new nation. Anti-white pogroms followed. In Cap Français, 90 per cent of the French population were killed in a single day. In Port-au-Prince, 800 were killed in a week. Dessalines justified these massacres as righteous revenge, a repayment of 'war for war, crime for crime, outrage for outrage'. 'Yes', he declared, 'I have saved my country. I have avenged America.'

BELOW *The massacres in Haiti, from Marcus Rainsford,* An Historical Account of the Black Empire of Hayti *(1805).*

The Haitian Revolution sent shockwaves throughout the Atlantic world, especially in the Caribbean societies which had good reason to fear subversion among their enslaved populations. To prevent it, the British and Spanish tried to isolate Haiti from contact with their colonies, as did the slave owners of the United States. This was successful in so far as slave rebellions were nowhere repeated on the scale of Haiti. In fact, the plantation economies of Brazil and Cuba that operated entirely on enslaved labour were strengthened by the destruction of Saint-Domingue, which boosted demand for their sugar and coffee. That said, the Haitian Revolution contributed to ending slavery by revealing its dangers and highlighting its immorality. In 1807, the British Parliament abolished the slave trade and much of Spanish America abolished slavery during the 1820s.

SPANISH AMERICAN INDEPENDENCE

At the time of the American War of Independence (1776–83), symptoms of discontent with imperial government also appeared in Spanish America. Under King Carlos III (1759–88), Spain's efforts to reform colonial military systems, commercial regulations and taxation generated strong regional opposition. The first sharp reaction against these Bourbon reforms occurred in 1765, when people in the city of Quito rebelled against tax changes imposed without negotiation or conciliation. More formidable rebellions followed when Carlos III initiated a general overhaul of government, aimed at exerting closer control and taking more taxation.

ABOVE *The rebel Gabriel Condorcanqui, who took the title Túpac Amaru II, 1780.*

In 1781, rebellion broke out in Andean areas of New Granada (modern Colombia), with armed inhabitants, or *comuneros*, insisting that the crown retract its reforms. Without arms to suppress the rebellion, the authorities negotiated with the rebels, agreed to their terms and let the uprising end peacefully. More threatening rebellions took place in the Andean highlands of southern Peru and in neighbouring Upper Peru (now Bolivia). Led by Túpac Amaru, an Andean leader who claimed descent from the last of the Inka, these rebellions mobilized large indigenous communities in a war against whites. They were, however, only a temporary challenge to Spanish rule. Resistance faded when it was confronted by military repression, followed by a purge of indigenous leaders and the systematic suppression of Inka culture.

Dissent found other channels, too. During the later decades of the 18th century, fresh ways of thinking drawn from the European Enlightenment broadened political horizons and sharpened political ambitions among the educated elites. Exposure to innovative ideas about science, political economy and education stimulated a new quest for knowledge and spurred creole critiques of Spanish government. In the closing decades of the century, criticism took a new turn when the examples of the American and French revolutions inspired rebellions. In Brazil, creole conspirators at Minas Gerais were arrested in 1789 for plotting to set up an independent republic modelled on the United States. A decade later, a group of Blacks and free people of colour, some of whom had read French revolutionary writings, decided that it was 'necessary for all to become Frenchmen', so that 'everything being levelled in a popular revolution', racial privilege and

Francisco de Miranda (1750–1816)

Miranda was born into a wealthy family and educated in Caracas. He went to Spain in 1771 to complete his education and joined the Spanish army. As a Spanish officer, he fought in Morocco and against the British in the American War of Independence. His career in the Spanish army ended when he was accused of espionage on behalf of the British and in 1783 he fled to the United States. There, he mixed with some of the most important politicians of the time, including Washington, Jefferson and Hamilton, before moving on to London in 1785. In London, his American contacts provided introductions which facilitated extensive travel in Europe, including visits to the courts of Prussia, Sweden and Russia. Catherine the Great provided him with a Russian passport and diplomatic cover that allowed him to evade his Spanish pursuers. From 1791, Miranda took part in the French Revolution, serving as a general at the Battle of Valmy and in the Flanders campaign. Amid the power struggles of the Paris revolutionaries, he was arrested and narrowly escaped execution before taking refuge in Britain. In London, he lobbied politicians and government ministers to give British support to his plans for revolution in Spanish America. Without much backing, he launched a private expedition to liberate Venezuela in 1806, with volunteers recruited in New York. After its failure, he again sought refuge with the British, first in Trinidad and then in London. As soon as rebellion broke out in Caracas in 1810, he joined with fellow revolutionaries such as Simón Bolívar in declaring Venezuela's independence. He was a leader among the coterie of creole revolutionaries who founded the first Venezuelan republic and was given dictatorial powers when it began to fail. In 1812, the republic collapsed and Bolívar and other revolutionary leaders blamed Miranda. His capitulation to the royalists was regarded as a cowardly act of treason, and his colleagues blocked his escape from Venezuela. He was arrested by the Spanish authorities and taken to a prison in Cádiz, where he died four years later.

LEFT *Francisco de Miranda.*

LEFT The Oath of the Cortes de Cádiz in 1810 *by José Casado del Alisal (1863).*

discrimination would end and 'all would be rich'. The conspiracy was betrayed and several conspirators were hung, drawn and quartered. In Spanish America, small and abortive revolutionary conspiracies also occurred in the 1790s, among both whites and free people of colour who dreamed of applying American and French revolutionary principles in their own societies. The Venezuelan creole Francisco de Miranda even landed an armed expedition on the shores of Venezuela in 1806, hoping it would trigger revolution in his homeland.

These outbreaks showed the penetration of revolutionary ideas from America and France, but they lacked any substantial social base and had no serious prospect of overthrowing colonial rule. When change came, it was a consequence of collapse at the centre rather than insurrection in the colonies. Revolution stemmed from the crises caused by Napoleon's invasions of Portugal and Spain in 1807–8, events that caused colonial elites to question the viability of the systems of governance which they had accepted for so long and which had provided them with an unprecedented opportunity to seize autonomy.

Napoleon's overthrow of the Bourbon monarchy had far-reaching repercussions. When he deposed the Bourbon king Fernando VII in 1808, Napoleon put his brother Joseph on the throne, as King José I, and envisaged a smooth transition to French suzerainty. The contrary occurred. Many Spaniards recoiled against French rule, declared their loyalty to the exiled Fernando VII, and supported emergency governments (juntas) raised in cities and provinces. Some also joined in guerrillas, local wars fought by irregular troops against the French occupiers. Military resistance was paralleled by political revolution. The

juntas consolidated in a single Central Junta, followed by a Council of Regency which convened a Cortes in 1810 and thus initiated a period of radical reform.

The Cortes was a historic parliamentary body, made moribund by the Habsburgs and Bourbons but now reconstituted by Spanish liberals who claimed that the sovereignty of the monarch had reverted to the 'people' in the absence of the king. They set up the Cortes to express the people's will, in the form of a modern national assembly composed of deputies who represented the 'Spanish nation'. The Cortes met at Cádiz in September 1810, in one body with members who represented the entire Spanish world, including Spanish America. Its deputies demanded that Fernando VII return to the throne at the head of a new constitutional monarchy, designed to govern Spain and its overseas dominions as one 'Spanish Nation', in which American provinces would be equal to those of Spain.

ABOVE *Miguel Hidalgo.*

Their promulgation of a constitution in 1812 was an extraordinary political moment. It turned subjects of the crown into citizens with individual rights, including the right to elect representatives to make laws on their behalf. Freedom of expression and a free press were also guaranteed by law. In Spanish America, these changes had even more radical implications than in Spain, as they extended citizenship to indigenous people and to free people of colour. People of African descent were excluded, except for the special few who showed 'merit and virtue'. The obligation of indigenous people to pay tribute and provide forced labour was also ended, though slavery remained legal. However, despite their liberal intentions, the deputies at Cádiz recognized that Spain's economic future depended on colonial resources. They therefore made sure that Spanish American representation in the Cortes was smaller than Spain's, despite having a larger population.

While the Cádiz Cortes debated, many towns and cities in Spanish America were moving towards independence. In the absence of the king and amid uncertainty about the fate of Spain's new regime, many creoles decided in 1810 that they should have their own governing juntas, like those in the mother country. Numerous towns and cities set up juntas to govern in the king's name, and though not all were successful some became the bases of autonomous governments. In Venezuela, New Granada (Colombia), Río de la Plata (Argentina) and Chile, royal officials were thrown out and replaced by creole leaders who, though they initially proclaimed loyalty to Fernando VII, soon broke with Spain.

BELOW *José Maria Morelos.*

Spanish officials held on to the oldest viceroyalties. In Peru, loyalism was strengthened by military force and fears of revolt by indigenous people, and the Viceroyalty became a bastion against revolution. Its viceroys repelled incursions by armies sent by revolutionary Buenos Aires and protected royal rule in Peru, Bolivia and Chile. In New Spain, loyalism also prevailed in embattled conditions. In 1810, the creole priest Miguel Hidalgo raised a formidable insurrection among indigenous people and free people of colour in northern-central Mexico. Though ended by his defeat and execution, Hidalgo's rebellion sparked a widespread insurgency led by the mestizo priest José Maria Morelos, which posed a serious challenge to viceregal government. However,

ABOVE *Battle of the Palo River, New Granada, 1815.*

Mexico City and other important cities remained in loyalist hands and the viceroy's larger and better-organized forces succeeded in defeating Morelos in 1815 and repressing the remaining pockets of insurgency.

Beyond Peru and Mexico, meanwhile, movements for independence sprang up throughout South America. Nascent republics first appeared in Venezuela and several regions in Colombia. They were mostly small city-states and soon fell prey to internal discord and civil war, caused by resistance from loyalists and by rivalries between themselves. These divisions undermined their military effectiveness and by 1815 royalist forces, made mostly of Americans, had defeated most of them. Buenos Aires was unconquered but its future looked bleak, as armies advanced into Argentina from the royalist stronghold in Peru.

Changes in Europe also hindered movements for independence. Fernando VII returned to the Spanish throne in 1814 and quickly overturned the constitutional regime set up at Cádiz. This was in tune with the times. After Napoleon's defeat, the European

Simón Bolívar

Bolívar was born, on 24 July 1783, to wealth and privilege, the son of an old creole family in Venezuela, who owned plantations, mines, houses in Caracas and many enslaved people. His liberal education and travels in Europe introduced him to the political thinkers of France and Britain and inspired his fight for liberty against Spain in the name of reason, freedom and progress. Without formal military training, Bolívar became a great general who played a prime role in the liberation of South America, from his first rebellion in Venezuela in 1810 until the surrender of the last Spanish viceroy in 1824. Such was his influence that his aide and chronicler, the Irishman General Daniel F. O'Leary, likened his death to, 'the last embers of an expiring volcano, the dust of the Andes still on his garments'.

LEFT *Simón Bolívar.*

powers favoured the restoration of monarchy in Spain and the return of its colonies, while the end of war in Spain also released armies for deployment in America. In these new circumstances, the king planned to reconquer his overseas territories, beginning with Venezuela and New Granada in the north, and Buenos Aires in the south. In 1816, General Pablo Morillo landed a large army in Venezuela and proceeded to reconquer New Granada. The expedition to Buenos Aires was delayed, for lack of sufficient resources.

RIGHT *José de San Martin.*

Ferdinand's plan to combine reconquest and reconciliation was unsuccessful. The arrival of a Spanish army stalled independence movements in northern Spanish America, but military occupation was insufficient to overcome them. From 1815, revolutionary leaders in Venezuela and Argentina launched wars of liberation which gradually loosened Spain's grip on its colonies. In Venezuela, Simón Bolívar emerged as a paramount political and military leader.

Together with other Venezuelan warlords, he built disciplined and capable military forces, reinforced by imported arms and foreign soldiers of fortune (such as his 'British Legion'). In 1819, Bolívar defeated the viceroy of New Granada near Bogotá, then consolidated the liberation of Venezuela and New Granada by creating the Republic of Colombia. From there, he moved south against royalist governments in Ecuador, Peru and Upper Peru (later Bolivia).

The revolutionaries of Buenos Aires also participated in the liberation of South America. In 1817, José de San Martin, a veteran of war against the French in Spain, assembled an army which he led from Argentina across the Andes to conquer the royalist army of Chile. He placed Bernardo O'Higgins in command of government, while mounting a seaborne assault on royalist Peru. From the shores of the Pacific, San Martin fought his way to Lima, where he proclaimed Peruvian independence in 1821. However, this was an incomplete revolution, as the Spanish viceroy had retreated to Cusco and still controlled Andean Peru. To overcome this final hurdle, San Martin agreed to leave Bolívar to command the campaign against the remaining Spanish strongholds in the southern Andes and withdrew to exile in France.

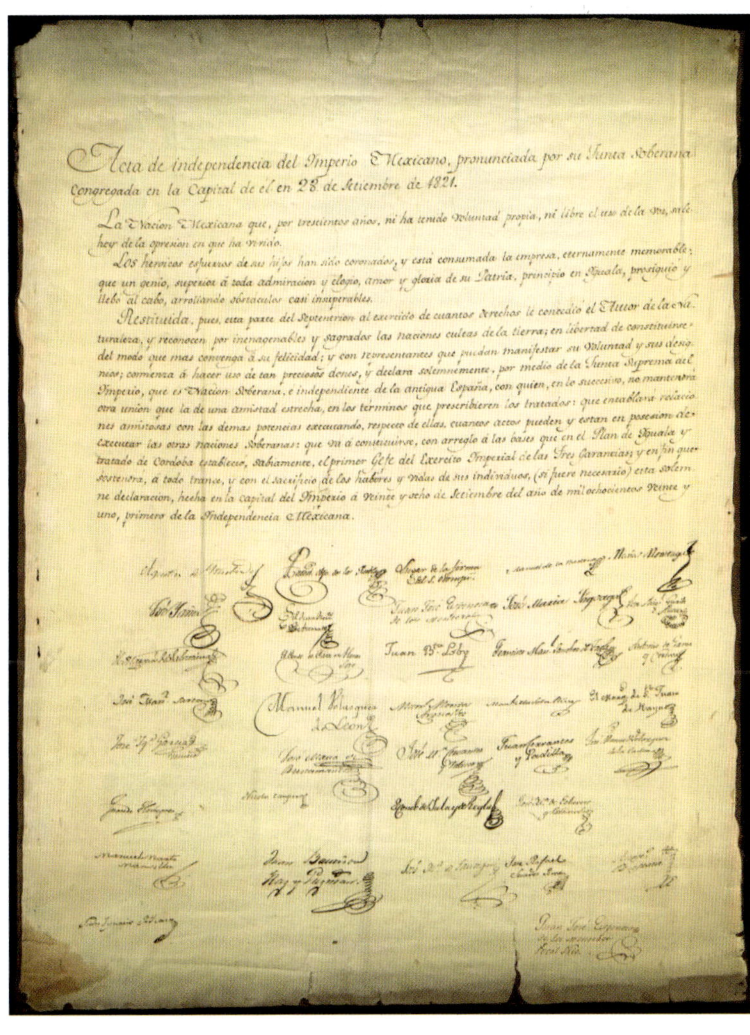

Acta de independencia del Imperio Mexicano, pronunciada por su Junta Soberana Congregada en la Capital de él en 28 de Setiembre de 1821.

La Nacion Mexicana que, por trescientos años, ni ha tenido voluntad propia, ni libre el uso de la voz, sale hoy de la opresion en que ha vivido.

Los heroicos esfuerzos de sus hijos han sido coronados, y está consumada la empresa, eternamente memorable, que un genio, superior á toda admiracion y elogio, amor y gloria de su Patria, principió en Iguala, prosiguió y llevó al cabo, arrollando obstáculos casi insuperables.

Restituida, pues, esta parte del Septentrion al exercicio de cuantos derechos le concedió el Autor de la Naturaleza, y reconocen por inenagenables y sagrados las naciones cultas de la tierra; en libertad de constituirse del modo que mas convenga á su felicidad; y con representantes que puedan manifestar su voluntad y sus designios; comienza á hacer uso de tan preciosos dones, y declara solemnemente, por medio de la Junta Suprema del Imperio, que es Nacion Soberana, é independiente de la antigua España, con quien, en lo sucesivo, no mantendrá otra union que la de una amistad estrecha, en los términos que prescribieren los tratados: que entablará relaciones amistosas con las demas potencias executando, respecto de ellas, cuantos actos pueden y estan en posesion de executar las otras naciones Soberanas: que va á constituirse, con arreglo á las bases que en el Plan de Iguala y tratado de Córdoba estableció, sabiamente, el primer Gefe del Exército Imperial de las Tres Garantías; y en fin que sostendrá, á todo trance, y con el sacrificio de los haberes y vidas de sus individuos, (si fuere necesario) esta solemne declaracion, hecha en la capital del Imperio á veinte y ocho de Setiembre del año de mil ochocientos veinte y uno, primero de la Independencia Mexicana.

ABOVE *Declaration of Independence of the Mexican Empire, 1821.*

Bolívar's actions exemplified the importance of military leadership in South American independence, for he played a key role in Spain's defeats. His armies were small by European standards (never more than 6,000 men), but they gradually gained an edge on royalist forces, helped by the influx of arms and men after the demobilization of European armies in 1815. And, as they gained territory, Bolívar and his lieutenants had new platforms for advance, built on local bases of support and resources. The liberators were helped, too, by events in Spain. In 1820, the army regiments which concentrated at Cádiz (for the long-delayed expedition against Buenos Aires) mutinied, sparking a series of provincial revolts that forced Fernando VII to reinstate the Cortes and the 1812 Constitution, together with other liberal reforms. This sudden change of regime provoked disagreement among officials in the colonies which were still under Spanish control and, as Madrid became an increasingly weak and unstable centre, the balance of opinion and power in Spanish America shifted away from Spain.

The final stages of the struggle were played out in Mexico and Peru. In 1821, Spain lost Mexico, when the creole army commander Agustín de Iturbide reacted against the introduction of Spanish liberal reforms by seeking independence. Backed by elements in the royalist army and supported by various political allies, Iturbide planned to replace Spanish rule with a constitutional monarchy under a European prince. On achieving

ABOVE *The Battle of Ayacucho.*

independence, Iturbide decided to take the throne himself and in 1822 was crowned Emperor of Mexico. His reign was short. In 1823, he was ousted and succeeded by Mexico's first republic.

The fall of Spain's largest and richest colonies was followed by the remaining redoubts in South America. In 1824, Bolívar's compatriot José de Sucre defeated the last viceroy of Peru at the Battle of Ayacucho; in 1825, his armies took Upper Peru, the last regional bastion of Spanish rule, which Sucre promptly renamed 'Bolivia' in his commander's honour. A pocket of resistance remained in the fortress at Callao on the coast near Lima. When gone, Spain's American empire was whittled down to Cuba and Puerto Rico.

BRAZILIAN INDEPENDENCE

Brazil's independence, like that of Spanish America, sprang from the crisis caused by Napoleon's overthrow of Iberian governments. But, unlike Spanish Americans, Brazilians did not immediately challenge imperial rule. The arrival of the Portuguese prince regent, Dom João, together with the royal family and royal court, took Brazil in an entirely new direction. The prince regent's willingness to make concessions to the land- and slave-owning elites – such as free trade with Britain, aristocratic titles and posts in royal government – helped secure their loyalty, as did fears, natural to a slave society, that political disturbance might trigger rebellions of the kind that occurred in Haiti. In these circumstances, Portugal's crisis did not foster Brazil's independence. On the contrary, the transfer of the Portuguese court to Rio de Janeiro effectively turned Brazil from a colony into its own metropolis. In 1815, Dom João decreed that Brazil was a kingdom equal in importance to Portugal, a move that underlined how important it was for Portugal's survival.

The new regime did not satisfy all Brazilians. In 1817, it was challenged by a republican uprising in Pernambuco, which reflected provincial resentment towards the many immigrants and soldiers who had arrived from Portugal. However, when independence came, it was precipitated by events in Portugal rather than republican rebellion in Brazil. Portugal's revolution of 1820, which introduced a constitutional monarchy similar to Spain's, disrupted the existing arrangement in which the Portuguese monarchy had its headquarters in Brazil. Fearing they would lose their position of influence, the elites in Rio de Janeiro resisted inclusion in the liberal constitutionalist regime run by the Cortes in Lisbon, which promised unpalatable reforms. The catalyst for independence came when João returned to Lisbon and left his son Dom Pedro to act as temporary regent in his place. When the Cortes pressured for his return too, Brazilians saw this as a signal that Portugal intended to return them to a colonial status. The leading provinces united in opposition and, after much manoeuvring, Pedro bowed to their will and declared the independence of Brazil in September 1822. After a short war against Portugal, which lacked the means for military conquest, he was acclaimed Pedro I, Emperor of Brazil.

If Brazil's transition to independence avoided the prolonged warfare which afflicted much of Spanish America, it was mainly because the Brazilian elites were more united than their Spanish American counterparts. Their solidarity rested on similar economic interests, based in the plantation economy and sugar trade, and they were acutely aware that political disunity at the top might unleash the discontents of much larger populations of Blacks and people of colour. Elite unity was compounded by the advantages of institutional continuity, embodied in the bifurcation of the Portuguese monarchy. When King João returned to Portugal, he was able to pass his authority to his son Dom Pedro, who used it to secure his own position as a fully fledged independent monarch.

CONCLUSION

The establishment of independent American states between 1776 and 1825 had historic effects. The emergence of new states not only ended great empires and relegated Spain and Portugal to the ranks of minor European powers, it also created a group of republican American states which stood apart from the reactionary monarchies of post-Napoleonic Europe and were free to pursue their own purposes.

The European presence did not disappear completely. While France faded from the American scene, Britain kept territories in Canada and the Caribbean and continued to exert a strong influence over the United States. Portugal maintained cultural and social ties with Brazil, which drew its monarchs from the same royal family. Spain kept Cuba and Puerto Rico and harboured hopes of restoring parts of its lost empire, although schemes for retaking its colonies came to nothing. Spain's cultural legacy was nonetheless immense and did much to shape the Hispanic American republics after they had broken away from colonial rule.

RIGHT *Pedro I proclaims the independence of Brazil.*

CHAPTER 5

THE CHALLENGE OF INDEPENDENCE

On achieving independence, political leaders in the Americas faced a common challenge: how to create a new future from a colonial past. Should they become republics or monarchies? Should they centralize or disperse national political power? Who should be citizens, who should vote and what kinds of civil liberties should they enjoy? What was the place of indigenous nations? Should slavery be abolished, and if so, how? These issues were made more problematic by the unstable conditions that arose from the dispersion of authority during the wars of independence, the widespread use of violence for political ends and the emergence of military men as powerful figures. Unsurprisingly, many independent states witnessed internal power struggles, as competing groups disputed over where power should be concentrated, a problem which often led to civil wars.

FIRST CONSTITUTION, FIRST REPUBLIC

The United States was the first to confront the problems involved in establishing a new country. After claiming the right to rule themselves, Americans began to create new institutions for self-government during the war with Britain. The legislative assemblies of rebel states adopted their first constitutions and came together in a confederation to coordinate political and military resistance. Their constitutions set out the basics, in texts which defined the institutions of government, the relationship between the executive, legislature and judiciary, and explained the rights and responsibilities of citizens.

Although the state constitutions varied, they shared a dislike of centralized authority and a preference for liberty exercised locally. In reaction against the power of the crown, they reduced the power of the executive, increased that of the legislature and introduced the principle that all political office should be subject to elections. Most followed British traditions by establishing legislatures with upper and lower houses. But they also innovated. State constitutions clearly defined the legal rights of the citizen, guaranteeing freedom of speech and assembly, freedom of religion, the right to bear arms and so on. They also made politics more socially inclusive by giving the vote to men who had previously been unqualified and ruling that representatives in both houses should be chosen by vote. The degree of democratization varied. In most states existing property requirements for voting were lowered; in some they were abolished completely.

After the war, the states faced another crucial decision, concerning their relationship with each other. Under British rule, the colonies had separate governments and identities and had closer connections with London than with their neighbours. In their fight against Britain, this began to change, as they struck up a coalition framed by the Articles of Confederation. Under this agreement, the Continental Congress had authority to act in matters of foreign policy and sought some coordination in military matters. It was, however, not a national government. Congress could not, for example, raise taxes or regulate commerce, and had to rely on individual states to provide both money and military manpower. Nor could the Congress easily transform itself into a more effective instrument of central authority. All the states had an equal vote in important matters, and

Establishing a Government

'The American war is over but this is far from being the case with the American revolution. On the contrary, nothing but the first act of the great drama is closed. It remains yet to establish and perfect our new forms of government; and to prepare the principles, morals, and manners of our citizens, for these forms of government, after they are established and brought to perfection.'

Benjamin Rush, Address to the People of the United States, January 1787.

amendment of the Articles of Confederation required unanimity among states which disagreed on many issues. Nor was military influence strong. Washington's success as a general was a platform for his political career, but he had no ambitions to dominate. Americans also inherited the English aversion to standing armies and were quick to replace their wartime forces with locally recruited militias.

The question of how to achieve lasting unity came to the fore at the Philadelphia Constitutional Convention in 1787. Here, the delegates divided over two interpretations of government. The Federalists – who included George Washington, Benjamin Franklin, James Madison, John Jay and Alexander Hamilton – argued that a strong federal government was essential for defence against foreign states, for dealing with possible disagreements between the new American states and for the creation of economic and monetary policies which would serve them all. The Anti-Federalists, on the other hand, were wedded to the idea that the states should be independent of each other and free to pursue their own interests without central oversight or interference. Thomas Jefferson, for example, backed states' rights, thinking that a large, centralized government had too close a resemblance to the recently overturned British monarchy.

The Federalists prevailed, thanks to widespread recognition of the urgent need to oversee the distribution and government of western lands, and to deal with post-war economic problems. The result was the Federal Constitution of 1787, ratified in 1789, which brought into existence a national government that shared sovereignty with the states. The Constitution drew inspiration from Britain's 'mixed constitution', which balanced a legislature, an executive and an independent judiciary. Executive power was embodied in the president, who was chosen by indirect election and endowed with powers, exercised

LEFT *Alexander Hamilton.*

LEFT *James Madison.*

LEFT *Benjamin Franklin.*

ABOVE *Signing the US Constitution, 1787.*

in conjunction with the Senate, to conduct foreign policy, veto acts of Congress and appoint public officials. He was also commander-in-chief of the United States' armed forces, including the state militias when they were mobilized. The legislature consisted of a House of Representatives (chosen by the voters of the states in proportion to the size of their population) and a Senate (in which each state would have an equal number of representatives). The new Congress was invested with powers which the Congress of the Confederation had lacked, such as the right to levy taxes and regulate commerce for all the states of the Union. The federal government was of course also responsible for foreign relations.

The federation was not entirely stable, as the relationship between states' rights and the powers of central government was not definitively settled. And, in one key respect, the Constitution was deeply flawed. The institution of slavery, a contradiction of the principles of freedom which Americans espoused, remained untouched. Although the Constitution proclaimed all men to be free and equal before the law, slavery not only remained legal in the American South but entered a new phase of growth, linked to the expansion of cotton cultivation. Thus, while the creation of the United States included increasing numbers of white people in political life, it simultaneously deprived most Black people of basic human rights.

REPUBLIC, MONARCHY AND MILITARISM IN HAITI

Like the United States, Haiti made the transition to independence under the banner of a new constitution, designed to announce the emergence of a sovereign nation and to redistribute political power. Haiti's problems in forging a new state were greater than those of the United States, however, largely because its revolution had been more violent, divisive and destructive. At independence, Haitian politics had been thoroughly militarized by prolonged warfare. All of Haiti's leaders were military men who had fought in the rebellions and wars that preceded independence, and those who took power following the declaration of independence in 1804 were unwilling to lay down their arms. While they promulgated constitutions imbued with republican and liberal values, they preferred to exercise authoritarian control, backed by their armies.

Haiti's first independent government, led by Jean-Jacques Dessalines, reflected this authoritarian inclination. He aimed to build the state on the back of his army, and in 1805 created the Empire of Haiti. He placed himself at its head as the Emperor Jacques I and divided the state into six military departments run by governors appointed by himself. The new autocracy was short-lived. Dessalines' megalomania alienated his chief officers, including Henri Christophe and Alexandre Pétion, and their rebellion brought about his downfall. In 1806, Dessalines was assassinated by his own troops and his corpse dragged through the streets in a gesture of contempt.

ABOVE *Jean-Jacques Dessalines.*

Dessalines' death ended the empire. A new constitution issued in 1806 instituted the Republic of Haiti, with a president elected for four years and a legislative power invested in the Senate. Henry Christophe, the one-time slave who had become general-in-chief of the army, was chosen as president but decided to create his own state in the north, where he pronounced himself President and Generalissimo of the State of Haiti. In 1811, Christophe went a step further, crowning himself Henri I, hereditary king of Haiti, with autocratic powers and a full aristocracy. Meanwhile, Pétion, the French-educated freeman of colour, took over as president of the Republic of Haiti in 1807 and began a period of low-level war against Henri's northern kingdom.

Despite their constitutional differences, the two states shared a key similarity. Both concentrated power in the office of a central executive, who was also commander-in-chief of military forces; both were run by military men; both gave short shrift to democratic politics. Henri's monarchy proved to be the more fragile of the two. Weakened by dissent among his subjects, Henri precipitated the end of his dynasty by killing himself in 1820, leaving his hopes of dynastic succession to be obliterated by the execution of his son and heir a few days later. This ended Haiti's experiment with monarchy, but not its tendency towards centralized, authoritarian government.

When Pétion's named successor, Jean-Pierre Boyer, took over in 1818, his military-

Henri Christophe, King of Haiti

'Henry, by the grace of God and constitutional law of the state, King of Haiti, Sovereign of Tortuga, Gonâve, and other adjacent islands, Destroyer of tyranny, Regenerator and Benefactor of the Haitian nation, Creator of her moral, political, and martial institutions, First crowned monarch of the New World, Defender of the faith, Founder of the Royal Military Order of Saint Henry.'

1 April 1811

LEFT *Henri Christophe, king of Haiti.*

style command led him to suspend the legislature and make himself president for life. He then used his powers to extend Haitian territory into Spanish Santo Domingo in 1822, spreading throughout the island what Jonathan Brown, an American visitor in the early 1830s, described as 'a sort of republican government sustained by the bayonet ... where civil authorities were subordinate to army officers'. In 1844, after the war for Dominican independence, the island reverted to its historic French- and Spanish-speaking components and, after further vicissitudes, divided into the modern Dominican Republic and the Republic of Haiti which we know today.

Post-independence Haiti experienced far greater difficulty in creating a functioning democracy than the United States, due to the legacies of slavery and war. After slavery ended, deep social division remained, separating Blacks and people of mixed race.

The End of Slavery

Haiti was the pioneer of anti-slavery and independence in the Caribbean. In the British West Indies, slavery was abolished by the British colonial government in 1833 and the islands long remained under colonial rule. France retained its islands in the Lesser Antilles and abolished slavery in 1848. Spain kept Cuba and Puerto Rico and allowed slavery until 1886. Both Cubans and Puerto Ricans made several attempts to become independent between the 1860s and 1890s, culminating in the Cuban War of Independence (1895–8). After the United States defeated Spain in the Spanish–American War (1898), Puerto Rico became a US possession and Cuba was brought under American military government until it became an independent republic in 1902.

The devastation of war was also difficult to overcome. The production of sugar and coffee, Haiti's leading exports, had been seriously disrupted during the war and the international environment after independence did little to help recovery. On the contrary, the United States and the leading European powers all treated Haiti as a pariah and their refusal to recognize the new state blocked access to international trade and credit. In these circumstances, Haiti never recovered its prominent position in transatlantic trade. The European markets that underpinned its colonial prosperity were lost and the plantation labour force was decimated. For, once they were free, formerly enslaved people preferred life as independent peasant farmers to the dangerous and ill-paid drudgery of the plantations.

ABOVE *Jean-Pierre Boyer is sworn in as president of Haiti.*

When France finally recognized Haiti in 1825, it brought no significant economic change. On the contrary, the imposition of exorbitant reparations imposed a crippling long-term debt. Its economic outlook blighted, Haiti was shackled by the poverty and illiteracy that were the legacies of slavery, and by divisions of colour and class that continued to inhibit state- and nation-building throughout the 19th century.

CENTRIFUGAL FORCES: THE EARLY SPANISH AMERICAN REPUBLICS

Like the United States and Haiti, the states that emerged from Spanish rule faced problems of defining their territories and forms of government. The first proved relatively simple. Post-independence governments tended to delimit their territories by reference to structures laid down under Spanish rule. These were, first and foremost, the viceroyalties and *audiencias* which provided the framework and overarching authority for smaller units of government run by provincial and district officials and by town councils. They were regarded as separate 'kingdoms', and their long life as autonomous entities was reflected in the territorial definition of the first independent states. Thus, the Viceroyalty of New Spain was the template for Iturbide's Mexican Empire; the Viceroyalty of New Granada for Bolívar's Republic of Colombia; the Viceroyalty of Río de la Plata for the

United Provinces of Río de la Plata; the defunct Viceroyalty of Peru for that country's first republic.

There was never any possibility that these would become a 'United States of Spanish America'. Not only did their inhabitants see their countries as discrete entities, but they were separated by great distances and formidable physical obstacles which made integration impossible. In fact, the first large states soon fragmented into smaller entities, as cities and regions within them asserted their own claims to independence. Thus, the Republic of Colombia split into three sovereign states in 1830 (New Granada, Ecuador and Venezuela). Central America seceded from Mexico in 1823 and became the United Provinces of Central America. Independent Peru retained the heartlands of the old viceroyalty, while new republics arose in Bolivia and Chile. Nor did the process of disaggregation end there. Powerful centrifugal forces remained, reflected in civil wars within the new states. In the River Plate region, Paraguay and Uruguay refused to join the United Provinces of Río de la Plata, led by Buenos Aires, which went through decades of civil strife before becoming the Republic of Argentina in the 1860s. In the 1840s, the Union of Central America splintered into the independent states of Guatemala, Nicaragua, El Salvador, Costa Rica and Honduras.

ABOVE *Map of independent states in South America, 1826.*

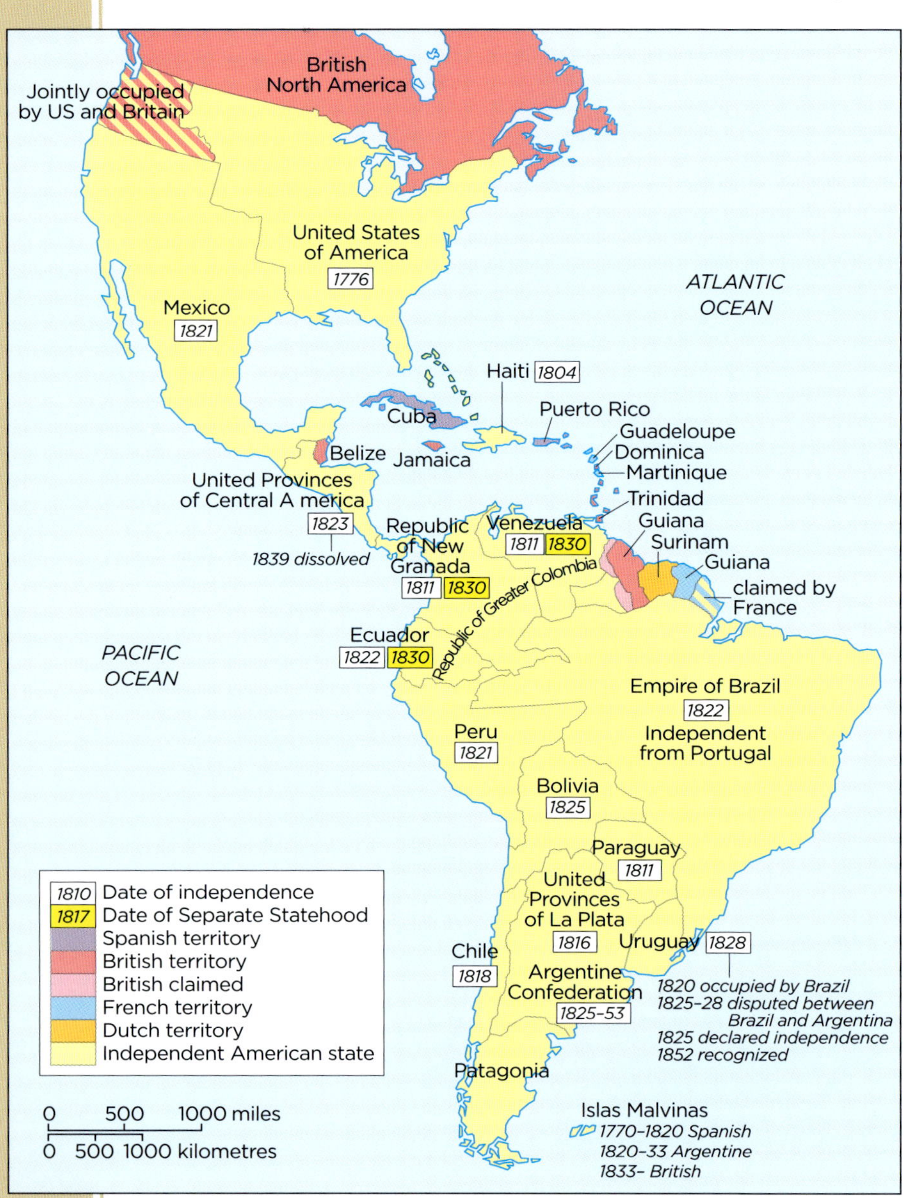

Nonetheless, the territorial shapes of Spanish government still bore marks of the colonial past, for at the end of the 19th century, most republics had territories which broadly resembled the *audiencias* and governorships which had existed under Spanish rule. They had also retained Spanish as their primary language and Roman Catholicism as the official religion. This colonial legacy did not impede radical change in political culture, however. Most post-independence political leaders embraced a liberal agenda of constitutional government, with equality before the law for all citizens, freedom of speech, and freedom for production and commerce. Many took the United States as a model and built representative systems in which electors (usually propertied men) could choose their governments. They hoped for economic progress through freedom to trade, and, amid greater prosperity, aimed to create an educated, responsible citizenry, free from slavery and other forms of racial inequality. They frequently adopted

Enlightenment ideas, which inspired reforms in administration, public order, education and the dissemination of news, as well as policies aimed at stimulating economic activity. Overall, their liberal standards were notably higher than in much of Europe, where many states remained in the grip of repressive monarchies for much of the 19th century.

While Spanish American political leaders generally agreed on the desirability of representative government, they differed over the forms it should take. A few wanted constitutional monarchies headed by a European prince, but such schemes went nowhere. Apart from two brief experiments in Mexico, none of the Spanish American states followed Brazil into constitutional monarchy.

There were, however, several attempts to create governments with strong executive powers, often proposed by the military men who had led armies in the wars for independence, on one side or the other. Bolívar's 1826 Bolivian Constitution is a prime

ABOVE, LEFT *Cavalry fighting in the Argentine Confederation, c.1839.*

ABOVE, RIGHT *Coin celebrating the independence of Guatemala.*

LEFT *A painting celebrating the abolition of slavery in Argentina, 1839.*

ABOVE *Juan Manuel de Rosas, ruler of the Argentine Confederation 1829–32.*

example. In his draft of the constitution, Bolívar identified tyranny and anarchy as 'two monstrous enemies' which had to be defeated. He feared that Spanish Americans were abusing their new-found freedom in factionalism, military uprisings and provincial rebellions, and it was with this in mind that he drafted the Bolivian constitution. Based on British constitutional monarchy and Napoleonic consular constitutions, the Bolivarian model aimed at a 'republicanized monarchy'. In other words, a paternalistic republican government in which life-presidents and hereditary senates constrained the democracy of elected legislatures.

Spanish America's other constitutional blueprint came from Spain's 1812 constitution, which attracted those who wanted large, centralized states with representative systems in which legislatures dominated. Río de la Plata in 1826, Chile and Peru in 1828, and New Granada, Venezuela and Uruguay in 1830 all aimed at republics of this kind.

Strong central governments were difficult to achieve and sustain, however. The relationship between centres and provinces was a great source of friction, leading to endless conflicts over the form that national government should take. Some wanted a national state led by a strong central government; others wanted federations composed of equal states, in which central government was relatively weak. In most places, central governments had insufficient income from taxation to impose themselves, and political life tended to become provincialized. In Mexico, for example, municipal politicians discharged key functions of government, such as enforcing laws, tax-collecting, holding elections and raising militias, and often led resistance to control from Mexico City. Local militias also became a new feature of political life. Members were 'citizens in arms', able to oppose attempts by central governments to impose unwelcome laws.

Military men played a prominent role in post-independence politics, using arms to achieve political goals. Mexico, for example, witnessed 50 coups between 1822 and 1847, many of them led by General Antonio López de Santa Anna, who became the nation's

Bolívar's Disillusionment

'This liberator who scorned liberalism, soldier who disparaged militarism, republican who admired monarchy', Bolívar 'the Liberator' is central to the history of Spanish American independence. He was a sophisticated political thinker, determined to bring political and social order. Committed to representative government but fearful of democracy, he inclined towards centralized government guided by a strong presidency. He hoped to unite Colombia (composed of Venezuela, New Granada and Ecuador) with Peru and Bolivia in a Federation of the Andes. When Bolívar tried to apply the Bolivian Constitution to Colombia, he was opposed by old friends and allies and, after an assassination attempt in Bogotá, he retreated from politics, terminally ill and deeply disillusioned. 'Independence is', he lamented, 'the only benefit we have gained, at the cost of everything else.'

leader no fewer than 11 times. And Mexico was not the only country where authority frequently moved from elected representatives into the hands of strong, personalist leaders ready to use armed force. 'Caudillos' of this kind (whether army officers, local warlords, or leaders of peasants who wanted citizenship on their own terms) appeared in several other regions, too, including Central America, Peru, Bolivia and, most of all, Río de la Plata (later Argentina). Chile was an exception. Its 1833 constitution endured for over a century and a succession of decade-long conservative governments managed to escape civil wars, rapid changes of power and social upheaval.

As privileged groups clung to their wealth and power, the republics did not benefit all their citizens. In Latin America, like the United States, republican and liberal values were compatible with deep social inequality and even slavery, which persisted in Venezuela, New Granada and Peru until mid-century. However, independence generally allowed greater popular political participation, at least in the early decades of the republics, when Indigenous populations, Blacks and free people of colour entered into political debate and action, and joined with whites to claim rights as citizens.

ABOVE *General Antonio López de Santa Anna.*

REPUBLICANIZED MONARCHY: THE EMPIRE OF BRAZIL

In Brazil, independence was a less abrupt departure from the past, as the shift from being a kingdom of the Portuguese monarchy to becoming an independent empire took place without the large-scale or prolonged warfare of the kind that affected Spanish America. Once installed, however, the new monarchy faced the usual problems of imposing authority over historically disparate regions and their restive elites. Indeed, the first constitutional crisis appeared almost immediately after the accession of the first emperor, Dom Pedro I (1822–31). Pernambuco and adjacent provinces (which had shown secessionist signs in 1817) refused to accept this succession and instead joined the short-lived Confederation of the Equator in the northeast of the country that broke away from the rest of Brazil in 1824. Their project for an independent republic was stopped, however, by the emperor's superior military forces, and Pedro continued with plans to enhance his power over Brazil's government. Thus, while his 1824 constitution offered all the essentials of a liberal state, with an elected bicameral legislature, the separation of powers and so on, he made the emperor a 'moderator', with decisive powers of appointment and adjudication.

This did not guarantee stability, however. The emperor's position was weakened by Portuguese demands that he return to Portugal and further weakened when his war against the United Provinces for control of Uruguay ended in stalemate. Pedro I took

ABOVE *The Paço de São Cristóvão, Brazil's Imperial Palace, 1862.*

the blame and was forced to return to Lisbon in 1831, leaving the succession to his five-year-old son. This solution soon came under strain. Until Pedro II came of age in 1840, his authority was exercised by regents, whose authority was challenged by provincial rebellions which, once again, strained the bonds of Brazilian unity. Fortunately for the monarchy, the provincial rebellions did not present serious separatist challenges or impede the continuity of central government. Pedro II acceded to the throne and, backed by the landed classes, took up the role of firm centralized leadership designed by his predecessor. Under the cloak of constitutional government, powerful continuities prevailed. For decades, Brazil would retain its slave-holding social base, its Portuguese-related dynasty, and its long-standing trading relations with Britain. Gradually, Brazilians diversified their economy and population, but modernity was always tempered by links with the colonial past.

DIVERGENT ECONOMIES

During the half-century or so after independence, the United States entered on a path of development that reshaped American life. It was increasingly a commercial and industrial economy, in which most people were involved in producing goods for sale rather than family consumption. Along with this 'market revolution' went revolutions in industry, agriculture and transportation, all of which made the United States exceptional among the independent states of the Americas.

An outstanding feature of the early decades of the United States before the Civil War was a huge expansion in its territory and population. After the Louisiana Purchase, the republic expanded to fill half a continent. Driven by a combination of natural increase and immigration, the population rose from around 4 million in 1790 to almost 32 million in 1860 (including the enslaved, but excluding indigenous Americans). About 4.25 million migrants arrived between 1840 and 1860, many more than went to the whole of Latin America.

With this rapid rate of population growth (roughly 3.5 per cent annually) went significant changes. First, the United States' balance shifted westwards, beyond the Appalachian Mountains and into the many new states created after independence. State and federal policies that offered cheap land drew settlers to western frontiers and laid the foundations for the rapid growth of agricultural production. By 1860, more than half of the population were living in the West, and many more followed.

The competition among East Coast cities for the commerce of the interior accelerated another kind of economic development in the 1840s and 1850s. An early factory system appeared in the 1830s, notably at Lowell in Massachusetts, where water-powered cotton mills were copied from those of Manchester in England.

Another key component of industrialization was the design and manufacture of the machine tools needed for generating and transmitting power used in factory

Immigration

Between 1820 and 1840, over 250,000 Irish immigrants arrived in the United States, mostly to settle in northeastern cities and towns, where they performed unskilled work. The infamous Irish Famine (1845–52) sparked a massive exodus. Between 1840 and 1860, nearly 2 million Irish fled starvation in their European homeland and settled in the coastal cities of the United States, where they became unskilled manual workers in gruelling occupations. Over 1.5 million immigrants from the various German states also arrived in the United States during the antebellum era. Most used American ports and cities as temporary waypoints before moving to rural areas, where they took up farming.

The sudden influx of immigrants, especially the Irish in the cities, triggered a backlash among many Anglo-Protestant Americans, who tried to limit European immigration. The strongholds of their nativist movement were in northern cities such as Boston, Chicago and Philadelphia, and in the 1850s they formed the American Party, more commonly known as the Know-Nothing Party.

LEFT *Anti-Catholic riots in Philadelphia, 1844.*

production, and for making interchangeable parts which simplified assembly and repair. The engineers who made cotton gins, muskets, rifles, spinning machinery and power looms played a key part in launching the Industrial Revolution in the United States. Colt firearms, agricultural machinery (McCormick's reaper), locks, woodworking machinery, machine tools and textile machinery attracted great interest at London's Crystal Palace Exhibition in 1851. They showed that the United States was on the brink of becoming a major manufacturing nation and, though it could not yet compete with British and European manufacturers in the world market, it could supply a wide variety of manufactured products to its own, growing home markets.

Fast economic development was closely linked to improvements in transport networks, boosted by state governments which subsidized road, canal and railway construction. The application of steam technology brought a revolution in transport and communication, by lowering costs and increasing speed, particularly on great inland waterways such as the Mississippi and Ohio rivers. Towns and cities were also multiplying fast, extending urban growth into the interior, far beyond the big ports of the Atlantic coast.

The Lowell Mills

The Lowell cotton mills centralized the process of textile manufacturing under one roof, using female labour. Working conditions were hard but the lure of wages was strong. As a worker observed, 'very many Ladies . . . have given up millinery, dressmaking and school-keeping for work in the mill'. Lowell's vision brought a rush of capital and entrepreneurs into New England and played a key part in America's first era of industrialization.

LEFT *The Lowell cotton mills, Massachusetts.*

The transportation and communication revolutions fostered a process of commercialization that altered American lives. Farmers who previously produced crops mostly for family consumption now turned to the market, where they could earn cash to spend on goods they had previously made or done without. They also accessed credit through eastern banks, which provided them with money to expand and to invest in new technologies. Between 1815 and 1850, patents on agricultural technologies multiplied, with important effects on productivity. John Deere's steel-bladed plough, for example, allowed unbroken ground to become fertile farmland, while McCormick's horse-drawn mechanical reaper helped to mechanize wheat harvesting.

Frontier expansion promised freedom and prosperity for settlers, who poured in from Europe in the hope of improving their lives, but it came at great cost to indigenous peoples,

The Erie Canal

New York State completed the Erie Canal in 1825, connecting the Great Lakes with the Hudson River and the Atlantic Ocean. Its success launched a canal-building boom, which pushed inland. By 1840, Ohio had created two navigable all-water links from Lake Erie to the Ohio River.

LEFT *Lockport, Erie Canal, 1839.*

Steamboats

The first commercial steamboat service appeared on the Hudson River in New York in 1807. Soon, steamboats filled the waters of the Mississippi and Ohio rivers. By 1830, more than 200 moved up and down western rivers and what had been downstream-only routes became two-way highways.

LEFT *Steamboats on the Mississippi River outside St Louis, Missouri, 1859.*

who were forced off their traditional lands in a government-backed process akin to ethnic cleansing. Expansion also had a price in terms of American liberty, as the spread of cotton plantations in the south and southwest brought a concomitant expansion of slavery.

From the 1790s until the Civil War in the 1860s, the cotton boom made an outstanding contribution to American economic growth. After Eli Whitney invented the mechanical cotton gin in 1794 (speeding up the processing of cotton fibre), cotton became a very profitable crop. When new lands for cultivation became available, cotton planters rushed to take them. This began during the 1820s and 1830s, when the federal government forced eastern indigenous Americans to migrate to reservations west of the Mississippi River and auctioned off their lands. Henceforth, the South took on a new life producing cotton to meet the demands of industrial mills in Britain. The cotton crop doubled in size in the 1820s, then doubled again in the 1830s. By 1860, cotton was not only the key export of the South; it also provided two-thirds of all the United States' exports and 75 per cent of the world's cotton.

BELOW *Eli Whitney's patent for the cotton gin.*

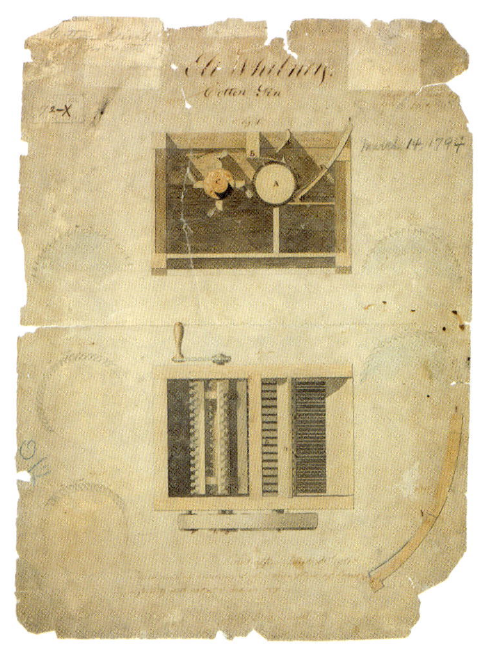

The cotton boom was not only crucial to American growth; it also meant that the South's tradition of slavery became more deeply ingrained. By 1860, there were 4 million slaves in the South, and, as the southern states were enriched by cotton exports, so their leaders came to see themselves as a different civilization. They regarded their way of life as very different from that of the more mercantile and urban northern states and became convinced of their right to exist as a separate nation. In fact, it was another kind of capitalism, in which humans were treated like machines, forced to produce profit for small groups of investors without any recourse to the rights given to white people, however impoverished. Here, in

ABOVE *Cotton pickers on a Georgia plantation, c.1900.*

the opposition of different forms of capitalism, one wedded to slave labour and the other to wage labour, were the seeds of the greatest internal political crisis since independence, the American Civil War.

Latin American leaders hoped to emulate the economic transformation of the United States. At independence, many believed that free trade would unleash economic potential unrealized under Iberian rule and bring growth comparable to that of the United States. Bolívar, for example, foresaw a future in which the Republic of Colombia, with its Atlantic and Pacific ports and control of the Isthmus of Panama, would become a new crossroads for global trade. Others believed that the huge lands available for settlement would attract Europeans and bring new knowledge and energy. In fact, the idea that freedom from imperial control would automatically open pathways to prosperity was overly optimistic. Most economies saw little growth in their output or international trade before 1870. Brazil was an exception, thanks to expanding external markets for sugar and, especially, coffee. Mexico, on the other hand, ceased to be the largest and richest economy of the Americas and was overtaken by the United States. Unlike the United States, where economic development was dynamic and transformative, Latin America was less open to commercial capitalism and saw very limited change.

This economic stagnation had several causes. One was the physical damage inflicted by internal wars on large regions and some important economic sectors. Silver mining in Mexico and Peru was especially hard hit by the destruction of machinery and infrastructure, and decades passed before silver mining returned to its pre-independence levels. Population growth slowed during and after the wars of independence (to about 1 per cent per year between the 1820s and 1850s) and migrants to Latin America were few. Some created small agricultural colonies in Argentina, Uruguay and southern Brazil but they had little impact on economic activity.

Patterns of production and trade also remained much the same. Throughout the colonial period, Spanish American trade relied heavily on payments of silver and gold, which were low bulk, high value commodities which did not require any great transport infrastructure. At independence, poor transport links kept internal markets small and isolated producers from external markets. Some attempts were made to stimulate the manufacturing industry, notably in central Mexico, where cotton spinning mills were set up in the city of Puebla. But the use of tariffs to provide protection for industry invariably failed, because of limited demand and the lack of start-up capital. As for exports, they remained much the same, with only modest growth. The Río de la Plata did well from exports of salt beef and hides through Buenos Aires, and Chile developed its first copper mines in the 1830s. But the only large new export was guano – bird excrement – dug up by Chinese workers on islands off the Peruvian coast and sold for fertilizer throughout Europe, usually through British companies. An offshore niche economy using unfree labour, guano did much to improve the finances of Peru's government in Lima but had very little effect on Peru's economy as a whole.

To grow, Spanish American countries needed capital, expertise and new channels for trade. At first, British investors showed great enthusiasm, mainly for loans to governments and mining ventures. Several defaults on loans to governments and investment in over-ambitious mining projects soon curtailed such enthusiasm, however, and investors' losses gave Spanish America a bad name on the London stock market. Political turbulence was another disincentive to investment by overseas banks and businesses, which feared that rebellions and civil wars would impose 'the law of force rather than the force of law'. In these circumstances, British investors in the Americas turned to the United States, where industry, canals and railways offered more profitable prospects. Brazil and Cuba (both sugar exporters using enslaved labour) were exceptions. British commerce injected money in payment for sugar and coffee, and banks provided funds for government, thanks to Brazil's reliability in servicing its debts. Cuba also benefitted from a boom in sugar production, underpinned by slavery and overseas capital. By the mid-1830s, it had the first railway in Latin America and had introduced steam-driven machinery for processing sugar. While under Spanish rule, Cuba was a greater economic success during the first half of the 19th century than any of its independent counterparts.

ABOVE *Plaza de Mayo, Buenos Aires, 1854.*

A common trend throughout 19th-century Latin America was towards economic dependence on Britain. Some say that this marked the first step in a transformation from being colonies of Spain and Portugal to becoming informal colonies of Britain. It is certainly true that Britain did much to shape the Latin American economies, especially in the later 19th century, when British commerce and investment facilitated closer integration into world trade. After mid-century, economic activity generally quickened, stimulated by the industrializing economies of western Europe, led by Britain, which wanted imports of food, such as sugar, grains and beef, wool and leather, guano and nitrates for fertilizer, and non-ferrous metals. Faced with these opportunities, the political elites became committed to free trade, which accelerated commodity exports and brought a new wave of growth in mining and agricultural production. However, although the creation of links with Britain brought economic benefits, they also perpetuated old structures. Most of Latin America continued to rely on the production of primary products for export, which fed industrialization in Europe while blocking it in Latin America. In short, economic development increasingly diverged from that of the United States, to Latin America's long-term detriment.

SISTER REPUBLICS?

Relations between the United States and Spanish America republics started well. During the Spanish America wars of independence between 1810 and 1824, politicians and public in the United States showed sympathy for their southern neighbours in several ways, ranging from sending men and arms, toasting Latin American independence in Fourth of July celebrations, naming towns and babies after Bolívar, and applauding the differences of the New World from the Old. For a time, politicians and public indulged their ingrained dislike of Spanish Catholicism and embraced an image of a shared republican future, in which the United States would be the hemisphere's model and mentor.

BELOW *James Monroe.*

The idea of a republican bloc, distinct from the corrupt, war-torn world of European monarchies and able to defy the powers of Europe, took a brief hold on the American political imagination. In 1822, the United States became the first nation in the world to recognize Spanish American independence and in 1823 President Monroe underlined a policy of separate hemispheres. 'The American continents', not just the United States, were, Monroe declared, to be kept free of any future attempts at European colonization. The 'Monroe Doctrine', as this declaration became known, warned Europeans against intervening in the Americas and asserted the right of the United States to defend itself and other American states against such intrusion. It also staked out the rights of whites against indigenous Americans, who were allowed no rights to states of their own.

This idea of a republican alliance against Europe

RIGHT *Manifest Destiny.*

OVERLAND MAIL
US

Manifest Destiny

'Do not lounge in the cities!' cried the American newspaperman Horace Greeley in 1841. 'Go west, before you are fitted for no life but that of the factory.' More strategically, the *New-York Tribune* that he founded and edited repeatedly propagated the idea that American exceptionalism required the spread of American capitalism and democracy across the continent. This disregarded the indigenous Americans who controlled much of the land east of the Mississippi River and almost all of the west. Their place in Manifest Destiny was to suffer the effects of a federal policy of removal that came close to genocide.

was welcome in Latin America, where many admired the United States, borrowed from its constitutional texts and hoped to emulate its example. During the wars of independence, this sense of solidarity was strengthened by trade, especially in arms and ammunition. The United States was, however, also seen as a nation apart. Thus, when Bolívar organized the Congress of Panama in 1826, with a plan to create a league of Latin American states with a common military, a mutual defence pact and a supranational parliamentary assembly, he did not initially include the United States, which he saw as a potentially competing power. The annexation of Florida in 1821 by the United States, he warned, showed the dangers of a northern neighbour that was 'very rich, very warlike, and capable of anything'. American politicians were also wary of links with the Spanish American states and so, when Bolívar conceded an invitation for two representatives of the United States to attend, they were delayed by pro-slavery politicians who feared that Spanish America might become a base for outlawing slavery, even encouraging slave rebellions in the United States. In fact, the Panama Congress was a damp squib. The delegates promulgated a 'Treaty of Union, League, and Perpetual Confederation', but it was unfulfilled. The only state that ratified it was Colombia, which itself broke into separate states soon after. Bolívar's dream of supranational unity then collapsed irretrievably, among civil wars and wars between emergent states across Latin America.

The Monroe Doctrine was more of a vision than a reality, as the United States lacked the military means to keep 'America for the Americans'. Its assertion was nonetheless a signal that North Americans saw their republic as an empire in the making, destined to compete for power by territorial expansion and diplomatic manoeuvre. And, when Spanish America fragmented in the 1820s and 1830s, politicians in the United States increasingly stressed how different their nation was from Latin America, especially in religion and racial composition. Republican universalism was thus replaced by a sense of exceptionalism in the United States, embodied in the idea that the nation had a 'manifest destiny' to occupy all of North America.

In the north, the US prevailed on Britain for rights over Oregon and negotiated a treaty which set the border with British North America at the 49th parallel (excepting Vancouver Island and British Columbia), a border which later marked the permanent boundary between Canada and the United States. In the south, on the other hand, the intrusion of settlers from the United States into Texas (which they declared an independent state in 1836) led to war over lands that Mexico had inherited from Spain. In 1846, President

Polk ordered the annexation of Texas and, after seizing Mexico City in the Mexican–American War (1846–8), forced the Mexican government to give up a huge swathe of territory, including Texas, California and other lands north of the Rio Grande.

Other signs of the ambition of the United States to gain new territories surfaced in the 1850s, in proposals to take Cuba and Nicaragua (the latter as a site for an interoceanic canal), but these did not materialize. For most of the 19th century, the United States realized its Manifest Destiny on internal land frontiers, where migrants occupied vast reserves of unploughed land, dispossessed indigenous peoples and expanded the markets that drove industrialization forward.

BELOW *General Winfield Scott's entrance into Mexico City, 1847.*

CHAPTER 6

DIVERGENCE

The United States had moved on to a fast pathway to economic growth during the early 1800s and avoided the political fragmentation that affected many Latin American states. It was not, however, free from the problems of unity and order common in those countries. By the 1850s, the addition of new states imposed growing strains on the federal political framework, as did growing opposition to Southern slavery in the industrializing and rapidly modernizing North. Differences over the moral issue of slavery were not the sole cause of conflict, but they played a key part in triggering the greatest civil war in the history of the Americas.

THE AMERICAN CIVIL WAR

The question of whether slavery should be allowed in the United States was long left unresolved for fear that any decision against it would fracture the federal union. Thus, the framers of the American Constitution accepted that states which already had slavery should be allowed to continue with it while assuming that new states created by westward expansion would be free. But this did not prove to be the case. The advocates of slavery insisted that new states should be allowed into the Union without facing any federal restrictions, and in 1820 Congress allowed the admission of Missouri as a slave state in return for recognizing the entry of Maine as a 'free' state. The Missouri Compromise, as it was called, did not settle the matter, however. Indeed, the fault lines deepened when the United States added more territory from its war with Mexico in 1846–8, which opened potentially new spaces for slavery.

ABOVE *Jefferson Davis.*

Discord over the issue sharpened in the mid-1850s, with the emergence of the Republican Party as an anti-slavery coalition, and came to a head when the Republican Abraham Lincoln won the presidential election of 1860. Along with the mainstream of the anti-slavery movement, Lincoln aimed to bring about the gradual abolition of the institution – but the southern states rejected his authority. The first to move against him were the leaders of seven states (South Carolina, Mississippi, Florida, Alabama, Georgia, Louisiana and Texas), which announced their secession from the Union over what they described as 'state rights'. They declared themselves the Confederate States of America (The Confederacy), drew up their own constitution, established a capital at Richmond, Virginia, and appointed Jefferson Davis as their president. Before long, eight more states would join them.

The secessionists were confident that a strong military showing would allow them to go their own way. They took the initiative in April 1861, with an attack on the federal fortress at Fort Sumter, near Charleston, South Carolina. Lincoln responded by calling for 75,000 volunteers to serve in the Union army for three months, while also ordering a naval blockade to cut off the Confederates' access to overseas trade.

BELOW *The attack on Fort Sumter, 1861.*

For Lincoln and the Republicans, the primary purpose of their action was to prevent the break-up of the Union rather than to abolish slavery, on the grounds that the Union was essential to the idea of an American nation. Southerners, on the other hand, defended states' rights to override federal laws, primarily to protect slave ownership and the plantation economy, but also because of a belief

LEFT *A Confederate battle flag.*

in the South's distinctive culture. Not all southerners were planters or slave owners, but there was little difficulty in raising a fighting force from non-slave-owning men. They fought to defend a way of life which, by sustaining slavery, gave them a privileged position as whites, however poor.

The South had a substantial economic base, with about 30 per cent of total US wealth, but the Union had more, together with a greater ability to mobilize its resources for war. It had advantages in productive capacity, with six times as many factories and 97 per cent of firearms production, greater bullion supplies, and larger food production, plus a greater capacity to raise taxation to pay for the conflict. The Union also had 70 per cent of the country's railroads, available for moving men, supplies and arms, and a powerful presence at sea, cutting the South's communications and trade. It also had an edge in manpower, at a ratio of around 4:1, which was supplemented by the recruitment of African Americans. This put the South at a clear disadvantage for, despite its propaganda about the 'loyal' slaves that lived in the region, southerners were afraid to arm their enslaved people, of whom growing numbers fled to freedom behind Union lines.

BELOW *The Emancipation Proclamation.*

African American participation was not immediately welcomed by the Union, until military needs forced a change of policy. In January 1863, Lincoln's Emancipation Proclamation promised to free all enslaved people in areas not under Union control. Over 180,000 African Americans joined the Union army and 20,000 the navy, despite being paid less than whites and risking torture, death or a return to slavery if captured by the Confederates. Concerns about their treatment were raised with Abraham Lincoln by the former enslaved man and Black abolitionist Frederick Douglass, who became a trusted advisor to the president. However, although poor treatment of Blacks suggests that northerners shared the racist attitudes of the South, the Union army was an agent of emancipation. Indeed, the African American exodus from the southern slave system developed a momentum which the Confederacy could not stem and contributed much to its defeat. Northern soldiers were, by contrast, often reluctant recruits. While some immigrants saw the war as a chance to bind themselves into their new society, many resented forced enrolments in what they regarded as 'a rich man's war and a poor man's fight'.

Frederick Douglass

Frederick Douglass escaped enslavement in 1838, aged 20, and progressed to become one of its foremost critics. He was both a gifted orator and writer, publishing three autobiographies, including *Narrative of the Life of Frederick Douglass: An American Slave* (1845), which provided the funds for him to secure his freedom. Douglass supported the Union cause during the Civil War; two of Douglass's sons fought with the all-Black 54th Massachusetts Regiment. Following the introduction of Black Codes restricting Black freedoms after emancipation, Douglass campaigned for civil rights and permission for Black people to purchase land. Through his writings, speeches and many photographs, Douglass confronted prevailing racial stereotypes of African Americans and demanded their inclusion in public life and society. He also connected with Black radicalism in the Caribbean, praising the Haitian Revolution for its overthrow of slavery and lauding Toussaint Louverture as the 'Black Spartacus'. He persistently championed the Republic of Haiti, where he served as the US resident consul general in 1889–91.

LEFT *Frederick Douglass.*

At the outset of the war, public opinion anticipated a short, sharp conflict, in which one big battle would decide the winner. However, the first battle, fought at Bull Run–Manassas in 1861, did not produce victory by a single show of strength. The war continued for four more years and proved to be far more destructive of lives and property than either side had foreseen. The South's General Robert E. Lee tried to advance into Union territory but was pushed back at Antietam in 1862 and Gettysburg in 1863, with huge losses on both sides. From 1864, the Union's military strategy shifted towards an emphasis on 'hard war', designed to demoralize southerners and destroy their economy. This culminated in General William T. Sherman's advance across Georgia, which left a great trail of destruction in its wake. By 1865, Sherman's occupation of Confederate territory and harsh treatment of Confederate supporters had undermined civilian belief in the war, while desertion diminished its army. In January 1865, Lincoln claimed moral victory by pushing the Thirteenth Amendment to the Constitution through Congress, to abolish slavery in the Union. Shortly after, the South accepted defeat. On 9 April, Lee surrendered at Appomattox Court House, Virginia, bringing the war to an end. At least 600,000 soldiers had died in the conflict.

A long road to reconciliation stretched ahead, with many questions still unanswered, about how the nation would be reunited, who would be responsible for rebuilding the South, and what part African Americans might now play in a free society. The Civil War had, nonetheless, solved one key problem. The United States was now definitively unified as one nation under a federal government, a unity that would ensure its continued growth and emergence as a single great power.

ABOVE *The aftermath of the Battle of Gettysburg, 1863.*

Abraham Lincoln

Born in the southern state of Kentucky in 1809, Lincoln progressed despite little formal schooling to become a lawyer and politician in Illinois. He gained a national reputation when he stood against Stephen A. Douglas for senator in 1858 and won the Republican nomination and election for president in 1860. Lincoln was a man of limited military experience but took executive control during the Civil War, overseeing military strategy and naval blockades. His Emancipation Proclamation of 1863 was a turning point in American history, for it promised to end slavery and rallied Black southerners to the Union side. While seeking legal equality for Black people, Lincoln believed them to be socially inferior to white people, awaiting education and integration. On 14 April 1865, just five days after the South surrendered, Lincoln was assassinated at a theatre by the actor and secessionist John Wilkes Booth. The Gettysburg Address, a brief but stirring oration he gave in November 1863 at the dedication ceremony of a cemetery to the fallen, is today recognized as one of the finest and most significant political speeches ever delivered.

LEFT *Abraham Lincoln.*

INDIAN WARS

While the Civil War raged, the expansion of white settlement continued in large regions of the West. This ensured conflict in another form, as indigenous peoples fought to preserve their traditional lands. While Lincoln at Gettysburg had envisaged a nation 'conceived in liberty, and dedicated to the proposition that all men are created equal', he often disregarded the rights of indigenous peoples, signing laws that gave away millions of acres of tribal land. Lincoln shared the common opinion that Native Americans were a foreign people who should accept the purchase of their land and move aside. Some Native Americans wanted separation from the United States, so that they might preserve their own cultures, but they invariably found that peace treaties were ignored by settlers and politicians, creating disputes that often flared into local warfare as both sides took the law into their own hands.

The Homestead Act in 1862, which promised titles of land west of the Mississippi, aggravated conflict. As settlers moved in, they took over land and exploited other resources that until then had been controlled by indigenous peoples. Several native nations, including the Comanche and Seminole, allied with the Confederacy, while others sought to protect themselves by aligning with the Union. Some efforts at building peaceful co-existence were made in the Reconstruction years, but the continuous encroachment of settlers led to more frequent war. A gold rush in South Dakota, for example, coupled with settler demands for land, provoked resistance from the Sioux and Cheyenne, in an alliance which the US army failed to break. Lieutenant Colonel George C. Custer's attempts to do so collapsed at the Battle of Little Bighorn in 1876, where his forces were wiped out. By then, however, the foundations of indigenous life were disastrously depleted. The population of bison, an animal whose existence was essential for indigenous life, had plunged from 30 million to a few thousand, killed for food by settlers and for hides by professional hunters, backed by an American industry that provided powerful rifles designed for buffalo hunting and chemicals for processing bison remains. Gradually, indigenous people were compelled to live on reservations, government-controlled settlements in remote and unproductive areas plagued by poverty and disease. In the meantime, under the terms of the Homestead Act, some 400,000 settler families were handed access to free or low-cost land – as were the railroad companies, speculators and financiers who in fact benefitted the most from this vast process of territorial redistribution.

ABOVE *A depiction of the Battle of Little Bighorn of 1876 by Lakota artist Amos Bad Heart Bull.*

LEFT *The ruins of Richmond, Virginia, 1865.*

RECONSTRUCTION

After the Civil War, Congress passed a series of Reconstruction Acts to restore southern states to the Union and assure African Americans of their place as citizens in American society. The legal end to slavery did not erase the economic and social system associated with bondage, however. Lincoln's replacement, Andrew Johnson, favoured southern interests and opposed civil rights for the formerly enslaved, while many southern governments impeded the political and social emancipation of freed people. A number of restrictive laws, known as the 'Black Codes', prevented Black men from bearing arms or testifying against white people in court and made them vulnerable to arrest if found to be without a home or work. Opposition to emancipation also involved violent terrorism, notably with the appearance of the Ku Klux Klan, whose gangs of hooded Confederate veterans attacked and lynched black people with impunity from the law.

Congress's introduction of a Fourteenth Amendment in 1866 gave all Americans – regardless of colour – equal protection under the law and reversed some of the South's discriminatory Black Code decrees. The amendment also allowed many Black people to vote and engage in democratic politics for the first time. For a short while the South was transformed from a white stronghold into a collection of Republican-led states in which African Americans held positions of local power. When recession in the North ended Reconstruction in 1877, white Democrats returned to power in the South. They quickly reversed Black integration into the political system, and, though unable to restore slavery, they did much to perpetuate old inequities and injustices. Thereafter, most Black southerners had access to land only by working on plantations, or as tenant farmers or sharecroppers subject to exploitative terms. Social discrimination and segregation were normalized.

BELOW *November, 1867. The US journal* Harper's Weekly *commemorates the first black vote.*

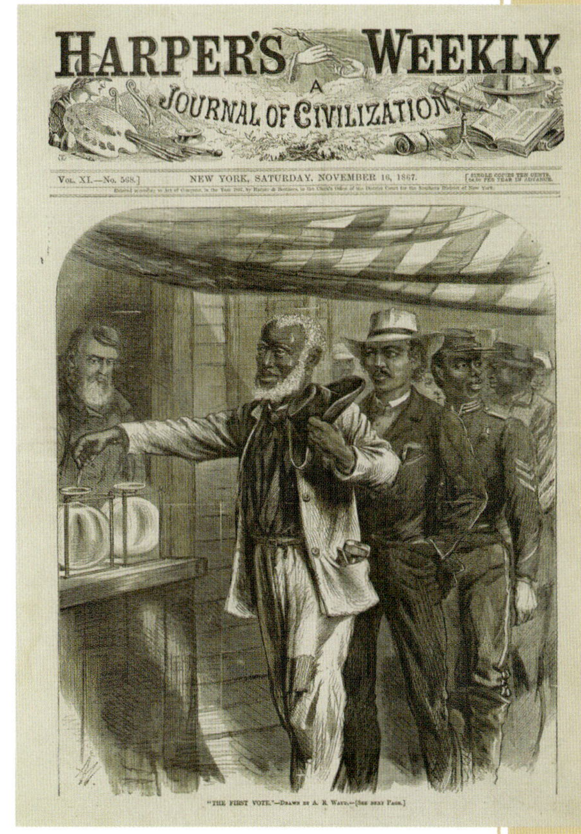

HARPER'S WEEKLY.
A JOURNAL OF CIVILIZATION.

Vol. XI.—No. 568.] NEW YORK, SATURDAY, NOVEMBER 16, 1867.

"THE FIRST VOTE."—Drawn by A. R. Waud.—[See next Page.]

THE GILDED AGE

BELOW *Golden spike ceremony, completing the Union Pacific Railroad.*

In United States history, the years between the conclusion of the Civil War and the turn of the 20th century are often referred to as the 'Gilded Age'. It's a name taken from an 1873 Mark Twain novel of the same title and was a period that saw great economic and technological advances as America transformed from a rural and agricultural society into an increasingly urban and industrialized polity. Millions of immigrants arrived from Europe and the nation 'shrank' as railroads linked the East and West coasts and all points in between. But it was a period that was also marked by political corruption and by great and growing inequalities between rich and poor. By 1900, half of the US working population would be labouring for company wages rather than for themselves.

The United States from the 1860s onwards recast itself as a nation built on business and manufacture, the signs of which were most visible throughout the North. Hundreds of tonnes of steel were produced every day to satisfy the needs of the expanding railroad network and the rise of 'sky-scraping apartment houses'. With the backing of Congress, the Union Pacific Railroad received permission to lay a rail track eastward from California to reach Iowa, where it connected with the rest of the railway system and produced the first transcontinental railway in 1869. In the early 1870s, Thomas Edison's improvements in telegraph operations brought more efficient communications, and the self-taught engineering genius invested his profits in an industrial research lab that churned out a stream of inventions, a thousand of which were patented under Edison's name. The Edison Electric Light Company illuminated city streets with incandescent light bulbs from 1882. Another potent symbol of growth was in urban centres, where the deployment of steel girders and safe elevators allowed architects to design taller and taller buildings, especially in Chicago and New York City. At the start of the 20th century, 66 'skyscrapers' were under construction in Lower Manhattan, some up to 25 storeys high, including the Flatiron Building, completed in 1902, and the Woolworth Building, the world's tallest edifice between 1913 and 1930.

BELOW *The Flatiron Building under construction, 1902.*

The boom in production owed much to a new wave of immigration, with Irish and German workers joined by Italians, Russians and Poles. Between 1890 and 1914, an estimated 15 million new arrivals landed in the United States, though not all of them stayed. These migrants transformed American society. The influx of many nationalities brought new languages, culture, food and religion and, unsurprisingly, stirred up fears that the country was being overwhelmed by people who would not adapt to an 'American' way of life. By 1900, the US had the largest population of European origin of any country except Russia. This was a far cry from the nation's mostly British origins. Immigration from China also grew rapidly on the West Coast, where Chinese labourers found work in railway construction, agriculture and industry until their immigration was curtailed in 1892.

Manhattan's Wall Street became the financial centre of the nation, with the offices of J.P. Morgan, the biggest name in banking, next door to the New York Stock Exchange. The greatest profits were to be found in the production of steel and, increasingly, oil, whose industries were respectively dominated by the Scottish American entrepreneur Andrew Carnegie and the self-made John D. Rockefeller. By the beginning of the 20th century, the latter's Standard Oil company had such complete control of US oil production and distribution that it was forcibly broken up by law in 1911. Much of Standard's success was underpinned by the rapidly increasing demand for gasoline that accompanied the huge growth in automobile ownership from around 1900.

ABOVE *Immigrants arrive at Ellis Island, 1915.*

Robber Barons

Cornelius Vanderbilt

ABOVE *Cornelius Vanderbilt.*

Cornelius Vanderbilt (1794–1877) made money by buying and selling water rights before investing in shipping. He operated his first ferry between Staten Island and New York City aged 16; by 40 he was running a line of steamships up the Hudson and to Boston, gaining himself the nickname 'the Commodore'. His service undercut government-subsidized shipping to the extent where he ultimately accepted money from his rivals to not sail his vessels against them in competition. Deals like this led to Vanderbilt and other US tycoons of the time to be labelled as 'Robber Barons' by the press. In 1862, Vanderbilt sold his ships and made a second fortune as a financier of railroads.

John D. Rockefeller

ABOVE John D. Rockefeller.

John D. Rockefeller (1839–1937) initially made his wealth through the buying and selling of agricultural products during the Civil War. He later moved into the oil business, refining crude oil into kerosene and other petroleum products and turning his company Standard Oil into a virtual monopoly that controlled prices from the oil well to the refinery and on to the consumer. In 1916, Rockefeller became the first US dollar billionaire.

Robber Barons (cont.)

Andrew Carnegie

ABOVE *Andrew Carnegie.*

Andrew Carnegie was born in Dunfermline, Scotland, in 1835. Financial struggles led his family to move to Pittsburgh, USA, when Andrew was 12. There, he progressed from working as a telegraph operator to running the Western Division of the Pennsylvania Railroad Company and turning over $50,000 a year ($968,000 today) by the end of the Civil War. Carnegie changed his focus to steel production and cannily bought into iron operations too. He teamed up with the coal- and coke-processing magnate Henry Clay Frick to ensure he could control the supply of raw materials to his foundries. Carnegie chose to retire in 1901 and sold his company, the first to be valued at more than $1 billion, to John Pierpont Morgan. He died in 1919.

J. P. Morgan

ABOVE *J. P. Morgan.*

The buyout of Carnegie's steel enterprises by J. P. Morgan (1837–1913) was the largest industrial takeover in US history to date and was one of the many major mergers between railroad, shipping, electricity and steel companies that benefitted the Connecticut-born mogul's banking business. Pierpont Morgan & Co. began trading during the Civil War and profited from the sale of Union bonds and arms. As a financier and manager, Morgan took active control of railroad corporations and helped the US Treasury and New York banks to avoid bankruptcy on more than one occasion.

In response to exploitation and inequality, workers began to organize in labour unions, and new populist political parties were created to represent the burgeoning working class. American unions were less committed to socialist agendas than their European equivalents. This was in part due to the more comfortable living standards enjoyed by workers in the US, and to the influx of immigrants happy to settle into the American way of life without complaint.

American capitalism had its setbacks, however. In 1885, a stock-market collapse triggered by a banking failure caused a squeeze on wages and 10 per cent unemployment. Farmers were also at the mercy of the markets and rising railroad charges. Many were in debt and faced interest payments on their land. One solution was to form alliances. By 1890, the National Farmers' Alliance had grown to accommodate more than a million members and was ready to tackle the two big political parties with the founding of the People's Party in 1892. Known more informally as the Populists, the new party incorporated white and Black farmers within its ranks, as well as women, and stood in opposition to a government which, it claimed (not without reason), colluded with big business. Among the Populists' demands was a graduated income tax, a shorter working day and nationalization of the railroad, telegraph and telephone systems. James B. Weaver, the party's presidential candidate in the 1892 election, won just over one million votes (representing 8.6 per cent of ballots cast). While this was significant, it also represented the peak of the party's popularity as an independent entity. It would ally, unsuccessfully, with the Democratic Party in subsequent elections.

ABOVE *James B. Weaver's 1892 election poster.*

DOMINION OF CANADA

At a time when the United States was divided by war, its northern neighbours were coming together. In 1864, a group of representatives from the colonies of Nova Scotia, New Brunswick, Prince Edward Island, Ontario and Quebec assembled at Charlottetown on Prince Edward Island to discuss an integrated British North America, the first step in the formation of modern Canada. The British North America Act – an agreement to establish a general federal union – was passed and quickly approved by the British government, which wanted to preclude any attempt by the USA to absorb Canada. The Dominion of Canada was officially formed on 1 July 1867 (a date now celebrated as Canada Day), consisting of the provinces Ontario, Quebec, Nova Scotia and New Brunswick – Prince Edward Island chose to remain a British colony for the time being. Canada was now a self-governing polity of the British Empire, dividing power between the federal government and the provinces.

One of the confederation's first acts was to acquire Rupert's Land, a vast territory that stretched from the border with the United States and surrounding Hudson's Bay. The land, now known as the Northwest Territories, was sparsely populated by indigenous

LEFT *Delegates at the Charlottetown Conference, 1864.*

communities and Métis (descendants of indigenous women and European fur traders), who were not consulted in the deal. Led by Louis Riel, the Métis forced the Canadian government to negotiate and to create the small province of Manitoba. The Dominion continued its spread westward, with New Caledonia and Vancouver Island being accepted into Canada as British Columbia in 1871. Prince Edward Island finally joined the confederation in 1873. A series of treaties with the indigenous people between Ontario and the Rocky Mountains removed their claim to territory in return for subsidies, medical care and land on reserves.

ABOVE *Louis Riel's provisional Métis government.*

Canada stretched between the Atlantic and Pacific Oceans. Helping bridge this broad territory was the Canadian Pacific Railway, completed in November 1885. In 1896, gold was discovered along the Klondike River in the northwestern region of Yukon, bordering the US state of Alaska. Prospectors from the United States were just some of the new wave of around 4.5 million immigrants entering Canada around this time, which also included many eastern Europeans from Ukraine who found agricultural work on the prairies. By the turn of the century, Canada was able to sustain its de facto independence from Britain, funded by its reserves of gold, a burgeoning industrial sector, and the successful export of wheat and timber. Despite this, questions about its absorption into the United States remained.

THE LATIN AMERICAN EXPORT BOOM

BELOW *Rubber plantation in Brazil, c.1925.*

Before the 1850s, Latin American countries had experienced far less social and economic change than the United States. Wealth and power tended to concentrate in the hands of landowning elites who dominated the rural economy, while an urban upper class shaped political discourse. Change accelerated in the latter half of the century, when Latin America's exports expanded and diversified in response to the needs of the industrializing world.

The growth of export markets was evident everywhere. The spread of electrification in the industrial countries generated a need for Chilean, Peruvian and Mexican copper; Bolivian tin was required to plate the steel cans used for preserved food; nitrates from Bolivia, Peru and Chile supplied fertilizer to European farmers. Rubber from Amazonian Brazil, Peru and Bolivia became vital for car tyres and electrical insulation. Mexican

henequen, a type of agave, provided twine for American farmers to bind their bales of hay. Chilled and tinned beef, wool and wheat from the plains of Argentina and Uruguay were exported to Europe. More countries engaged in Latin American trade, too, with the US becoming a major partner in some regions. By mid-century, Britain had taken the lead in providing markets and supplying imports, a lead which it long retained in the Southern Cone (the bottom part of South America comprising Uruguay, Argentina and Chile). By 1913, the US was a leading market and supplier of goods, especially for Mexico and Central America, which were now increasingly seen as America's 'back yard'.

ABOVE *Conquest of the Desert.*

The high growth rate of exports, encouraged by free trade, brought unprecedented wealth into Latin America, reflected in the accumulation of individual and family fortunes and the renovation of towns and cities. The benefits were unevenly spread, however, and the growth of national wealth did little to improve general living standards. Between *c.*1850–1910, the United States achieved an increase in gross national product of about 1.5 per cent a year; in Latin America, only Argentina and Chile reached that level and most countries fell far below. Living standards were accordingly low. Employers seeking rural labour often used devices such as retaining workers by debt, for example by paying wages in advance or overcharging for goods bought at company stores, or resorted to outright intimidation. Brazil and Cuba continued to rely on slavery. From 1800 to 1850, Brazil benefitted from the free labour of around 1.5 million enslaved people while the Spanish Caribbean, mainly Cuba, exploited the efforts of around half that number. Semi-coerced labour, mostly Chinese, also played a part in boosting export production, not only in Peru's guano industry and coastal agriculture but also in Cuban sugar and Mexican henequen plantations.

The largest contribution to the labour force came from a massive influx of European immigrants, mostly into Argentina, Uruguay and Brazil. Argentina alone absorbed about 2.5 million Europeans from 1871 to 1915, 80 per cent of whom were from Italy and Spain. By 1914, about a third of the Argentine population was foreign born. As many lived in Buenos Aires, the country's capital began to resemble a European city. The

immigration boom transformed Argentina and Uruguay, which joined the world's richest economies, with their production of beef, wool and wheat adding to the great expansion of global food supplies that had started on the prairies of the United States and Canada.

When they stood in the way of agricultural expansion, indigenous peoples came under attack. Some regions saw deliberate government-backed military campaigns designed to clear them from areas required for ranching and settlement, notoriously in Argentina's so-called 'Conquest of the Desert' in the 1870s and 1880s that was aimed against semi-nomadic communities. Indeed, throughout the far south, indigenous people were driven off the land to make way for Chilean and Argentine livestock farmers, including the Mapuche people of the Pampas and the Selk'nam and Yaghan people of Tierra del Fuego.

ABOVE *Porfirio Díaz.*

LATIN AMERICAN POLITICS DURING THE EXPORT BOOM

Prosperity built on commodity exports changed the political scene. The idealistic liberalism of the early 19th century, focused on the rights of man, was increasingly overtaken by a new strain of politics based on the positivist belief in science, which stressed the link between order and progress, and the need for strong and interventionist government to achieve it. Increasingly, the groups who held economic power formed

BELOW *The Battle of Arica, 7 June 1880, part of the War of the Pacific.*

oligarchies which ran regions and nations. Like their predecessors, they embraced economic liberalism, allowing free trade, but focused on strengthening the state and imposing authoritarian government.

Two patterns stand out. One was 'oligarchic democracy', in which the formal framework of liberal democracy remained in place but voting was restricted and elections manipulated from above. In Argentina and Chile, for example, political parties that represented factions of the oligarchy competed for power but agreed on basic issues and prioritized order over most other concerns. Typically, such states were dominated by powerful families linked in extended kinship groups, which might include families with land and urban property, wealth from commerce, agriculture and export commodities, as well as members with military and political influence, and professionals such as lawyers, doctors and priests. A second pattern resembled dictatorship. Here, upper-class rule was more indirect and was applied through strong men, often military officers, who imposed law and order on behalf of the economic elites. A prime example was Porfirio Díaz, the Mexican leader who held power for almost 40 years, but the pattern also appeared in Peru, Venezuela and other countries. In both cases, the fundamental aim was to create centralized nation-states and impose social control in the interests of the privileged classes. Political stability was seen as essential to attract foreign investment to boost growth and strengthen the state. Investment in railways was particularly welcome, as it not only improved the economic infrastructure but also helped governments impose their rule.

ABOVE *Maximilian I of Mexico.*

Chile was a notable example of an oligarchic republic created by leading families who benefitted from the export boom. In the 1870s, Chilean companies secured rights to mine nitrates on Bolivian territory in return for tax payments. When Bolivia increased the tax, their legal conflict escalated into war. Peru tried to mediate but, having signed a mutual defence treaty with Bolivia, was drawn into the conflict. Chile's well-organized army and navy prevailed in the War of the Pacific (1879–84), soundly defeating its adversaries and winning control of the mineral-rich coastal strip, taken from Peru and Bolivia. Bolivia, by contrast, suffered a lasting setback, by losing its access to the sea as well as important mineral resources. It was now landlocked, with its navy confined to the waters of Lake Titicaca, high in the Andes.

Another instance of war arising from conflict over returns on investment, in this case entangled with internal political conflicts, occurred in Mexico. The 1860 'War of the Reform' was fought between liberals determined to extend civil rights and reduce the power of the Church and conservatives determined to preserve a more traditional society. It ended with the victory of the liberal Benito Juárez, who was elected president in 1861. When Juárez then declared a moratorium on Mexico's foreign debts, he immediately aroused the animosity of foreign creditors. While the US was distracted by its own Civil War, France tried to establish a client state in Mexico, by placing the Austrian Archduke Ferdinand Maximilian on the throne of a new Mexican empire between 1864 and 1867. The French intervention was short-lived, however. Faced with strong resistance in Mexico, the French ruler Napoleon III withdrew his forces, leaving Maximilian to be deposed and executed. Juárez restored the republic, implemented extensive economic and educational reforms, and dominated politics until his death in 1872.

A quite different war occurred at around the same time in the Río de la Plata basin, where the territories of Paraguay, Bolivia, Argentina, Uruguay and the Empire of Brazil met. The border lands were poorly defined, which encouraged dissent over territorial rights. After some preliminary skirmishes in 1864, in which Paraguay supported Uruguay against Brazil, the conflict widened into the War of the Triple Alliance in 1865, when Brazil, Argentina and Uruguay took up arms against Paraguay. The Alliance invaded Paraguay in spring 1866, leading to some of the bloodiest battles in Latin American history. The fighting ended in 1870, when the Paraguayan dictator Francisco Solano López was killed in battle and a provisional government was put in place. The war was an unmitigated disaster for Paraguay. It lost between nine and 19 per cent of its population, mostly males, and about 40 per cent of its pre-war territory to Brazil and Argentina.

RIGHT
Proclamation of the Republic of Brazil.

BRAZIL, THE OLD REPUBLIC (1889–1930)

Brazil's monarchy oversaw a period of prolonged prosperity thanks to the export of coffee and rubber from the Amazon basin. Dom Pedro II, Emperor of Brazil, had outlawed slavery in 1888 and the country had seen a huge population increase, with 100,000

Pedro II and the Belle Époque

Pedro II (1825–91) came to the Brazilian Imperial throne following his father's abdication in 1831. He gained full power aged 14, in 1840. Dom Pedro II's early years were spent stabilizing the country and seeing it thrive as an exporter. Brazil's boom period was epitomized by the construction of the Amazon Theatre in Manaus. This Renaissance-style opera house was built in the heart of the rainforest but had cast-iron columns that came from Scotland, an auditorium based on a Parisian interior and 198 crystal chandeliers from Italy. The theatre was completed after the reign of Pedro II and inaugurated five years after his death in exile in Paris, France.

LEFT *The Amazon Theatre in Manaus, Brazil, constructed between 1884 and 1896.*

immigrants entering the country in 1889 alone. Despite this prosperity, Pedro II was ousted by a coalition of landowners and the military. Brazil's first republican government was founded in November 1889, with the coup leader General Manuel Deodoro da Fonseca taking charge.

Within two years the republic had agreed a constitution and had a directly elected president at the head of a federal government that incorporated 20 self-governing states. Oligarchs still held power in the regions and only literate men were allowed to vote (a mere 3 per cent of the population). Wealthy landowners dominated regional governments, while the São Paulo coffee plantation owners and cattle barons of Minas Gerais provided almost all of the republic's presidents in a policy dubbed *política do café com leite* ('coffee with milk'). Coffee accounted for more than half of Brazilian exports by the turn of the century.

THE UNITED STATES IN THE CARIBBEAN

Spain retained its grip on Cuba after the first wars of independence around mid-century and continued to oppose all attempts of the island's inhabitants to achieve independence. To eliminate rural insurgency, colonial governments adopted draconian methods, which

included *campos de concentracion* (the confining of rural people into government-controlled settlements) and a scorched-earth policy in the countryside. The reports of Spanish atrocities carried by US newspapers (especially Joseph Pulitzer's *New York World* and William Randolph Hearst's *New York Journal*) stimulated public indignation at colonial oppression and increased the periodicals' circulations by inciting war. United States President William McKinley was reluctant to intervene, but had little choice when, in February 1898, the US battleship *Maine* blew up in Havana's harbour, killing most of its crew. It is likely that the explosion was an accident, but rabid press reports claiming that it was a Spanish plot forced an official

ABOVE *American artillery hoist the flag at Fort Malate, Philippines, 1898.*

American response. McKinley duly declared what was dubbed a 'splendid little war' on Spain that was brief and one-sided. American warships sank and disabled a Spanish flotilla in the Philippines, while land forces defeated Spanish forces in Cuba. The ensuing peace treaty granted independence to Cuba, albeit as a virtual protectorate of the United States, and gave America responsibility for Puerto Rico, Guam and the Philippines. Although both wars are now largely forgotten, they were important conflicts in that they pointed towards the development of a new imperialism. Trade rather than territory, commercial ambition not colonialism, underpinned the United States' challenge to Spain, as well as the country's annexation of the Hawaiian islands in 1898, which linked American trade with China and Japan.

RIGHT *Theodore Roosevelt.*

'A SQUARE DEAL'

The shift towards a more aggressive external policy became more pronounced during the presidency of Theodore Roosevelt (1901–9). Roosevelt was a reformer who alarmed his Republican Party colleagues with plans to raise taxes from monopolies and confront corruption. While the Populists saw big government as the problem, Progressives like Roosevelt believed that America's issues were best addressed by more and better regulation of business and a check on the power of plutocrats. Nominated as vice president alongside William McKinley for the 1900 election, Roosevelt took the presidency when McKinley was assassinated in 1901 and set about pursuing policies aimed at strengthening the United States within and without.

The key to Roosevelt's domestic policy was reform that promised greater economic and social equality – what he called 'a square deal' for all – enacted by a stronger central state. While not anti-business, Roosevelt aimed to curb the accumulation of power by America's richest – and unelected – men. One of his first acts was to prevent the banking magnate J.P. Morgan from forming Northern Securities, a large trust that would have put almost all of the western rail and shipping lanes into his hands. Roosevelt also pressed Congress for legislation to protect food quality and conserve woodland, adding 81 million hectares (200 million acres) of national park land.

Roosevelt was equally committed to asserting American power abroad. He fought as a volunteer in Cuba during the war against Spain and was an enthusiastic proponent for extending US authority in the Caribbean Basin. Indeed, in 1904 he added the 'Roosevelt Corollary' to the Monroe Doctrine by announcing that only the US could intervene to deal with misdemeanours by independent states in and around the Caribbean, if necessary on behalf of foreign powers. Roosevelt believed, too, that the United States should live up to its status as a world power on a par with the large European nations and build up its navy to ensure that it was respected overseas. When, in 1904, the United States took over construction of the Panama Canal, assuming control from the French-led consortium that had abandoned the project in 1889, this reflected Roosevelt's thinking

The Panama Canal

At 82 km (51 miles) long, the Panama Canal took ten years to complete at a cost of $350 million ($11 billion today) and 5,600 workers' lives. The US army played an important part in planning and supervising its construction and in fighting disease among its mostly immigrant workforce. The first ocean-going ship to pass through the canal was the *Cristóbal* on 3 August 1914. The celebrations, however, were muted; that same day, Germany had declared war on France. World War I had begun.

LEFT *A ship passes through the Panama Canal, 1915.*

that the waterway would help his country assert its naval dominance and trading interests in the Pacific. Panama before 1904 had been under the jurisdiction of Colombia, and when that country's Senate rejected Roosevelt's initial offer to purchase the French-owned rights to cut across the isthmus of Panama, the US president secretly encouraged Panamanian separatists to revolt. When Panama duly won its independence in November 1903 the United States lost little time in securing permission to complete the canal and operate it in exchange for an annual fee of $250,000 ($8.86 million today) payable to the Panamanian government.

Roosevelt's successor, the Democrat Woodrow Wilson, would prove equally successful in delivering progressive policies. He strengthened anti-trust laws, introduced the Federal Reserve Act to stabilize the US banking system and a scaled income tax that demanded more from the country's top earners. He also looked to improve conditions for workers by mandating an eight-hour workday and restricting child labour. Wilson would, however, make his most significant mark in international politics by steering the United States through World War I and the Paris Peace Conference that followed it, successfully advocating for the creation of the League of Nations, a multinational organization designed to prevent fresh conflict (but which the United States itself did not join).

THE MEXICAN REVOLUTION, 1910–20

While the United States emerged as a global power at the turn of the century, neighbouring Mexico went through one of the greatest upheavals in its history following the fall of the dictator Porfirio Díaz, a military man who held the presidency from 1897 to 1911. His extraordinary longevity in politics owed something to his control of the army but rested primarily on his relationship with an oligarchy that favoured order and progress and wanted good relationships with both the United States and Great Britain, for the capital investment they brought. This was a classic positivist regime. Public health, communications and transportation were improved, while the liberal freedoms of elections and a free press were curtailed and political opposition crushed.

The catalyst for change came with the election of 1910. In the preceding years, Mexico suffered widespread immiseration, caused by inflation, falling wages, poor harvests and unemployment. Workers and middle-class voters welcomed a new challenger to Díaz in Francisco Madero and his Anti-Re-electionist Party. Madero was a wealthy liberal with business concerns in cereals, cattle and mining, but he came out in support of workers and against the suppression of strikers. He was arrested ahead of the election but, on his release shortly after, fled across the border and denounced the ballot from the safety of Texas. An anti-Díaz coalition gathered momentum, including lower-class insurrections in several regions. In Chihuahua, farm labourers led by Pascual Orozco and Francisco 'Pancho' Villa took up arms against the wealthy elites that controlled the land. To the south, Emiliano Zapata led the peasant communities of the Morelos region in a fight to regain their ancestral lands. Under pressure from his wealthy supporters, Díaz was forced out of office and Madero installed, on the understanding he would disarm the peasant rebel groups. But Madero proved unable to control Zapata or to prevent industrial action. He then lost US support when he raised an oil-production tax. He was removed from power and killed in 1913 during a coup led by one of his generals, Victoriano Huerta.

BELOW *Francisco Madero arrives during the coup dubbed the Ten Tragic Days, February 1913.*

Huerta was unable to defeat Zapata and Villa, however, or to win US support. Woodrow Wilson sent troops to occupy the port of Veracruz for six months and supplied arms to various factions. Huerta resigned and was replaced in 1917 by a Madero supporter, Venustiano Carranza, a leading light of the liberal-centrist Constitutionalist faction, who presided over Mexico's first revolutionary constitution. Carranza's rule did not lead to a great change in Mexican governance, but the 1917 constitution was a radical document which made social reform possible. It empowered government to redistribute land, announced workers' rights that far exceeded those in the United States, and provided a challenge to the old system of property and power. These gains were more fully realized in the 1920s and 1930s.

Zapata and Villa

Emiliano Zapata

ABOVE *Emiliano Zapata.*

Emiliano Zapata (1879–1919) was a peasant's son arrested in his teens for joining protests against the large commercial landowners (*hacendados*) who were forcing peasant smallholders off the land. After a brief period in the army, Zapata returned to supporting peasant farmers and took back *hacendados*-occupied land by force in order to redistribute it. Zapata backed Francisco Madero in the aftermath of the disputed 1910 election and led a guerrilla force of 5,000 men to take Cuernavaca, the state capital of Morelos. Madero failed to act on Zapata's demands for communal land ownership, so Zapata returned to the countryside to continue his independent attacks on the *hacendados*. As well as redistributing land, Zapata set up a Rural Loan Bank, to provide credit to farmers. His reforms were popular but unacceptable to Venustiano Carranza, whose soldiers assassinated him in 1919.

Francisco 'Pancho' Villa

ABOVE *Pancho Villa.*

Francisco 'Pancho' Villa (1877–1923) was a *hacienda* worker, muleteer, rustler, miner, trader and bandit before joining the Madero-led revolution against Porfirio Díaz in 1911. When General Victoriano Huerta removed Madero in 1913, Villa joined Carranza's side against the coup leaders and proved himself to be a very capable military leader. He then joined Zapata in opposing Carranza and seeking land reform. On Carranza's death in 1920, Villa laid down his arms and received a pardon. He was assassinated by his political enemies in 1923.

CHAPTER 7

THE AMERICAS IN THE AGE OF GLOBAL CRISIS

Before 1914, the global order built during the later 19th century showed signs of strain, as growth in international trade and investment slowed and social unrest disturbed the stability of the great states. The question of how to accommodate the United States in a world dominated by Britain and other European powers was also unresolved. However, in 1914, these developments were still in play when the international order was shattered by the outbreak of a global war. World War I ended peaceful co-existence among the imperial powers and destroyed the Austro-Hungarian, Russian and Ottoman empires. After a short respite in the 1920s, the post-war order fractured during the 1930s, opening new political fissures both within and between nations, and initiating new, more aggressive forms of imperialism in Germany, Italy and Japan. These were also tumultuous times for the Americas. For, though they were distant from European power politics, the United States and the Latin American countries were battered by the Great Depression and the repercussions of two global wars.

THE GREAT WAR

At the outbreak of war in August 1914, President Woodrow Wilson affirmed that the United States would remain neutral, on the grounds that the European war was one 'with which we have nothing to do, whose causes cannot touch us'. Even after a German U-boat sank the British ocean liner *Lusitania* in May 1915, with the loss of 1,198 crew and passengers, including 128 Americans, Wilson stayed out of the war for almost another two years. American reluctance changed in 1917, when Germany showed its willingness to infringe US neutrality. First, the German foreign minister Arthur Zimmerman took secret steps to form an alliance between Mexico and Germany, should the United States enter the war, with the promise of support to regain territory taken by the US in the Mexican–American War. And, weeks after the telegram was sent, Germany resumed submarine warfare on enemy or neutral ships, including those bearing the American flag. Unable to ignore these affronts, the United States Congress formally declared war on Germany on 6 April 1917, with President Wilson pronouncing that 'the world must be made safe for democracy'. Railroads in the United States were temporarily brought under federal control and conscription was implemented. In 1918, 2 million US troops sailed to France in support of the Allies, at a point in the war when German forces were moving towards Paris. Although they were late arrivals, the vast number of fresh soldiers, plus the finances and military supplies promised by the Americans' entry into the war, changed the balance of the conflict.

BELOW *The RMS* Lusitania.

BELOW *The Zimmermann Telegram.*

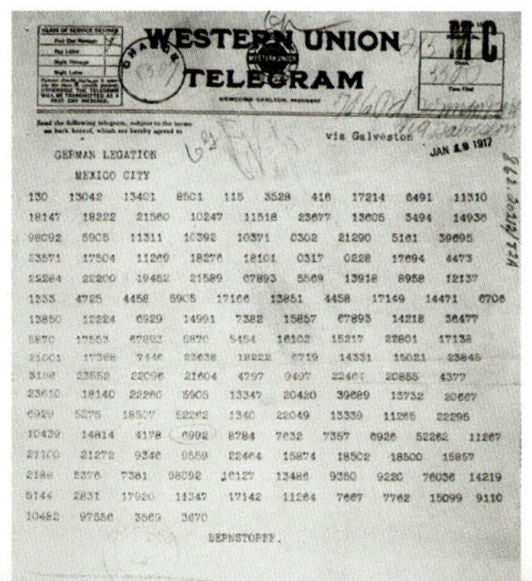

WESTERN UNION TELEGRAM

via Galveston JAN 19 1917

GERMAN LEGATION
MEXICO CITY

130 13042 13401 8501 115 3528 416 17214 6491 11310
18147 18222 21560 10247 11518 23677 13605 3494 14936
98092 5905 11311 10392 10371 0302 21290 5161 39695
23571 17504 11269 18276 18101 0317 0228 17694 4473
22284 22200 19452 21589 67893 5569 13918 8958 12137
1333 4725 4458 5905 17166 13851 4458 17149 14471 6706
13850 12224 6929 14991 7382 15857 67893 14218 36477
5870 17553 67893 5870 5454 16102 15217 22801 17138
21001 17388 7446 23638 18222 6719 14331 15021 23845
3156 23552 22096 21604 4797 9497 22464 20855 4377
23610 18140 22260 5905 13347 20420 39689 13732 20667
6929 5275 18507 52262 1340 22049 13339 11265 22295
10439 14814 4178 6992 8784 7632 7357 6926 52262 11267
21100 21272 9346 9559 22464 15874 18502 18500 15857
2188 5376 7381 98092 16127 13486 9350 9220 76036 14219
5144 2831 17920 11347 17142 11264 7667 7762 15099 9110
10482 97556 3569 3670

BERNSTORFF.

Charge German Embassy.

Once the United States entered the war, many Latin American states followed suit. Cuba, Haiti, Panama, Costa Rica, Nicaragua, Honduras and Brazil declared war on the Central Powers in 1917. Bolivia, Peru, Uruguay and Ecuador broke off relations with Germany, while Mexico, Argentina, Chile, Colombia, El Salvador, Paraguay and Venezuela remained neutral. No Latin American state took a direct part in the war, however, at sea or on land. British Americans had no such luxury, as they were expected to join the war effort as soon as hostilities began in 1914. The West Indies sent volunteers and Canada made a substantial contribution, second only to India. More than

650,000 Canadians and Newfoundlanders were transported to Europe's battlefields, while Canadian factories provided large amounts of munitions. As volunteers tapered off, the government introduced a draft in 1917, a move that was especially unpopular with French Canadians. Nonetheless, Canadian troops and pilots made a significant contribution to the Allied victory, particularly in major offensives in 1918 known as 'Canada's Hundred Days'. Canada's involvement in the war also had major political repercussions. Debates over participation sharpened Canadian nationalism and disputes over the supply of troops for Britain's wars eventually led to the signing of the Statute of Westminster in 1931, which gave Canada full legal autonomy and the right to make its own laws.

The United States' intervention in World War I was decisive. First, it helped to defeat Germany on the European front, including at Meuse-Argonne, the deadliest campaign in US history, in which more than 26,000 soldiers were killed. Over six months of combat, the American Expeditionary Force suffered 255,000 casualties, many of whom died due to an influenza pandemic that probably started in army training camps in the US and, on reaching Europe, became the deadly global pandemic known as the Spanish Flu. Secondly, President Wilson played a key part in negotiating an end to the war in 1918, backing the Allies' demands that German troops withdraw from all occupied territories and that Kaiser Wilhelm II abdicate. The acceptance of these terms in November 1918 led to the armistice that ended the war.

ABOVE *American soldiers at Meuse-Argonne.*

Wilson was also instrumental in the post-war settlement. He was the first US president to spend any time outside the Americas while in office, passing six months in Paris during peace negotiations on which he exerted a strong influence. The Fourteen Points that he composed included the restoration and adjustment of European borders, a reduction in arms and the establishment of a League of Nations, an international body intended to intervene in and settle disputes between countries. The peace treaty that

BELOW *Canadian soldiers at the Battle of Vimy Ridge, 1917.*

ABOVE *President Woodrow Wilson.*

was eventually agreed at Versailles demanded Germany accept responsibility for starting the war and pay crippling reparations. Wilson received the Nobel Peace Prize in 1919 for his work in establishing the League of Nations, but the desire among the people and the politicians at home to not involve themselves further in European affairs ensured that the United States never joined it.

Engagement in a global war had a powerful impact on American politics. The US was not as badly damaged physically as the leading European powers, but the war had a palpable effect on the American state and its citizens. Political power, for example, became much more centrally concentrated. To support the war effort, the federal government had legislated on most areas of industry and business, and many progressives welcomed the standardization, efficiencies and increased social mobility that this brought. However, although the nation appeared united in grief over the loss of more than 100,000 soldiers, it soon showed itself to be deeply divided. After the war, a wave of labour strikes swept through American cities, bringing with it a 'Red Scare' that followed hard on the Russian Revolution of 1917. By the end of the decade there was a palpable belief that the forces of socialism were behind the industrial unrest. The wartime patriotism that had produced anti-German prejudice now transformed into a fear of and an opposition to radical – that is left-leaning – forces. This was reflected in the imprisonment of the socialist leader Eugene Debs in 1918, and, much more powerfully, in the trial in 1920 of the Italian immigrant anarchists Nicolo Sacco and Bartolomeo Vanzetti. Charged with armed robbery and murder, they were painted by their supporters as innocent victims in a class war that was biased against immigrants and radicals, and by their enemies as dangerous revolutionaries intent on destroying the United States itself. The latter party saw its arguments prevail and both men were executed in 1927. Writing just a few years after the event, the American novelist John Dos Passos argued that the US had become 'two nations', comprised of 'oppressors' and 'the beaten crowd'.

RIGHT *Opening of the League of Nations.*

LEFT *Crowd of supporters following the hearses of Sacco and Vanzetti during their funeral, 1927.*

Whatever the true motives of Sacco and Vanzetti, there were a small number of genuine anti-government groups who plotted deadly acts of violence. Anarchists were responsible for sending homemade parcel bombs to congressmen. One Italian-born anarchist was killed by his own explosive which he planned to use against the US

Eugene V. Debs

One of the most prominent and charismatic US radicals of his day, Eugene V. Debs (1855–1926) was a former railroad worker, leader of the Socialist Party and co-founder of the international labour union, the Industrial Workers of the World. Debs came to prominence in 1894 when leading the American Railway Union in a strike over pay. A year later, he was jailed for six months and spent his time in prison reading Marx and socialist pamphlets, cementing his political views. Debs ran for president on behalf of the Socialist Party in 1900, the first of five unsuccessful campaigns, though he received almost a million votes in 1912. In 1918, Debs made a passionate speech against the military draft, which led to his arrest for violating the Espionage Act. He was sentenced to ten years but was released early by President Warren G. Harding on Christmas Day, 1921.

LEFT *Eugene V. Debs in 1921, after his release.*

ABOVE Disposal of illegal liquor during Prohibition.

attorney general, A. Mitchell Palmer, in the summer of 1919. A few months later, Palmer formed a Bureau of Investigation to hunt down radicals, leading to the arrest of a thousand socialists and anarchists, the first of several drives to eradicate leftist radicals. J. Edgar Hoover, the man Palmer placed in charge of his agency, would remain at the head of the new department as it evolved into the Federal Bureau of Investigation (FBI) and became a leading persecutor of the American left.

Concerns about foreign threats also motivated new legislation restricting immigration, which was also fuelled by prejudices about racial purity and perennial anxieties about influxes of 'aliens' who were incapable of becoming the true 'Americans' defined by nationalist mythology. The National Origins Act of 1924 introduced quotas for certain countries. Annual numbers from Europe were reduced to 150,000, and, while there were no limits on immigration from Latin America, immigrants from China and Japan were effectively banned. High walls were being built around the 'city on a hill', now narrowly construed as a sanctuary of Anglo-Saxon values. However, America was already a highly diverse society and culture, committed to democratic ideas of equality and opportunity and, as failed attempts to outlaw the consumption of alcohol showed, it was resistant to the imposition of social discipline from above. The Eighteenth Amendment to the Constitution of January 1920 prohibited the manufacture and sale of alcohol, but to no great effect. The demand for alcohol continued and production and consumption went underground. The illegal trade in alcohol benefitted organized crime and gangsters such as Chicago's Al Capone as well as smugglers operating along the Canadian border. Clandestine drinking venues known as speakeasies became an integral part of city life during America's 'Jazz Age'.

THE ROARING TWENTIES

The 'Roaring Twenties', as this era became known, saw unparalleled expansion and innovation. In the decade 1919–29, gross national product rose from $72.4 billion to $104 billion and the United States became the richest country in the world per capita. Skyscrapers increased in number and scale, symbolizing the nation's ascent, while consumer markets flourished. By 1927, 63 per cent of American homes had electricity and could use new appliances such as cookers and refrigerators. By the end of the decade, more than 40 per cent had radios and around 80 per cent of the population enjoyed the entertainment provided by the new technology of cinema. Thousand-capacity theatres opened in the cities, showing silent movies accompanied by pipe organ music. By 1926, 20,000 movie theatres had opened across the country. The motion picture industry received a massive boost the following year when the first 'talkies' were released – motion pictures with synchronized sound. In the home, radio brought families together for nightly news reports, music and drama. In 1922, President Warren G. Harding demonstrated the medium's political potential by addressing the nation directly by radio. This removed the need for campaigning politicians to tour the country by rail. In 1927, this new audience listened excitedly to live radio reports from Paris describing the first successful non-stop flight across the Atlantic by the pilot Charles Lindbergh, publicizing a new form of technology whose popularity and use would develop from a rich person's pursuit to a means of mass transportation in the years to come.

ABOVE *Charles Lindbergh takes off on his transatlantic flight.*

Another innovative feature of economic and social life was the growing use of cars. The car industry did much to drive the American economy throughout the 1920s, helped by massive investment in new highways. Annual automobile production rose from around 9 million at the start of the decade to 27 million at its end, providing work not only in the motor industry itself but also in the rubber, steel, oil and other industries. Its central figure was Henry Ford, who became internationally renowned for his success as a carmaker and for showing how standardization could yield productive efficiency. 'Fordism' was regarded as the economic model of the future, an essentially American future of mass production and consumption and burgeoning economic power. Ford also represented another feature of contemporary capitalism: its opposition to organized labour. Like his fellow industrialists, Ford sought to prevent the unionization of his workforce by all possible means, including violence and intimidation.

Wheels for All

Thanks to the innovations of Henry Ford, automobiles became affordable to ordinary Americans. The first Model T went on sale on October 1908. A simple vehicle, it was started with a hand crank and had a middle pedal for reverse and a top speed of about 70 km/h (45 mph). Ford's use of the assembly line, with workers focusing on one part of the assembly process as the vehicle moved along a conveyor, was central to its success. Through this process, Ford's production lines reduced the time it took to produce a Model T from around 14 hours to approximately 90 minutes. This allowed for a greater number of automobiles to be built and sold at relatively low prices.

LEFT *The Ford Model T.*

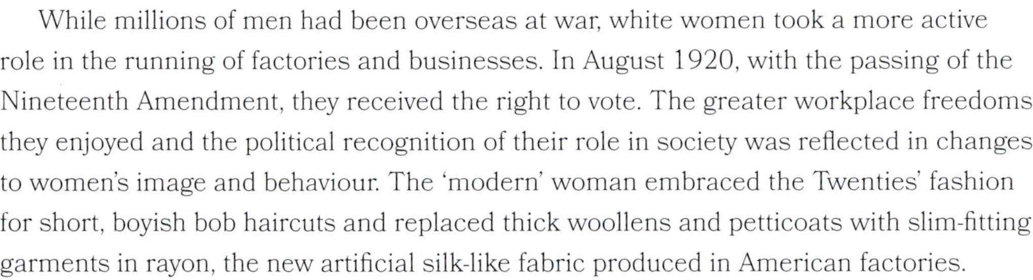

While millions of men had been overseas at war, white women took a more active role in the running of factories and businesses. In August 1920, with the passing of the Nineteenth Amendment, they received the right to vote. The greater workplace freedoms they enjoyed and the political recognition of their role in society was reflected in changes to women's image and behaviour. The 'modern' woman embraced the Twenties' fashion for short, boyish bob haircuts and replaced thick woollens and petticoats with slim-fitting garments in rayon, the new artificial silk-like fabric produced in American factories. Women were also more socially active and visible. They could drive cars, smoke cigarettes and drink alcohol and, in the ubiquitous speakeasies of cities such as New York, Los Angeles and Chicago, dance to jazz, the new upbeat, brass-led music developed by Black musicians such as the trumpeter Louis Armstrong.

BELOW *Actress Louise Brooks, displaying classic Twenties' fashion.*

When the writer F. Scott Fitzgerald coined the term 'the Jazz Age' to describe this period it was meant as much as a sign of disillusionment as a celebration of exuberance. In novels such as *The Beautiful and the Damned* and *The Great Gatsby*, Fitzgerald described a culture of hedonistic excess, led by the idle rich. This was played out against a jazz soundtrack, proof that what had begun as a folk music among Black communities in the South had entered the mainstream to become an enduring phenomenon. The rise of jazz was part of a wider social change that had seen more than a million Black people move in search of work and better life opportunities from the South to the cities of the North. There, they joined poor European immigrants in an eclectic social mix.

THE CRASH AND THE GREAT DEPRESSION

The economic environment of the Twenties was, however, based on the optimistic assumption that the nation was capable of unstoppable growth. This created a situation which stimulated over-production. When the inevitable correction came, it was more than simply a cyclical downturn of the kind which had previously occurred. A deeper crisis began when the mania for speculative investment in company shares gave way to a widespread panic, starting on 24 October 1929, when rumours of falling values prompted a rush to offload shares. This caused a dramatic crash on the New York stock market, which soon spread throughout the financial system and into the wider economy. Savers rushed to banks to withdraw their funds. People lost trust in the market and, as shares plummeted in value, small, uninsured local banks found that they did not have the funds to return deposits. Thousands of banks with insufficient reserves closed between 1930 and 1932, and, although only about 10 per cent of US households owned shares, the loss of confidence in financial services initiated a downward spiral. People spent less and businesses responded by tightening their belts and reducing their workforce – at one point at a rate of around 100,000 employees a week. By 1932,

LEFT *Crowds gather outside the New York Stock Exchange on 24 October 1929.*

The Dust Bowl

In addition to the financial problems that plagued the nation, American farmers suffered from the extended droughts and storms that swept across the Great Plains of Kansas, Oklahoma and Texas, lifting the dusty topsoil and dumping it on distant cities. Farming methods played a part in this disaster, as crops such as corn and wheat did not have roots long enough to bind and nourish the soil. Ploughing unsettled the arid earth while dry weather desiccated it, transforming fertile agricultural land into a dust bowl. Unable to grow and sell a harvest, many farmers packed their belongings and headed to the cities in a forlorn hope of better fortune, an exodus vividly depicted in John Steinbeck's 1939 novel, *The Grapes of Wrath.*

LEFT *A farmer and his children walking in a dust storm in Oklahoma, 1936.*

12 to 13 million citizens were out of work. The stock market crash had metastasized into a full-blown crisis of American capitalism and provoked a prolonged depression throughout the world.

In the face of the crisis, President Herbert Hoover reiterated the principles set out in his 1928 election campaign. He adhered to the Republican Party creed that America's strength lay in the 'rugged individualism' of its citizens, who would restore prosperity by their own efforts. He inaugurated new infrastructure projects to generate employment, such as the Boulder Dam (now known as the Hoover Dam) on the Colorado River, and he encouraged private charities and state authorities to alleviate the worst effects of job losses. It was not enough. Shanty towns erected on the outskirts of cities for poverty-stricken families were mockingly dubbed 'Hoovervilles' and the president's inadequacy in dealing with the crisis ensured that he was voted out of office in 1932. The newly elected Democrat president, Franklin Delano Roosevelt, adopted an entirely different approach. While Hoover regarded government intervention as un-American, Roosevelt took the opposite view and turned to state intervention on an unprecedented scale to get the nation back on its feet.

BELOW *Workers from the Civil Works Administration painting the Denver capitol building, 1934.*

A NEW DEAL

To address the economic slump and social distress that followed the crash, Roosevelt introduced the New Deal, an ambitious combination of legislation and public-works programmes aimed at short-term recovery and longer-term economic and social reform. Its first phase included the Federal Emergency Relief Administration, which provided direct relief to those who had lost their homes and lacked work and food, and a National Recovery Administration which aimed to bring business into a war on poverty. The government also financed the Civil Works Administration and Civilian Conservation Corps, which hired millions of unemployed people in new infrastructure and outdoor projects, including the building of 40,000 schools, 1,000 airports, new transport links and 800,000 km (500,000 miles) of road surfacing. A second phase of the New Deal took

Franklin Delano Roosevelt

A distant cousin of former president Theodore Roosevelt, Franklin Delano Roosevelt (1882–1945) became assistant secretary for the navy during the presidency of Woodrow Wilson and vice-presidential candidate for the Democrats in 1920. A year later, aged 39, Roosevelt contracted polio, which left him paralyzed from the waist down. Confined to a wheelchair in private, he hid his infirmity from the public by wearing steel leg braces and struggling to walk upright. Like his cousin, FDR, as he was known, became governor of New York (1929–33) ahead of a successful presidential campaign.

FDR is renowned for his New Deal, which supported banks and sponsored extensive work programmes to revive the US economy, for his leadership during World War II and for his contribution to post-war economic reconstruction plans for Europe and Asia. Famous for his regular 'fireside' radio broadcasts, Roosevelt was supported by his wife Eleanor, who travelled the country widely and delivered hundreds of radio broadcasts herself, representing the president and promoting women's rights and civil rights. FDR died from a cerebral haemorrhage on 12 April 1945, just three weeks before Germany's surrender in World War II.

LEFT Franklin Delano Roosevelt.

these reforms a stage further. The 1935 Social Security Act provided for unemployment insurance and pensions, and the Works Progress Administration, which eventually employed almost 9 million people, commissioned creative work of many kinds, from writing, painting, photography, theatre and music. Roosevelt's New Deal required vast borrowing but, by bringing people back into work, his deficit financing ploughed money back into the economy.

Roosevelt's strategy for relief, recovery and reform changed the role of the federal government in the American economy. While conservatives criticized it as creeping state socialism, it was in fact more a reaffirmation of American principles. When Herbert Hoover attacked the New Deal as 'the most stupendous invasion of the whole spirit of Liberty that the nation has witnessed since the days of Colonial America', Roosevelt argued (rather as Lincoln had done during the Civil War) that it reflected the need for a 'broader definition of liberty', one that would provide both 'greater freedom' and 'greater security for the average man than he has ever known before in the history of America'. In times of economic and social emergency, Roosevelt declared, government had to 'assist the development of an economic declaration of rights, an economic constitutional order' designed 'not to hamper individualism but to protect it'.

In proposing 'the new terms of the old social contract', Roosevelt transformed American politics. The promise of the New Deal created a coalition that brought together organized labour with southern whites, rural Protestants, urban Catholics and Jews. African Americans also moved away from the Republican Party – the party of slave emancipation – towards the Democrats. And, though not free from extremism and violence, the United States steered clear of the extreme political polarization found in Europe, where fascism and communism became forceful competitors for power.

Seen in the larger historical context, the New Deal stands as one of a series of major transformative shifts in the social and political development of the American Republic, all associated with the strengthening of the federal state. The first came during and after the Civil War, when the ending of slavery, redefining of citizenship and establishment of voting rights infused new meaning into the American concept of freedom. The second was the New Deal, which sought to use the power of the central state to widen the idea of freedom to include freedom from want, economic security and equal opportunity for all. The third would come with the equal rights legislation of the so-called 'Second Reconstruction' of the 1960s.

CANADA IN THE 1930S

Canada was also hard hit by the Great Depression. Like the big export economies of Latin America, which relied on international markets for foodstuffs and resources, Canada was badly affected by the collapse of global demand for agricultural goods and primary resources such as minerals. Prices plummeted for all its main exports (wheat, lumber, minerals and fish), and urban manufacturing fell as the domestic market shrank. By 1933, Canadian exports were halved, nearly a third of the workforce were unemployed and a government response was urgently needed. Policy now shifted from free trade

LEFT *Ottawa Conference, 1932.*

towards a system of 'imperial preference', proposed at the Ottawa Conference of 1932. This was designed to boost trade between Britain and its colonies, to protect British industries from foreign competition (especially the US), and thus to stabilize economies for the duration of the Depression. For Canada, imperial preference had short-term benefits but damaged trade relations with the US, which now had to face imperial tariffs. To restore these relations, Canada moved towards a more balanced approach in the mid-1930s, with a treaty aimed at strengthening its economic ties with the United States while maintaining links to Britain.

The 1930s was a politically turbulent decade in Canada, characterized by rising political discontent and the emergence of new political movements. The federal government faced considerable difficulty in dealing with the disparities of its regions, and the decline in the authority of the traditional Liberal and Conservative parties. At first, government responses were slow and tended to cling to the precepts of economic liberalism. The Liberal Party prime minister William Lyon Mackenzie King (1921–6, 1926–30, 1935–48) considered the economic downturn to be temporary and refused to provide federal aid to the provinces for unemployment relief. His Conservative successor, Richard Bedford Bennett (1930–5), hoped that imperial preference would stimulate economic recovery and it was only when Mackenzie King returned to power in 1935 that the federal government introduced relief programmes aimed at alleviating unemployment and hardship.

LEFT *William Lyon Mackenzie King.*

THE UNITED STATES IN WORLD WAR II

The outbreak of war in Europe opened another stage in American history, marked by its effects on the country's economy and its role in global politics. When the war in Europe started in 1939, the United States remained neutral, though Roosevelt hoped to defend democracy by supporting Britain and the Allies with arms and supplies. The Nazi advance across Europe in 1940 made this increasingly urgent, as it left Britain as the only remaining barrier to Nazi control of western Europe and the eastern Atlantic. Roosevelt responded with measures to strengthen the Allies' and US defences. He increased military spending and prevailed upon a reluctant Congress to pass the Selective Service and Training Act, America's first peacetime conscription. By 1941, the US was already involved in an undeclared war with Germany over U-boat attacks on American shipping, but public opinion was still divided over the desirability of becoming embroiled in a war that was not a direct threat to the nation. That attitude changed suddenly and dramatically when Japan declared war on the United States by launching an attack on its Pacific Fleet at Pearl Harbor, in Hawaii, sinking eight battleships and leaving 3,500 dead

BELOW *The attack on Pearl Harbor, 1941.*

LEFT *A woman working on plane construction, February 1943.*

and wounded. Roosevelt denounced the attack as 'a date which will live in infamy' and, in a near unanimous vote, Congress declared war on Japan. Four days later, Germany and Italy declared war on the United States, to which the US responded with its own counter-declaration on the same day.

Mobilization for war was a much more effective means of escaping from economic depression than the New Deal had been. American manufacturing moved into production at a new scale and pace. With three shifts, factories were kept running for 24 hours a day, seven days a week. Over its four years of involvement in World War II, the United States built huge numbers of military planes, vehicles and ships, and increased farming output by more than a third, in part to sustain its allies across the Atlantic. Built on lightly regulated capitalism rather than coercive state direction, and helped by the absence of direct enemy attacks on US cities and industries, the nation's overall capacity for production increased by about 50 per cent from 1939 to 1944.

Popular mobilization in support of the war was also large – 16 million Americans signed up to serve in the armed forces, including 400,000 women who were enlisted for non-combat duties, the majority as nurses. The breaking of gender barriers was even more notable in the wider industrial sphere, where women became indispensable members of the workforce. Six million women worked in plants producing ships, tanks, planes, weapons and ammunition. War also eroded racial barriers. African Americans and Native Americans were encouraged to join the fight against fascism, but many enlisted in the hope of overcoming prejudice and social marginalization at home. Over a million Blacks served in the military, albeit mostly in segregated non-combat units. Black GIs

stationed in Europe noted the striking contrast with their circumstances at home, and their wartime experience contributed to growing post-war demand for civil rights.

The United States played a central part in the defeat of Germany, not only by providing arms, supplies and ships but also by using its military forces on the European front, notably in bombing German industries and cities, and committing massive military resources to the liberation of Nazi-occupied Europe. The United States was even more crucial in the Asian war, where it took the lead against Japan. After fighting for strategic Pacific islands, including the Philippines, President Truman, who succeeded Roosevelt in April 1945, used the world's first atomic bombs to force Japan's unconditional surrender. The first bomb was dropped on Hiroshima on 6 August 1945, the second on Nagasaki three days later. Truman declared the results of the Hiroshima atomic bomb blast 'the greatest thing in history'. The first bomb alone killed 40,000 people in an instant. One hundred

ABOVE *The mushroom cloud over Hiroshima.*

The Atomic Bomb

Concern that Nazi Germany would master the technology to develop an atomic bomb compelled leading scientists, including Albert Einstein, to urge President Roosevelt to create America's own. The top-secret Manhattan Project was set up in Los Alamos, New Mexico, at a cost of almost US$2 billion ($35 billion today), led by the US physicist J. Robert Oppenheimer. The first successful atomic bomb test took place on 16 July 1945. As the original target, Germany, had surrendered just three weeks after the test, two atomic bombs were dropped on Japanese cities. The first bomb exploded 600 m (1,950 ft) above Hiroshima with a blast equivalent to 13 kilotons of TNT. After the second bomb exploded over Nagasaki a few days later, Japan surrendered unconditionally and World War II was brought to an end. After the war, Oppenheimer opposed development of the next level of thermonuclear device, the hydrogen bomb, and promoted the peaceful use of atomic energy. But, the United States continued its development of atomic weapons, which became the basis of a new strategy predicated on the idea that war with the Soviet Union could only be avoided by fear of 'mutually assured destruction'.

LEFT *J. Robert Oppenheimer.*

thousand more would die from burns and radiation over the following months and years. Japan surrendered on 15 August 1945.

The use of atomic bombs not only forced Japan's surrender. It also demonstrated America's technological capability, economic strength and pre-eminence as a world power. The Soviet Union and much of western Europe had been devastated by the global conflict, while the United States by contrast emerged as an even larger and more dominant economy at the end of the war than it had been at the beginning. From this position, US governments sought to rebuild the international economy and to decolonize the European empires.

LATIN AMERICA DURING THE GLOBAL CRISIS

During World War I and the Twenties, Latin American economies remained buoyant, held up by continuing demand for their exports. Boosted by US investment, some increased their share in world markets for several commodities, such as Argentine meat and grains, Colombian and Central American bananas, Cuban sugar, Chilean and Peruvian copper, Bolivian tin and Venezuelan oil. This consolidation of the export economies strengthened the urban middle and working classes and ended the political monopoly of the elites. In some countries, the elites responded to dissent by seeking the allegiance of the middle classes. In Argentina, for example, new voting laws made male suffrage more inclusive and permitted the middle-class Radical Party to win the presidency in 1916. In Chile, changes which had started in 1890 widened the political arena and made parliamentary government more representative of the population. In Brazil, the new republic that replaced the monarchy ushered in a phase of controlled electoral politics. And, in Mexico, the revolution that began in 1910 was initially aimed at broadening political participation, to give the middle classes a greater voice. Overall, these reformist movements aimed to replace oligarchic democracy with co-optative democracy, in which the middle classes achieved greater representation while the lower classes were kept on the margins. This adaptation worked well enough for the elites, who retained their dominant position while export economies continued to flourish during and after World War I. However, the 1929 Crash and the Great Depression of the 1930s changed everything. As prices tumbled and unemployment grew, social and political unrest multiplied and the governing elites had to find new ways to sustain their power. One response was military rule. In the early 1930s, army officers intervened in government or seized power in Argentina, Brazil, Chile, Peru, Cuba and several Central American states, all of them aiming to prevent popular protests from turning into revolutionary movements (inspired, perhaps, by the Russian Revolution). Argentina was among the first to see a military coup when, in 1930, the army cracked down on leftist movements and installed a coalition government (known as the Concordancia) in 1932, aimed at countering the Depression. It relied on fraudulent elections to remain in power, until support from the middle class dried up.

ABOVE *Guards outside the house of the deposed President Hipolito Yrigoyen of Argentina, 1930.*

The army stepped in once more in mid-1943, but it remained indecisive, awaiting the outcome of World War II. At this point, the army officer and politician Juan Domingo Perón began to plot his way to power, with populist promises of economic renewal and a nationalist rejection of foreign influence over key parts of the economy.

These military regimes were one sign of the end of the era of oligarchic democracy. Governments now began to shift away from the free-trade policies of the export boom and to adopt nationalist programmes designed to increase economic independence through state intervention. As protectionism swept the world and World War II disrupted the global economy, the larger Latin American states sought to stimulate the growth of national industries and shelter their societies from any repeat of the extreme contraction that began in 1929. They also recognized the need to allow labour to negotiate with employers to ensure industrial growth and permitted the formation of trade unions and labour organizations, which they had previously tried to block.

Broadly speaking, these changes promoted political changes of two kinds. One was the expansion of co-optative democracy, allowing workers access to elections and the right to form their own parties. Another was the development of multi-class political groupings, in parties portrayed as representative of society as a whole. These populist movements tended to appeal to the working as well as the middle classes, using an anti-imperialist, nationalist rhetoric. They were usually driven by and built around charismatic leaders who presented themselves as leaders of the entire nation and encouraged personality cults. Sometimes populism overlapped with another political novelty, known as corporatism, a concept developed in Mussolini's Italy.

A striking example of corporatism at work was found in Mexico under Lázaro Cárdenas (1934–8), when the political changes made during the Mexican Revolution were extended by integrating peasants and workers into a new state system. The roots of Mexican corporatism can be traced back to 1929, when the incoming president, Álvaro Óbregon, was assassinated before he could take office. In the power vacuum that followed Óbregon's murder, his predecessor, Plutarco Elías Calles (who was himself ineligible to become president once more), established a new political organization called the National Revolutionary Party (PRN) and used his leadership of it to oversee the terms of Mexico's next three presidents. This precipitated Mexico's conversion into what gradually became a one-party state, run by party bosses like Calles who guaranteed the election of their chosen presidential candidates. Calles was succeeded as Mexico's leading power broker by Lázaro Cárdenas, who in 1934 moved the PRN to the left and became the country's president. Once in office, Cárdenas implemented radical policies of a kind found nowhere else in the Americas. He redistributed twice as much land as all his predecessors, creating a communal system which apportioned their own plots to peasants that they could cultivate privately. He also gave the peasantry a voice in the political system. In 1938, he established a new Mexican Revolutionary Party (the PMR), built on groups organized by function (peasants, workers, military and the middle class) which the government could control through mediation. This was a concept borrowed from corporatism, which promised to end class conflict by bringing social groups into a system that allowed them representation within a centralized and authoritarian state. Cárdenas's other singular feature was his fervent nationalism, which was displayed most strikingly in his relations with the United States. Following a series of wage disputes between workers and the (mostly US) oil companies operating in Mexico, Cárdenas resolved the issue by nationalizing his country's petroleum industry. Although this aroused the fury of the oil companies and the US government, Cárdenas refused to back down when his stronger northern neighbour tried to pressurize him into reversing his decision. Instead, he paid compensation to the oil companies and used his country's ownership of its petroleum reserves to pay for his social and economic programmes. Despite a US boycott on Mexican oil that lasted for decades, Cárdenas and his successors were able to build a power base through the distribution of oil profits to allies and rivals alike that ensured their party always remained in control.

ABOVE *Lázaro Cárdenas.*

Brazil was another country in which corporatism played an important part in shaping politics. During the 1930s, two ideological movements dominated, both committed to mass mobilization and revolution. On the right was 'Integralism', a nationalist movement with affinities to European fascism. Its base was middle class, its ideology Christian, traditionalist and nationalist, and its organization was paramilitary, imitating the style of German and Italian fascists. They were opposed by a popular front movement, with some resemblance to European leftist anti-fascist organizations. The National Liberal Alliance – launched in 1935 – combined socialists and radicals, and was run by the Brazilian Communist Party, dedicated to following Moscow's line. When the communists attempted a revolutionary uprising in mid-1935, involving some army officers and rank-and-file troops, the government struck back with an attack on the left. The Integralists did not take power, however, as Getúlio Vargas, elected president in 1930 and sustained by the army, created the Estado Novo (New State) in 1937, a corporatist state styled on Mussolini's Italy. He was in turn deposed by the military in 1945, but not before he and his collaborators had created a centralized apparatus of government which promoted economic growth and pushed for industrialization, including ventures in steel and chemical production, mining and the manufacture of automobiles and aircraft. This was confined to a few major cities, but had a lasting political impact, evident in Brazil's combination of conservative, pro-business and technocratic governments that followed World War II.

ABOVE *Getúlio Vargas.*

CHAPTER 8

THE AMERICAS DURING THE COLD WAR

After World War II, with the fall of the old colonial empires and the collapse of recent German and Japanese imperialism, the United States emerged as the leading international power. After 1945, Americans who had long resisted foreign entanglements and stayed out of the League of Nations, now embraced responsibilities around the world and expanded their power at unprecedented speed. This transformation stemmed largely from the growing weight of American economic power during and after the war, which gave the US a huge material advantage over all other nations. By 1950, the US economy produced twice as much as Britain, Germany and France combined, and was far ahead of the Soviet Union, its chief rival. New American thinking about foreign policy was reinforced by the possession of nuclear weapons, together with a growing awareness (sharpened when the Soviet Union developed an atomic arsenal) that the US needed overseas alliances to solidify its primacy. The outcome was the creation of an American 'system' that was an empire in all but name. The 'American Century' was truly under way.

THE COLD WAR

American influence reached around the globe. In Europe, the US intervened to stave off Soviet expansion in Greece and Turkey, and provided Marshall Aid to restore the war-torn Western economies. In 1949, President Truman signed the North Atlantic Treaty, thereby establishing NATO (the North Atlantic Treaty Organization), and made parallel commitments to East Asia, with a security pact with Japan in 1951 and American control of the Philippines and Micronesia. Latin America was also subsumed in this great informal empire, while Britain's commercial presence all but disappeared. The Inter-American Treaty of Reciprocal Assistance (the Rio Treaty) of 1947 reflected US dominance, by offering military aid to Latin American states in case of armed attack or other forms of aggression – in other words, communist subversion. The other regions of the Americas were deeply affected by the growth of US capitalism and the determination of US governments to dominate the western hemisphere, economically and politically. In the immediate post-war world, most Latin American countries accepted US pre-eminence. They looked to the United States for trade and investment, though some of the richer countries such as Argentina, Mexico and Brazil sought to break from their dependence on exports and generate industrialization at home. Few had diplomatic relations with the Soviet Union and, aside from local communist parties, none looked to it as a social or cultural model. That was to change during the 1960s, when socialist revolution in Cuba acted as a catalyst for an upsurge of nationalist, anti-American feeling among a new generation of Latin Americans and triggered a wave of left-wing movements and insurgencies that brought a severe reaction from a US determined to defend its hegemony.

RIGHT *The Yalta Conference.*

At the Yalta Conference of February 1945, US President Roosevelt, British Prime Minister Winston Churchill and Soviet Union Premier Joseph Stalin mapped out plans for a post-war Europe. They agreed that Germany should be denazified, disarmed and deindustrialized to prevent any future empire-building, and they imposed their joint supervision by dividing the country into four zones occupied by the Soviet Union, Britain, France and the US. They also agreed that countries freed from Nazi control would have the right to hold free elections, and the United Nations created to provide international cooperation and prevent future wars.

ABOVE *The Berlin airlift.*

Cooperation was short lived. While Stalin moved to partition central and eastern Europe under communist governments subject to Moscow, the United States and its allies focused on reviving the capitalist economies of western and southern Europe, so that they might resist Soviet encroachment. Roosevelt's successor, Harry Truman, duly implemented the 'Truman Doctrine', built on two main elements. The first was to revive western Europe with a foreign aid programme devised by secretary of state, George Marshall. The $13 billion Marshall Plan provided support to help western European countries rebuild their factories and infrastructure. When Stalin reacted by blockading Berlin, the Allies kept the city alive with a largely US-financed airlift to sustain its independence from Soviet control. Stalin backed away from the prospect of war and ended the blockade in May 1949, but antagonisms were now clearly defined. The creation of NATO that year established an alliance of 32 countries designed to stand in opposition to the Soviet Union and its client states, in which the United States would play a vital political, financial and military role.

ABOVE *Harry Truman.*

During the 1950s, the United States was also drawn into East and Southeast Asia. After China fell to Mao Zedong's People's Liberation Army in October 1949, the country became a second front of communist influence which, while less threatening than the Soviet Union-dominated one in Europe, had the potential to block the advance of American capitalism and Western democracy. The new regime, like its imperial predecessors, sought to ensure that the land approaches to its borders were in friendly hands, and was soon drawn into conflict with the United States. When North Korea invaded the South in 1950, seeking to unify the country under communism, it received massive Chinese military aid. Conversely, as an ally of South Korea, America was quick to send in troops in what Truman described as a 'police action' on behalf of the United Nations. American soldiers not only faced North Korean forces but hundreds of thousands of Chinese soldiers sent in support. Truman hinted that the atomic bomb might be used to drive the North back, but the implicit threat did not materialize. The war dragged on for two years, at a high price. By the time Truman's successor Dwight Eisenhower ordered the return of US personnel, some 54,000 American troops had died in the conflict.

RIGHT *US troops during the Korean War.*

'REDS UNDER THE BED'

The US was secure in knowing it was the only power with the ultimate weapon – the atomic bomb – and Truman gave approval for development of its even more destructive replacement, the hydrogen bomb. But the advantage was soon lost. In 1949, American scientists found evidence that the Soviets had tested their own atomic bomb in the Pacific. The revelation that atomic bomb secrets had leaked to the Soviet Union not only changed American strategic thinking, it also led to a wave of paranoia at home, about subversion by 'Reds under the bed'. The House Un-American Activities Committee (created in 1945 to combat Nazi subversion) was redirected against the communist threat, supported by the FBI and newly created bodies, such as the Central Intelligence Agency (CIA), which took over the international side of American security, and the National Security Council. The resulting nationwide anti-communist hysteria came to be known as 'McCarthyism', after the Republican senator Joseph R. McCarthy, who, in early 1950, announced that he had a list of some 200 communists working in the State Department. Although never verified, McCarthy's lurid claims triggered witch-hunts against supposed communists in other areas, notably in the Hollywood film industry. In 1947, a string of Hollywood actors, directors, writers and technicians were called to testify and denounce any communist sympathizers they knew, amid a blaze of publicity. By 1954, McCarthyism had run its course – but not before exposing deeply entrenched anxieties about the vulnerability of the 'American Dream'. After Stalin's death in 1953, fear of communist infiltration subsided but the threat of atomic war kept the Cold War alive. Families built fallout shelters in their backyards and kept them stocked with canned food, while schoolchildren were taught to take cover should warning of a nuclear attack be issued. It was said that no nation possessing atomic weapons would risk using

BELOW *Joseph McCarthy questioning a suspect with the House Un-American Activities Committee.*

them, fearing equally destructive reprisals. The idea of deterrence based on fear of Mutually Assured Destruction (MAD) did not prevent US involvement in external conflicts, however, and successive governments intervened to support anti-communist client states and political leaders, often of an autocratic or dictatorial kind.

The Cold War between the US and Soviet Union also extended into a 'space race'. The Soviets led the way, launching the Sputnik 1 satellite into orbit on 4 October 1957, followed by Sputnik 2 with a dog aboard a month later. On 12 April 1961, Yuri Gagarin became the world's first cosmonaut, completing one orbit of the planet before returning to Earth via a safe parachute landing. The US astronaut John Glenn followed in his wake a year later. The rivalry compelled US president John F. Kennedy to declare, in September 1962: 'We choose to go to the Moon in this decade and do the other things, not because they are easy, but because they are hard.' The US succeeded in its mission, delivering the crew of Apollo 11 to the Moon and back in July 1969, effectively ending the Space Race.

ABOVE *Buzz Aldrin on the surface of the Moon, 1969.*

CUBAN MISSILE CRISIS

The United States did not delay in asserting its authority in countries where nationalist challenges arose, whether in Iran in 1953 to protect oil interests, or in Guatemala a year later, to prevent land reforms disrupting business for the US-owned United Fruit Company. But the most dramatic crisis in its relations with Latin America came in the unlikely setting of Cuba, long assumed to be friendly, not to say servile, to US interests. The crisis stemmed from what was initially a nationalist, democratic overthrow of a dictator who was widely disliked in Cuba for his corrupt and repressive regime. In 1959, Fidel Castro's guerrilla force, which was supported by peasants and a network of urban dissidents, removed Fulgencio Batista's military regime from power. True to Cuban nationalism, Castro immediately sought to curtail US interests, a move with unexpectedly dangerous repercussions. For, when the United States retaliated by boycotting Cuban trade, Castro sought to forge a partnership with the Soviet Union, which by then was under the control of General Secretary Nikita Khrushchev.

For the United States, this was an intolerable prospect. US President Dwight D. Eisenhower ordered covert attempts to supplant Cuba's new revolutionary leader and began planning for a CIA-backed invasion to overthrow Castro by rallying Cuban resistance. His successor, John F. Kennedy, inaugurated in 1961, continued this policy to disastrous effect. The plot to send 1,400 Cuban exiles to foment anti-Castro resistance failed miserably at the Bay of Pigs and served only to drive Castro and his colleagues to seek military aid from the Soviet Union. The dangers of Cuba's realignment in the Cold War soon appeared, when, in October 1962, the US discovered that nuclear missiles had been shipped to Cuba, within range of major American cities. Kennedy ordered a blockade of the island by the

Castro and Guevara

The son of a wealthy Spanish farmer, Fidel Castro (1927–2016) adopted anti-imperialist views while studying law in Havana, Cuba. In 1953, he was imprisoned for his involvement in an unsuccessful uprising against President Fulgencio Batista, who had taken power in a military coup. Released in an amnesty a year later, Castro left for Mexico before returning in 1956 with his brother Raúl, the Marxist revolutionary Ernesto 'Che' Guevara and a small armed force. Only 12 of the party escaped death or capture, but they were able to build strength and numbers in the backlands of Cuba's Sierra Maestra mountains. Following three years of guerrilla warfare, Castro's Cuban revolution succeeded in removing Batista from power in 1959 and Castro took over as prime minister. After expropriating foreign-owned farms and businesses, including US-owned oil refineries, Castro became the target of numerous, often bizarre, assassination attempts by American agents. Castro was, however, to become one of Latin America's longest lasting rulers, who not only defied the United States but also transformed Cuba into a one-party, socialist state, expanding public services while abolishing democratic institutions and a free press.

Che Guevara (1928–1967) was an Argentine medical student who travelled widely through South America in the 1950s. The poverty he witnessed on his tour prompted him to join anti-capitalist causes. After meeting the Castro brothers in Mexico, Guevara joined their Cuban Revolution and later took responsibility for land reform on the island. He left Cuba in 1965 to lead revolutions in Africa and South America. Guevara was caught and killed while leading a rural guerrilla group in Bolivia in 1967.

Fidel Castro survived an uninterrupted US trade embargo and the collapse of the Soviet Union in the 1990s. He handed over presidential duties to his brother Raúl in 2008, six years before his death from undisclosed causes.

LEFT *Fidel Castro and Che Guevara.*

US navy and threatened to sink any Soviet ships that crossed a quarantine line, a tactic that risked general nuclear war. In the event, Khrushchev backed down and the issue of the missiles was peacefully resolved. The Soviet Union offered to remove the Cuban missiles if the US withdrew its own from Turkey, to which Kennedy secretly agreed. The following year, the superpowers signed an agreement banning nuclear tests in the atmosphere, another step towards normalizing relations.

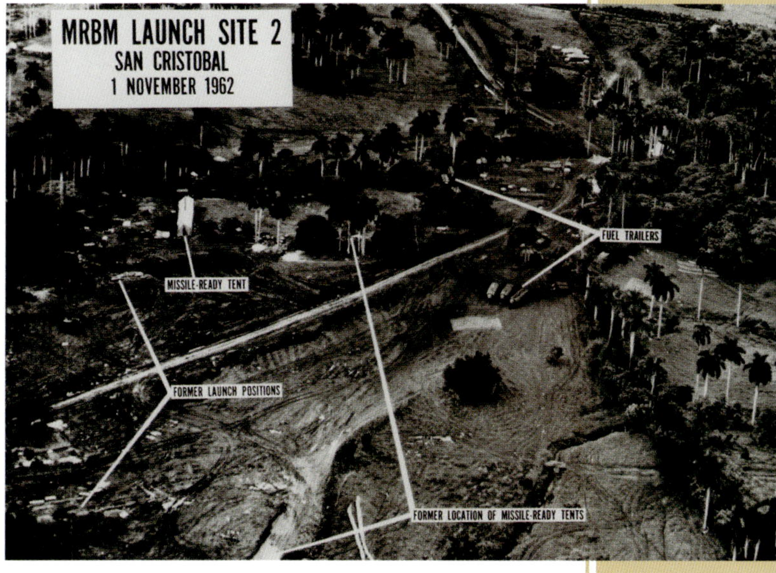

ABOVE *US areial reconaissance image of Cuban missile launch site, 1962.*

FIGHTS FOR RIGHTS

Within the United States, politics during the 1960s and 1970s was dominated by two issues. The first was the drive to deliver civil rights to African Americans, who still suffered social segregation and political exclusion in the southern states, and the movement to tackle other forms of prejudice elsewhere. Change came through the law courts and street protests. One such peaceful protest took place in Montgomery, Alabama, on 1 December 1955, when the seamstress Rosa Parks refused to give up her bus seat for a white man. A bus boycott ensued and over 5,000 (mainly African American) people took to the streets in demonstration. A Protestant minister, Martin Luther King, Jr, encouraged a non-violent response to intimidation, inspired by India's Mahatma Gandhi. King told the assembled crowd to 'stand up for their rights' but to refrain from retribution if attacked.

LEFT *Rosa Parks on the bus.*

ABOVE *Malcolm X.*

The bus boycott sparked a wider struggle for civil rights during the decade that followed. In November 1956, the Supreme Court backed Rosa Parks and segregation aboard the buses ended. King and fellow ministers formed the Southern Christian Leadership Conference to coordinate further protests. Non-violent actions included 'Freedom Riders' protesting segregated amenities at bus terminals, and sit-ins at segregated diners. The federal government was called in to enforce the law, as when US troops guarded a school in Arkansas to allow Black teenagers entry. When a major march through Birmingham, Alabama, was confronted by a large police force armed with dogs, batons and fire hoses, horrifying images of police brutality, televised across the nation, propelled Kennedy into action, with the promise of a civil rights bill, which became law in 1964, several months after his assassination.

This was not the end of the matter. The summer of 1964 witnessed more violent clashes between civil rights activists and southern segregationists in Mississippi. The catalyst was the issue of voting rights, the one thing that the Civil Rights Act had not directly addressed. While King continued to press for voting rights by peaceful means, the period after 1964 witnessed the rise of a new militancy, with the Black Power movement. The concept of Black Power had originated with the radical Black nationalist, Malcolm X, a leading figure in the Nation of Islam before he was assassinated in 1965, but it was popularized by the Trinidad-born Stokely Carmichael after Malcolm X's death. Black Power was more than just a political position. It went beyond a call for voting rights and integration and demanded an entire cultural shift towards self-sufficiency and autonomy for Black communities.

The Black Panthers

The Black Panther Party, founded in San Francisco in October 1966, formed neighbourhood patrols in a challenge to police, and set up free breakfast and education programs for their communities. Informed by Marxist philosophy, sporting black berets and leather jackets and bearing rifles, the Black Panthers provoked a negative response from the authorities. The FBI pronounced them an enemy of the US government and, through sabotage and clandestine means, undermined the organization. A five-hour shootout with police resulted in the death of the Black Panther Party leader Fred Hampton in December 1969.

LEFT *The Black Panthers at the California State Capitol on 2 May 1967.*

Martin Luther King, Jr

Martin Luther King, Jr (1929–68) was the son of a Baptist minister, with a PhD in theology from Boston University. After setting up his own ministry in Montgomery, Alabama, in the mid-1950s King was persuaded to lead boycotts and marches in a challenge to segregation laws in the South. King espoused non-violent protest but faced arrest, threats and physical attacks for his campaigning. He became the main leader of the civil rights movement and achieved widespread public recognition when, on 28 August 1963, he addressed a quarter of a million people gathered in the Capitol in Washington DC to back President Kennedy's civil rights bill. Standing on the steps of the Lincoln Memorial, he delivered his most famous speech: 'I have a dream that one day on the red hills of Georgia, sons of former slaves and sons of former slave owners will be able to sit down together at the table of brotherhood ... when we allow freedom to ring, when we let it ring from every village and every hamlet, from every state and every city, we will be able to speed up that day when all of God's children, black men and white men, Jews and Gentiles, Protestants and Catholics, will be able to join hands and sing in the words of the old Negro spiritual: Free at last.'

King led a voter registration drive in Alabama which helped secure the Voting Rights Act in 1965, banning literacy tests and other obstacles put in place to deter African Americans from voting. On 4 April 1968, while planning a campaign against poverty, King was assassinated by a petty crook in Memphis, Tennessee. Since 1971, his life has been celebrated with Martin Luther King, Jr Day, a federal holiday in January.

LEFT *Martin Luther King makes his speech at the Lincoln Memorial on 28 August 1963.*

Actions for equal rights extended to women, homosexuals, Hispanics and Indigenous Americans, who also faced discrimination. The publication of Betty Friedan's *The Feminine Mystique* in 1963 revolutionized the debate over a woman's place in society and, along with the Equal Pay Act of that year, spurred change in how women approached work and how employers treated women. The creation in 1966 of the National Organization for Women, led by Friedan, drew on the experience of civil rights activists to press for full female equality in all areas of American life. The introduction of the 'Pill', the first oral contraceptive, in 1967, was another reinforcement for the women's movement, after state laws against contraception were overturned by the Supreme Court in 1965 and 1972. Further rights for women followed in 1973 with the Supreme Court case, Roe

v. Wade, that established a federal right to abortion. The 1970s also saw the growth of the Gay Liberation Front, formed in July 1969 following a raid and confrontation with police at the Stonewall Inn in New York. A year later, Gay Pride marches began, along with demands for equal civil rights for homosexuals.

THE ANTI-WAR MOVEMENT AND THE COUNTERCULTURE

The second major political issue of the time arose from the war in Asia. When Eisenhower handed over power to Kennedy in 1960, the US was already supporting the pro-American government in South Vietnam in its struggle against communist North Vietnam, which was intent on uniting the two nations under its control. Kennedy accepted the need for intervention on the grounds of the 'Domino Theory', which held that if one nation turned communist, others would follow, eroding US influence across Asia and the

BELOW *American marines near Chu Lai during the Vietnam War.*

Middle East. Kennedy's turn towards deeper engagement in Vietnam did not end when he was assassinated in November 1963. Vice President Lyndon B. Johnson took charge and, after winning the presidential election by a landslide in 1964, pushed on with reform at home and anti-communist war overseas. At home, he committed himself to completing the Kennedy programme for civil rights, followed by pursuit of his own vision of a 'Great Society' that would extend America's prosperity to all its peoples. This did much to improve the living conditions of working-class Americans, notably through Medicare and Medicaid health insurance and higher-education student loans.

Despite his progressive social agenda, Johnson's record in office would be tainted by the effects of America's engagement in Southeast Asia. Shortly after his election in 1964, Johnson took the fateful decision to escalate the war. Following an incident in the Gulf of Tonkin where Johnson asserted that North Vietnam had committed acts of aggression against US navy vessels, Congress passed a resolution that permitted 'all necessary measures' to be taken against America's enemy. In March 1965, Johnson ordered bombing along supply lines used by the Viet Cong, the pro-North Vietnam communist guerrilla army operating in South Vietnam, and boosted the number of US troops deployed in the region. By 1968, more than 500,000 US soldiers were in place. The war became increasingly unpopular, however, as growing American casualties and a constant stream of televised images of the war shocked public opinion. While many still supported the war, the US was wracked by protests from a growing anti-war movement, which blended with other demands for social change that had been encouraged by Johnson's reforms. Various agendas for reform came together in an incoherent but compelling 'counterculture' that included hippies and the student-generated New Left. They had different and often competing aims, but they did reflect a fresh and distinctive efflorescence of the American Dream. Apart from some hard-left groups, they did not so much challenge the American way of life as call for a wider and more inclusive definition of it, for the benefit of all social groups. Like Johnson, the counterculture envisaged a Great Society, but of a more utopian kind.

ABOVE *Richard Nixon toasts Zhou Enlai during his visit to China.*

The war was slow to end, however. Aware of his unpopularity, Johnson chose not to contest the next presidential election, and the Republican Richard Nixon took office in 1968. With his secretary of state Henry Kissinger, Nixon tried a new approach. He made an unprecedented visit to communist China in February 1972 in the hope of pressuring the North Vietnamese into negotiations. Ultimately, Nixon was unable to deliver a peace deal. Instead, he signed a treaty ending America's involvement and leaving South Vietnam to fend for itself. Within two years, Saigon fell to North Vietnamese forces and was renamed Hồ Chí Minh City, in honour of the former North Vietnamese leader and

Watergate

The story of a break-in at the Democratic Party's Washington DC headquarters in the Watergate complex was first reported in the *Washington Post* on 18 June 1972. The burglars were caught attempting to place wire taps and had, apparently, been paid large sums from a pro-Nixon re-election group to do so. While the White House denied any involvement, there were widespread rumours that Nixon had tried to cover up the crime. When it was revealed that Nixon had made recordings of conversations about the affair, the Senate Committee set up to investigate Watergate made efforts to retrieve them. A case for impeachment was prepared and, in July 1974, the tapes were handed over and evidence of Nixon's attempted cover-up confirmed. Despite protesting that he was 'not a crook', Nixon resigned on 9 August 1974. He was pardoned by his successor, Gerald Ford.

LEFT *The Watergate building.*

revolutionary communist who had inspired his country's independence movement from France in the 1950s, and who had led North Vietnam's war effort until his death in 1969. After Vietnam, Laos and Cambodia also came under communist rule, with Cambodia suffering five years of genocidal misrule under Pol Pot's Khmer Rouge regime. By this point, Nixon was out of office following the Watergate scandal.

THE END OF THE COLD WAR

After the Democrat Jimmy Carter took the presidency in 1976, US ambitions to bend the world to its ideas and interests ran into new problems. During his four years in office, Carter supported a peace treaty between Egypt and Israel and agreed a deal with Panama in September 1977, handing over control of the Panama Canal from the end of 1999. However, his diplomatic successes were overshadowed by two major crises, both connected to the Middle East. The first was the energy crisis that stemmed from conflict in the Middle East. Oil prices had risen to unprecedented highs after the Yom Kippur War in 1973 and were then pushed up again following the Iranian Revolution in 1979. The second crisis also arose from the Iranian Revolution, when the American embassy in Tehran was captured and many hostages taken. Carter's attempt at a secret military rescue in April 1980 failed and he lost his campaign for a second term to Ronald Reagan, a former Hollywood actor, now a charismatic conservative.

ABOVE *Students burn an American flag outside the US embassy in Tehran, 11 November 1979.*

Reagan offered to revive American power and ambition. On taking office in 1980, he promised to swing away from 'big government' and to revive the individual liberty and enterprise which, he declared, had previously made America great. He came to power promising – and initiating – a wave of tax cuts, although his subsequent slashing of the budgets of public-support programmes did not recoup enough funds to cover the drop in fiscal revenue. Over the eight years of Reagan's presidency, the national debt went up by 188 per cent to hit $2.7 trillion. Once the world's biggest creditor, the US was now its biggest debtor, largely because of the vast growth of the military-industrial complex and government spending on increasingly sophisticated weaponry. Indeed, the Cold War continued to frame American identity and policy. Reagan appealed to American unity by denouncing what he called the 'Evil Empire' of the Soviet Union and launching a new military programme to intercept and knock out nuclear weapons from orbit. This Strategic Defence Initiative (SDI) was soon nicknamed 'Star Wars', given that the technology required to realize it was (and still is) unavailable. It did, however, provide Reagan with a useful political platform at home and some leverage during arms-reduction talks. He quickly established good relations with the Soviet premier Mikhail Gorbachev, who came to power in March 1985, and by the end of 1987 the two leaders had signed the first treaty to reduce their nuclear arsenals.

RIGHT *Ronald Reagan.*

Reagan's success in ending the Cold War was, however, handed to him by Gorbachev, whose radical economic and political reforms in 1985–6 accelerated the ongoing erosion of the Soviet Union. In 1989, the communist governments of Poland, Hungary and Romania were overthrown without Soviet interference, followed by the demolition of the Berlin Wall, which had divided the city for 28 years. The disintegration of the Soviet Union in 1991 finally ended the Cold War and, it seemed, marked the triumph of the United States in a new, unipolar world.

CANADA AND THE ANGLOPHONE CARIBBEAN

The aftermath of World War II saw the other English-speaking regions of the Americas move closer to the United States, economically and politically. The immediate post-war years for Canada, with its rich farming and mineral resources and closeness to US markets, produced a comparable prosperity, though with a different politics. Universal

BELOW *Independence supporters during the Quebec referendum of 1980.*

health care and pensions were introduced, and Newfoundland voted to become Canada's tenth province in 1949. The maple-leaf national flag was adopted in 1965, while Canada enhanced its economic power by lifting immigration restrictions to allow more arrivals from Asia and the Caribbean. The old fault lines between Anglophone and Francophone Canada had not disappeared, however, and during the 1970s Quebecois nationalists became more strident in their demands for independence. In 1970, militants kidnapped a diplomat and a minister, one of whom, the Labour Minister Pierre Laporte, was murdered. In 1976, the pro-independence Parti Québécois won the provincial election but failed to persuade voters to quit Canada in a 1980 referendum. As a country, Canada gained full sovereignty with the signing of the Canada Act in 1982. Seven years later, a Free Trade Agreement was agreed with the US, pledging closer economic ties between the nations, though Canada remained a member of the British-led Commonwealth.

During the 1960s, most parts of the British Caribbean finally secured their independence by mutual agreement and entered into the Commonwealth as independent nations. Although they kept strong ties to Britain, with the British monarch as titular head of state, their reliance on American markets and investments ensured that they were increasingly absorbed into the US sphere of influence. Economic development was limited by their small scale and limited resources – sugar still figured among exports, together with bananas and some minerals, notably Jamaican bauxite – and a new form of economic dependence replaced the old. Many emigrated, to Britain, the US and Canada, while the injection of cash from international tourism provided new sources of income. This was a valuable 'invisible import', made possible by turning the peaceful tropical environments of English-speaking countries into playgrounds for American and European tourists.

DEMOCRACY, DICTATORSHIP AND REVOLUTION IN LATIN AMERICA

Latin America enjoyed substantial economic growth from the 1940s into the 1960s. American and European demand for foods, minerals and raw materials led to the recovery of exports, and in some large countries growth was also generated by import substitution industrialization, where economic policies are designed to encourage domestic production of manufactures to replace imports. Electoral democracy strengthened too. From the mid-1940s to the 1970s, liberal democracies (in which citizens enjoyed rights to free speech, to join political parties and take part in free and fair elections) spread through nearly half of South American countries, where governing parties sought to modernize their societies and economies and to improve social justice. They enjoyed US approval and support, particularly after the Cuban Revolution. To counter Cuban influence, Kennedy instituted the Alliance for Progress in 1961. Over a

ABOVE *John F. Kennedy and Jackie Kennedy promote the Alliance for Progress in Venezuela, 1961.*

decade it provided aid for US-approved governments in Venezuela, Brazil, Argentina, Peru, Chile and Colombia.

However, when the post-war economic boom started to subside in the early 1960s, Latin American democracies faced opposition from landed and business elites that felt threatened by labour demands and inflationary pressures. In several South American countries, ruling elites imposed repressive regimes to sustain their preponderant share of wealth against restive labour forces. This often involved military coups, as in Brazil (1964), Argentina (1966) and Uruguay and Chile (1973). Military governments claimed to be the 'anti-political' representatives of national interests, against corrupt politicians and revolutionary elements (a position hardened by the Cold War climate which induced fears of communist subversion). Regimes of this kind are known as 'bureaucratic-authoritarian', for their tendency to place bureaucrats (military and civilian) in public office, while excluding the working classes and labour movements. Their anti-communist rhetoric and intention to strengthen foreign investment meant that they invariably enjoyed US support.

THE OIL STATES

Mexico did well during and after World War II, thanks partly to US support for industrialization and mineral extraction. The administration of Miguel Alemán (1946–52) invited both domestic and foreign investment in new infrastructure and encouraged tourism through the development of Acapulco, Cancún and Cozumel, and Mexico avoided high inflation until the 1970s. However, it did not dodge violent protests. Confrontations between students and soldiers resulted in a bloody clash in Mexico City in 1968, the year the country hosted the Olympic Games. The army's backing for the single-party state was unwavering, however, and in the 1970s, President Luis Echeverría sought to palliate social unrest by borrowing heavily to fund large social-welfare and housing programmes. A steep rise in oil prices and an international recession resulted in high inflation. Economic rescue came in the early 1980s when huge new oil reserves were discovered. With high oil prices, Mexico gained economic independence, but the windfall was wasted on fruitless development projects and further borrowing. When oil prices dropped and interest rates shot up, Mexico had to suspend interest payments on a foreign debt of $85.5 billion, which forced a reduction in social spending.

Venezuela was another state where oil revenues helped underpin the state, albeit in a considerably less complex economy than Mexico's. While second only to the US in oil production, Venezuela did not spread its benefits widely. The wealth generated provided the means to subsidize a growing middle class and some labour sectors, but many of the oil profits ended up lining the pockets of politicians and military leaders. Following World War II, Venezuela had a brief period of civilian government before a coup put the army

back in charge in 1948, with the predictable suppression of any opposition, the press and labour movements. In 1958, the armed forces struck again, but this time in favour of institutionalized politics. The Social Democrat and Christian Democrat parties now created a political network based on the exchange of favours, sustained by oil revenues. However, when oil prices slid downwards, the reduction in income forced the government to adopt austerity measures, inflation rose, foreign investment was withdrawn and violent protests took place. At the start of the 1990s, the government's grip on power seemed insecure.

ABOVE *Protestors and tanks in Mexico City, 28 August 1968.*

BRAZIL IN TURMOIL

In 1950, Getúlio Vargas returned for his third presidency. He invited foreign investment but struggled to balance the country's books and satisfy nationalist demands. Following a botched attempt by his bodyguard to kill one of his critics, the army demanded Vargas's resignation. He refused and, in August 1954, committed suicide. His successor Juscelino Kubitschek sought to boost the economy with a return to liberal capitalism, together with an ambitious plan to build a new capital in the interior and modernize the country's infrastructure. The strikingly modern Brasília was inaugurated in 1960, but the drive to modernize was shallow, leaving great inequities of wealth. João Goulart (1961–4) had no better luck improving the economy. In a measure that antagonized major landowners and the military, Goulart announced he was nationalizing the oil industry and seizing

RIGHT *Tanks on the streets of Rio de Janeiro, Brazil, during the 1964 coup.*

large estates. On 1 April 1964, the military moved in and seized power in a bloodless coup. Twenty years of military rule lay ahead.

On taking power, General Humberto Castello Branco was prepared to allow a quick return to constitutional government but, with no sign of a recovering economy, plans were put on hold. The country was opened up to greater foreign competition, which caused the bankruptcy of many domestic businesses. The cost of living rose, spurring a wave of protests, strikes and the emergence of urban guerrillas who brazenly kidnapped the US ambassador in September 1969 and committed a series of bombings and robberies. The concerted forces of the secret police and government-approved death squads eliminated them by 1973, and military rule continued while the economy made a surprising recovery. Manufactured goods finally overtook coffee as a

BELOW *Brazilian actresses protest the abuses of the military dictatorship, 1968.*

leading export and, with business booming once more, the junta saw no reason to return the country to democracy. The military gradually lifted its repression throughout the 1970s, with an end to the censorship of books and newspapers (though not radio or TV), the suspension of torture and the return of political exiles. Free elections returned the civilian politician Tancredo Neves to the presidency in 1985, though his death through illness before he took office meant that his place was taken by José Sarney, his vice president. Sarney soon faced spiralling debt and economic difficulties. Inflation rose to new heights, reaching more than 1,000 per cent in 1989.

PERONIST ARGENTINA

Argentina became a major exporter of food to an impoverished Europe following World War II. A healthy economy provided scope for the new president Juan Perón to nationalize railways, docks, the central bank and the telephone company and to proclaim Argentina's release from British imperialism. By 1947, the country's national debt was paid off. Agricultural exports were brought under state control, with profits helping fund welfare projects. The economy slowed from 1948, nevertheless, due to competition with the US and recovering European exports. As the economy stumbled, Perón tightened his grip on the country, silencing critics and taking control of unions and universities. His attempts to secularize society and legalize divorce put him in conflict with the Catholic Church and, with it, the armed forces. After a pro-Perón rally was bombed by military aircraft in June 1955, killing hundreds of supporters, several churches in Buenos Aires were set alight by Perónists. Two weeks later, Perón was ejected from office by an army coup and fled to Paraguay.

ABOVE *A man is 'disappeared' during the Dirty War in Argentina.*

The military government struggled to bring order to the country, under pressure from Perón supporters and while contending with student protests and civil unrest. In March 1970, Peronist guerrillas kidnapped and murdered a general and former president of the junta. The military chose to step aside, paving the way for the return of Juan Perón in 1973. His second term lacked the dynamism and confidence of his earlier time in power. He was now 77 years old and frail, but was fortunate in that his return coincided with an improvement in agricultural exports and a drop in inflation. He pressed ahead with a programme of nationalization and ordered a brutal crackdown on guerrilla factions. Less than nine months into his new presidential term, Perón died of a heart attack and his third wife and vice president, Isabel Perón, took over. Facing continued violence from guerrilla groups, she called a state of emergency in November 1974. From then until the end of the decade, the Argentine military were free to use any means to defeat the rebels. Tens of thousands of those deemed subversives were arrested and taken to their deaths in secret detention centres, during a period dubbed 'the Dirty War'.

The Peróns

Juan Perón (1895–1974) was part of a military alliance that removed the civilian Argentine president Ramón Castillo from power in 1943. He had spent all his adult life in the armed forces, moving up the ranks to become a colonel before the coup. He held several government positions, including minister of labour, minister of war and vice president, slowly building public and union support for his welfare policies. Established parties saw him as a threat and convinced the military hierarchy to arrest him in 1945. This drew protests from workers and union members, encouraged by Perón's partner, the actress Eva Duarte (1919–52), resulting in his release four days later and eventual election as president in 1946. Perón married Eva soon after.

As president, Perón improved social rights and introduced free university courses, but he ruled as an authoritarian, strictly controlling the press and arresting critics. His popularity was sustained through large rallies outside the presidential palace alongside his wife, who gained the affectionate name 'Evita'. She helped deliver female suffrage in 1947, while her work providing charity and affordable housing (and a 1978 musical based on her life) led to her gaining iconic status following her early death aged 33.

After a *coup d'état* pushed him out, Perón left Argentina. After almost two decades in exile, during which his country suffered under military rule, he returned in 1973. By this time, he was an aged, ailing figure, struggling to overcome divisions within the Peronist movement. He died in office in 1974.

LEFT *Juan and Eva Perón.*

Within two years, Isabel Perón's government was replaced by the military, who oversaw a return to a more free-market economy. Real wages fell as prices rose. Strikes were made illegal; union activists 'disappeared'. At the end of 1981, following another coup, General Leopold Galtieri took charge. Seeking wider public support, Galtieri planned an invasion of the Malvinas (Falkland Islands) in the South Atlantic. Argentina had disputed the sovereignty of the sparsely occupied islands since Britain claimed them in 1833. Contrary to expectations, Britain sent a military task force over 12,870 km (8,000 miles) to take back the territory. Galtieri's forces were removed within three months. Humiliated by the failed invasion and a deteriorating economy, Galtieri resigned and Argentina was returned to a democracy in 1983.

CHILE, FROM SOCIALISM TO DICTATORSHIP

Through the 1950s into the 1960s, a left-wing alliance of the socialist Salvador Allende and the communists seemed on the verge of winning presidential elections in Chile, but was kept from office by tactical voting on the right. Allende's Popular Unity party finally won by a small margin in 1970 but faced immediate resistance from the Chilean Senate and the US, which withdrew economic aid and began funding opposition groups.

BELOW *The coup in Chile, 1973.*

RIGHT *Augusto Pinochet.*

Popular Unity set out to break up large landholdings and release plots to poorer farmers and communal agriculture, as well as to nationalize large industries, including the country's profitable copper-mining businesses. A policy of holding down prices and increasing output did not stop runaway inflation. Illegal factory occupations and numerous strikes crippled the economy. Opposition parties appealed to the army to step in and, on 11 September 1973, General Augusto Pinochet Ugarte led a successful coup. Allende refused safe passage out of the country and died when the presidential place was bombed.

Pinochet began a ruthless eradication of socialists in the country, rounding up, locking up and exiling supporters of the Popular Unity party. Armed protesters and guerrillas were executed. Several thousand were killed; 30,000 people were banished. At the same time, Chile's economic focus switched to free-market capitalism and low tariffs to tempt foreign interest at the cost of less-competitive domestic suppliers. The economy improved but failed to pull almost half the population off the breadline. Unemployment was rife and real wages declined. Pinochet used repressive measures, but did face resistance. A depression in the early 1980s prompted protests and strikes. In 1986, Pinochet was almost assassinated by guerrillas firing at his motorcade. A referendum in 1988 voted against allowing him to remain in office, although Pinochet retained a good deal of power as commander-in-chief of the armed forces after he stepped down as president.

In the smaller Latin American countries, mainly in Central America and the Caribbean, political developments took a different form. With economies built around one or two agricultural exports (sugar, tobacco, coffee, bananas) produced on large plantations, they lacked the resources for import-substitution industrialization and were trapped in dependency and poverty. The main point of conflict was the problem of land distribution. As plantations sought higher profits, peasants were dispossessed and land became concentrated in fewer hands. Protests by landless or land-poor peasants were repressed in Guatemala, El Salvador, Nicaragua, the Dominican Republic and Cuba, where military dictators governed. Without the means to achieve social change through elections, dissidents tended to seek change by the only other means available, which was armed violence, increasingly informed and organized by Marxist-oriented revolutionaries. Similar movements appeared in some regions of South America, where the presence of an impoverished peasantry encouraged Marxist revolutionaries to see fertile ground for revolt. Peru is a striking case. In 1968, a military coup in Peru resulted in a government with more left-leaning nationalist policies, including land reform and the nationalization of privately owned plantations. But a fall in export prices and an international recession in 1973 put paid to this experiment. Elections were held in 1980, which led to the return of privatization, protests and guerrilla violence. The latter was supplied by Sendero

BELOW *The El Salvador Civil War.*

Luminoso (Shining Path), a shadowy Maoist group based in the Andean highlands.

Nicaragua, El Salvador and Guatemala all saw insurgencies in the 1970s and 1980s. Anxious about Marxist revolutions on its doorstep, the US government financially backed, equipped and trained the countries' armed forces to crack down on guerrilla armies. In the case of Nicaragua, the country had been ruled for 43 years by the dictatorship of the Somoza family either directly or through puppet presidents, with support from the US government and businesses. Elections were rigged and export profits siphoned to the family. In 1979, armed socialist guerrillas, called the Sandinista National Liberation Front, managed to overthrow the Somoza regime, the culmination of almost two decades of rebellion. US president Jimmy Carter offered the Sandinistas economic help towards the building of an open democratic system, but Marxists within the Sandinista Front tried to establish a socialist state based on the Cuban model. A split led to anti-Marxist Sandinistas uniting with former Somoza troops in opposition to the new Nicaraguan government. Known as the Contras, these rebels received support from the US under Ronald Reagan, in part through profits on illegal arms sales to Iran. The Sandinista government kept the Contras at bay and retained power through the 1980s despite a crumbling economy. They were ousted following free elections in 1990.

BELOW *Anti-Sandinista Contras training in Honduras.*

CHAPTER 9

THE US AND LATIN AMERICA IN THE AGE OF GLOBALIZATION

From the 1980s, the history of the Americas was closely related to the advance of 'globalization', a concept which refers to the increasing interconnectedness and interdependence of economies, cultures and societies across the world. This was not the first globalization. The expansion of 16th-century Europe into the Americas and Asia was an early example of a rapid expansion in the flows of trade, people, ideas and technologies, which forged new economic and cultural connections between societies previously isolated from each other. The advance of 19th-century industrialization and European imperialism into Africa and Asia was another example, of even greater reach, driven as it was by major innovations in industry, transport and communications.

THE UNITED STATES AND THE NEW WORLD ORDER

Globalization took on a new meaning in the 1980s, when a very rapid expansion of global trade began, driven on by US-inspired policies of free trade and market liberalization, promoted by institutions such as the International Monetary Fund (IMF), the World Bank and the World Trade Organization (WTO). These policies encouraged countries to open their markets to international competition and to create closer economic connections, as in trade agreements like NAFTA (North American Free Trade Agreement) in 1994 and the expansion of the European Union. Advances in technology, particularly the rise of the internet and digital communication, facilitated the movement of capital and services across borders. Outsourcing and offshoring became common practices as companies sought lower production costs in developing countries. China's economic reforms, beginning in the late 1970s, and its subsequent rise as a global manufacturing hub, played a crucial role in shaping modern globalization.

Some saw the disintegration of the Soviet Union as the 'end of history', closing the era of conflict between ideologies and opening new possibilities for encouraging international cooperation and the spread of democratic ideals in a world where the United Nations (UN) would play a larger role in addressing issues such as human rights, environmental policies and international security. Globalization has a powerful cultural dimension, too. The influence of Western media, particularly American movies, music and fashion, spread across the world, creating what some call 'cultural homogenization' or, more simply, the increasing spread of Americanization far beyond the United States.

As the Cold War came to a close, Ronald Reagan was replaced as president in 1989 by George H.W. Bush, his vice president, who took his predecessor's approach and focused on reshaping US foreign policy. Bush joined Soviet leader Mikhail Gorbachev in calling for the construction of a New World Order, which would strengthen the United Nations, increase cooperation between the superpowers, and deliver an integrated 'globalized' economy. Gorbachev was soon pushed aside, as the Soviet Union collapsed in 1991, but Bush continued with his plans to reshape the post-Cold War world in the interests of the United States, now the sole global superpower.

BELOW *George H. W. Bush.*

The subsequent growth of American power was accelerated by the triumph of neoliberalism. For neoliberals, the primary role of the state was to facilitate the free market and guarantee the rights of corporate capital. Under their influence, US military and political power was accordingly used to promote the free marketization of the globe. The aim was to do this peacefully, helped by transnational organizations such as the IMF or the World Bank, but US governments were also prepared to use threats or actions against regimes, such as Cuba, which refused to cooperate.

Another important effect of the end of the Cold War was the 'peace dividend' that came with the lowered threat of global nuclear catastrophe. Not only were wars thought to be less likely between countries that had

taken opposing sides in the conflict, but better relations between the US and its former Soviet enemy meant that they – and other nations – would be able to reduce the vast sums they spent on armaments. The nuclear threat did temporarily recede, and Bush assisted in the reconstruction of a post-Soviet Europe by allowing Germany to reunite in 1990 and join NATO. The peace dividend in Europe did not, however, bring an end to war in other regions. Instead, war was redistributed to new conflict zones, with the Middle East taking increasing prominence. Indeed, within a year of the fall of the Berlin Wall, the US was at war with Iraq, at the head of a UN coalition to reverse that country's invasion of Kuwait.

ABOVE *Desert Storm, 1991: US aircraft flying over burning Kuwaiti oil wells.*

Under Reagan, the US had become involved in an undeclared naval war with Iran over the security of oil flows through the Persian Gulf, while also providing arms for the Muslim mujahideen fighting the Soviet occupation of Afghanistan. Of these engagements on two fronts, the Iranian conflict had the most immediate consequences. During the Iran–Iraq War (1980–8), Iraq's leader Saddam Hussein strengthened his dictatorial authority and become a major US proxy in the region. After the war ended in stalemate, Saddam sought to cover his wartime costs by invading his oil-rich neighbour Kuwait, confident in US acquiescence. In fact, he faced a change of stance from Bush, who was concerned to sustain order among America's allies in the Middle East. So, when Saudi Arabia asked the US to provide troops to defend its borders, Bush secured UN Security Council approval for pushing Iraq out of Kuwait, using forces that incorporated US, NATO, Saudi, Syrian and Egyptian soldiers. America's former ally against Iran was now, according to Bush, 'a dangerous dictator ... who desires to control one of the world's key resources'. The allied forces drove Saddam from Kuwait in 1991, but the US refrained from forcing a regime change. Having converted an ally into an embittered enemy, the US left Saddam in place, weakened but still potentially dangerous.

ABOVE *Manuel Noriega arrested by US officials.*

While the 1989–93 Bush administration delivered a small peace dividend by cutting spending on its armed forces, the Pentagon retained a large budget on the grounds that the US still needed plentiful military resources to deal with potential threats from communist countries and others. One of the first disciplinary actions the US launched against the backdrop of the Soviet Union's terminal decline was against its erstwhile ally, President Manuel Noriega of Panama, a dictatorial general who had played a part in American anti-communist manoeuvres in Central America, especially in the war against the Sandinistas in Nicaragua. When Noriega blocked a US-backed candidate in Panama's election and showed other signs of independence from his American masters, he was accused of large-scale drug trafficking, captured by invading American troops in January 1990, and taken to the United States to be tried and imprisoned. Bush justified the invasion on the grounds that Noriega was corrupt, threatened US citizens and endangered American control of the Panama Canal; his overthrow was also an early instance of what became a wider 'War on Drugs' during and after the 1990s.

THE WAR ON DRUGS

BELOW *A drug bust, Los Angeles, 1986.*

The US federal government began regulating narcotics in the early 20th century, but the modern War on Drugs officially began in 1971, when President Nixon declared drug abuse 'public enemy number one' and launched a nationwide crackdown. He significantly increased funding and established the Drug Enforcement Administration (DEA) in 1973.

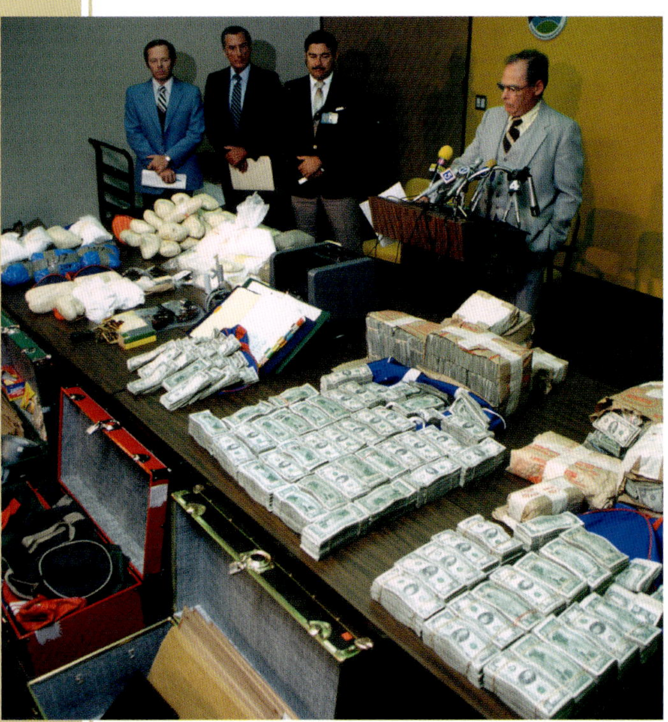

The policy took an even harsher turn in the 1980s under President Ronald Reagan, who expanded mandatory minimum sentencing and introduced the Anti-Drug Abuse Act of 1986. Funding for the FBI's drug-enforcement units jumped from $8 million to $95 million during his first term, and over the next decade-and-a-half, the number of drug offenders jailed would soar from 50,000 to 400,000, with African Americans disproportionately affected. Throughout the 1990s and early 2000s, the War on Drugs continued with aggressive policing and mass incarceration.

Despite tough policies on dealing and distribution, drug use rose dramatically. New forms of policing increased arrests and drug seizures but had minimal impact on the quantity of narcotics entering the US, as domestic demand reached new heights. Heroin, cocaine and crack (an intensified form of cocaine) were plentifully supplied, mostly from Latin America but also from Asian sources, such as heroin from Afghanistan. The problems caused by drug addiction widened and worsened with the misuse of methamphetamine and legal opioids, such as morphine and codeine, available as prescription painkillers. Synthetic opioids, such as fentanyl, have recently aggravated the social and health problems caused by drugs, while bringing huge profits to some large American pharmaceutical companies and to illegal suppliers in Asia and the Americas, who now manufacture opioids using chemicals originating in China and funnel them through the Mexican cartels.

ABOVE *A drug laboratory in Colombia, run by the Medellín cartel.*

The War on Drugs was not just internal. While attempting to deal with domestic drug abuse, the US tried to cut off supplies by providing foreign aid or military assistance in the countries identified as major sources, particularly in Latin America. Much of the aid was directed to support and train the police and armed forces assigned to arrest drug producers and traffickers. It proved a dispiriting undertaking; as one route closed, another opened. The US collaborated with several countries to crack down on local drug smugglers – notably Colombia, Mexico, Peru and Bolivia – but successes in disrupting the cultivation of coca and its trade were invariably temporary, as cartels developed new areas of supply and new channels for trade.

While efforts to extinguish the flow of illegal drugs continued, American public opinion began to shift towards other options in the 2010s. Critics argued that the War on Drugs failed to curb addiction, promoted crime and criminality, and tended to have disproportionate effects on minorities, especially African Americans. Supporters of decriminalization also claimed that legalizing the sale of drugs under government licences would deliver a considerable tax revenue. Decriminalization has not become a national policy, but to date 39 states have made the sale and purchase of cannabis for medicinal use legal, with 24 of them allowing its recreational use. Canada legalized the growing and use of marijuana for recreational purposes in June 2018, following the trend towards harm reduction, treatment and rehabilitation rather than strict enforcement, and signalling a shift away from punitive policies toward a more health-centred approach to drug policy.

US PARTICIPATION IN 'HUMANITARIAN WARS'

Another aspect of foreign policy during the 1990s, associated with the presidency of Bill Clinton (1993–2001), was a new willingness to engage in overseas interventions that were justified in moral terms, rather than by traditional realist notions of national interest. The Balkan wars exemplified the new approach, when US-led NATO powers were involved in an intervention to stop Serbian aggression against Bosnia in 1994 and Kosovo in 1999. Another instance of humanitarian, pro-democracy intervention followed a military coup in Haiti in 1991, in which thousands of Haitians were killed and even more attempted to reach the United States by boat, as refugees. The coup

leaders, led by General Raoul Cédras, refused to relinquish power and the United Nations authorized the use of force to restore democracy to the island. Sanctions and an arms embargo followed. In September 1994, the US joined a coalition of mainly Caribbean countries in preparation to invade Haiti. Threatened by overwhelming forces, Cédras allowed the return of ousted president Jean-Bertrand Aristide with barely a shot fired. There were, however, limits to the range of US humanitarian intervention, most obviously in the weak response to the Rwandan genocide in 1994, and this approach to foreign policy was discarded after 2001, as the US responded to the new priorities of the War on Terror.

ABOVE *Troops at the legislative palace in Haiti during the coup of 1991.*

THE WAR ON TERROR

As the shape of global alternatives to capitalism and state communism changed after the end of the Cold War, a new source of conflict arose from the emergence of political Islam as a serious competing ideology. With it came greater violence, a new kind of warfare, and the formation of networks of fundamentalist fanatics dedicated to opposing the West in general and the United States in particular. A key moment came on Tuesday, 11 September 2001, when two hijacked passenger planes were deliberately crashed into New York City's tallest building, the World Trade Center. Another plane hit the Pentagon, the headquarters of the US Department of Defense. A fourth was diverted and crashed before it struck its intended target, the White House. The Twin Towers of the World Trade Center both collapsed into a smouldering ruin. Almost 3,000 people died in what was by far the deadliest terrorist assault on American soil.

It soon became clear that the attacks were planned and coordinated by al-Qaeda, a group of Islamic fundamentalists led by Saudi millionaire Osama bin Laden, who was hiding in Afghanistan with the approval of its militant Taliban regime. The US responded by rallying an international coalition, invoking the collective defence clause in NATO's treaty for the first time since its signing in 1949. In October 2001, it then led an attack on Afghanistan with support from British, Canadian, Dutch, German, Norwegian, New Zealand and Australian troops. By the end of the year, the coalition succeeded in removing the Taliban from power (though they would regroup in Pakistan and take back control two decades later), and US president George W. Bush moved to extend the War on Terror against states which he defined as an 'Axis of Evil', including Iran, Iraq and North Korea. (Cuba, Libya and Syria were added later.)

Having declared a War on Terror with al-Qaeda in mind, Bush and his advisors were not content to confine themselves to attacks on terrorist networks. They also saw the September 11 outrages as an opportunity to fulfil larger goals, namely, to reconfigure the oil-rich Middle East and the surrounding region by replacing unfriendly governments with new ones, under leaders committed to market economies and Western-style democracy. With neoconservative hawks in his administration nudging Bush to action in

ABOVE *US soldiers in the Afghanistan War, 2001.*

Iraq, evidence was produced to suggest that Saddam Hussein was a leading sponsor of terrorist groups, with a stockpile of 'weapons of mass destruction' which could potentially end up in the hands of terrorists such as al-Qaeda. The proof was flimsy but enough to convince Britain, Spain, Portugal, Poland, Denmark, Italy and Australia to back the US in an invasion in Iraq that began on 20 March 2003.

Three weeks later, Baghdad had fallen and Saddam Hussein had fled. At this point, US casualties in the war were just 139. Three years later, they were around 3,000, with an estimated 150,000 Iraqis dead. When Saddam was caught in December 2003, the country was in turmoil. The US and its allies had made few plans for governing Iraq and, after the US administration disbanded the Iraqi army, civil war between rival Sunni and Shia Muslims made US and other foreign troops increasingly unwelcome. Weapons of mass destruction were never found, nor any links between Saddam Hussein and al-Qaeda. The war on Iraq had replaced a tyrant but at great cost in blood and treasure, and with an aftermath of ongoing instability and poverty.

The international image of the United States was also tainted by its departure from the laws of war, vividly reflected in images of prisoners being humiliated or tortured at Abu Ghraib prison, outside Baghdad, and incarcerated without trial at Guantánamo Bay, the US naval base in Cuba. Government lawyers argued that the detainees were 'unlawful combatants' from a failed state and were not covered by the Geneva Conventions; their legal rights could therefore be ignored. Nearly 800 people from 48 countries were incarcerated at Guantánamo and international protest against their imprisonment damaged America's reputation as a democratic society governed by the rule of law.

RIGHT *Camp X-Ray, Guantánamo Bay, 2002.*

THE DIVERSIFICATION OF AMERICAN SOCIETY

While the position of the US in the world was shifting, so too were some of the basic elements of American society. One of the most important areas of change was in the growth and diversification of immigration that followed the 1965 Immigration Act. The liberal provisions of the Act triggered accelerating change in both the scale and sources of immigration. Legal immigration went from 3.3 million in the 1960s to 4.5 million in the 1970s, a 40 per cent increase. By 1981, admissions had reached twice their 1965 level. They had also taken on a new character. For, despite efforts to maintain the predominantly European ancestry of the US population, emigration from Europe declined while pressures to leave parts of Latin America, Asia and Africa grew.

The ensuing shift in immigrants' countries of origin profoundly reshaped US society. Designed in accord with Cold War priorities for favouring US allies, the 1965 Act later allowed entry for large numbers of people displaced by American wars, particularly from Southeast Asia. Chain migrations from Asia, Latin America, Africa and the Middle East strengthened the trend towards a more diverse US society that had first emerged during World War II. In 1965, only about 5 per cent of the US population was foreign-born and the majority were from Europe or Canada. By the 2010s, 50 per cent of all immigrants in the United States were from Latin America and the Caribbean, and 27 per cent were from Asia. The majority resembled earlier immigrants, drawn to the United States by the promise of better economic opportunities. Many were driven to migrate by war, revolution, economic displacement or environmental disasters. Reflecting the changing international context, the streams of refugees slowly shifted from eastern Europe to Cuba, Central America and Southeast Asia. As members of these groups became permanent residents and citizens, they took advantage of the opportunities for family reunion allowed by the 1965 Act to bring in their relatives and did so in much larger numbers than their European-born predecessors.

The AIDS Crisis

The first reports of the disease later known as AIDS appeared in May 1981. The initial cases involved injecting drug users and gay men who showed signs of a rare form of pneumonia. More cases arose, with patients affected with a rare skin cancer. In 1982, the disease was given the name HIV/AIDS (acquired immunodeficiency syndrome) and it was understood to be passed on through contaminated blood. Campaigns to stop the spread of the disease were launched, promoting the use of condoms and the avoidance of shared needles. Though gay men and drug users were not the only people affected, their early association with the disease deluded some conservatives into accepting the irrational claim that AIDS was a retribution from God. The US government was slow to recognize this as a serious health crisis, partly because the stigma of contracting the disease led many to hide their diagnosis while the number of cases mounted up. An estimated half a million people died from the disease in the United States alone, and more than 39 million worldwide. Since the introduction of antiretroviral drugs in 1996, the number of deaths from AIDS in the US has dropped significantly; an estimated 1.1 million people currently live with HIV/AIDS.

LEFT *AIDS poster, 1994.*

DOTCOM BOOM AND BUST

With his victory in the election of 1992, Bill Clinton became the first American president born after World War II, a so-called 'baby boomer'. He won the election by shifting towards the centre ground of US politics, but, helped by his lawyer wife Hillary Rodham Clinton, he immediately sought to secure social benefits for the poor, by providing government-backed universal health insurance. Politically, the Democrat Clinton was stymied by a Republican-led Senate and powerful commercial lobbies, but the debates over health care reform also showed widespread popular reticence about expanding the social role of government. While Clinton invoked the legacy of Roosevelt, his attempts to benefit the poor (and improve the nation's health) were blocked by vested interests in the health care sector and the reluctance of many Americans to subsidize the needs of disadvantaged groups, especially when they were disproportionately Black. The strong conservative bias of the political system, reinforced by powerful commercial lobbies,

became apparent in the Congressional elections of 1994, when the Republicans took control of the House of Representatives for the first time in 40 years. Clinton's response was to adopt a moderate Republican agenda as a way of winning back the middle ground, with measures to reduce crime, restrict welfare and improve the nation's finances.

After his re-election in 1996, Clinton remained popular in the polls due to a thriving economy but was forced to waste political energy on resisting Republican attempts to impeach him for lying about his extra-marital affairs. His false statements to the House of Representatives resulted in the first impeachment of a president since Andrew Johnson, 130 years earlier. Clinton survived this Republican-driven assault, albeit at a high cost to his personal and political reputation. He spent much of his second term on foreign policy issues, notably in attempts to stabilize violent regions.

ABOVE *Bill Clinton.*

Much of the success of the economy during Bill Clinton's early years in office was the result of financial deregulation and the widespread adoption of information technology and the internet. Room-filling mainframe computers had been superseded by desktop machines. Apple, founded by Steve Jobs and Steve Wozniak, launched its first personal computer (PC) in 1977, offering word processing and spreadsheet programs. Four years later, new IBM computers ran Microsoft MS-DOS, an operating system developed by Bill Gates, which was even more widely adopted. Companies could communicate and transfer files internationally via email and the internet, much faster and more convenient than the fax machines and postal services they displaced. International business transactions could now be completed in the blink of an eye. Stocks and shares were traded through online brokerage systems and there was a lot of money to be made. Enthusiastic investment in new online e-commerce sites fuelled a 'dotcom bubble'.

BELOW *An IBM PC from 1981.*

By 1992, the number of websites had hit one million. Amazon launched in 1994 as an online book retailer. It quickly expanded to sell anything from music to clothing to food. Amazon's competitive pricing and convenience made it a significant challenge to traditional high-street shopping. Google went live in 1998, swiftly becoming the dominant search engine. Helped by a drop in interest rates, investors hurried to back new online (dotcom) start-up companies. Then, in 2000, following a recession in Japan, investors rushed to sell off their technology stocks and the dotcom bubble burst. Share values plummeted. Many big-name e-commerce sites stopped trading. Having had their fingers burnt, investors became more cautious about lending to the online sector.

Ominous signs of deepening social divisions in the United States appeared during these years, reflected in the emergence of an increasingly vocal social conservatism, fuelled by anger about positive discrimination, school curriculum changes and attempts to replace

LEFT *Aftermath of the Oklahoma City bombing, 1995.*

racist and sexist terminology with more acceptable language, a process described as 'political correctness'. The growing gulf between liberals and conservatives was helped by changes to rules governing the media. In 1987, Reagan had removed the requirement for licensed radio stations to provide balanced opinion, which left the AM airwaves open to extreme viewpoints and conspiracy theorists. Clinton blamed this surge of misinformation for the estrangement of Timothy McVeigh, a US army veteran, loner and gun obsessive who parked a truck bomb outside the main federal building in Oklahoma City in April 1995. It exploded, killing 168 people, including 15 small children in day care. Terrorist threats now came from within the United States, as alienated people took arms to fight against what they perceived to be an elite state that had departed from American values.

Clinton's successor, in 2002, was George W. Bush, the son of George H.W. Bush. His victory was contentious. A close vote in Florida led to demands for a recount from the Democratic candidate Al Gore. The Supreme Court voted against this by five votes to four; the five votes coming from Republican-appointed judges. Gore conceded. Despite his narrow victory, Bush reflected an underlying trend in the US towards oligarchic politics. Both he and Gore were sons of wealthy politicians who had attended Ivy League universities, and both reflected the drift towards a society in which wealth was

BELOW George W. Bush and Al Gore.

ABOVE
Lehman Brothers building in Times Square, New York.

increasingly concentrated in few hands. (In 2000, the wealthiest 1 per cent owned about 40 per cent of the nation's individual wealth, compared to 30 per cent a century earlier.)

While much of his presidency was taken up with foreign policy and the wars in Afghanistan and Iraq, Bush presided over a growing economy at home and rising immigration numbers along the West Coast and in the southwest and northeast, all areas of increasing electoral weight. More and more immigrants came from Latin America. In 1970, 5 per cent of the US population identified themselves as Hispanic; by 2020, the figure was 19 per cent. Bush's second term ended badly, however, as it coincided with a global economic collapse in 2008. American banks and other financial institutions were largely to blame, having speculated in risky loans to home buyers. When the resulting housing boom turned to bust, house values dropped by 20 per cent, interest rates rose and borrowers could no longer afford to pay for their mortgages. Amid rising unemployment, almost 900,000 properties were repossessed, leaving millions of Americans homeless. Banks and financial service companies suffered major losses. Several, including Lehman Brothers, Bear Stearns and Washington Mutual, the country's largest savings bank, went out of business or were bought out.

LATIN AMERICA IN THE AGE OF GLOBALIZATION

In Latin America, democracy became the norm during the 1990s and economic issues came to the forefront of politics, as governments sought to grow their economies by participating in the accelerating movements of goods, capital and people associated with globalization. A new wave of civilian presidents and their finance ministers sought to participate in the growth of global production and trade, and Latin American countries were invariably drawn into closer relationships with the United States. They joined a globalized market expedited by the introduction of affordable personal computers and the internet. The exceptions were Cuba, which became even more isolated as its Soviet sponsor disappeared, together with Nicaragua and Venezuela as they came under left-wing leaderships at the start of the 21st century.

After many Latin American countries defaulted on their massive foreign-debt payments, the US government offered a neo-liberal solution. The 1989 Brady Plan agreed to the cancellation of some debt and rescheduled the remaining payments on the condition that the debtor countries followed a programme of economic liberalization advised by the International Monetary Fund (IMF). The recommendations included major cuts in state spending, the privatization of state-owned industries and a reduction in import tariffs and subsidies paid to domestic producers. The measures opened up Latin

American countries' economies to more foreign trade, part of a globalization of world markets, but they put national suppliers under pressure.

More barriers to international trade were removed through the 1990s. In 1994, Mexico joined Canada and the US in signing the North American Free Trade Agreement (NAFTA). Argentina, Brazil, Uruguay and Paraguay (and, later, Venezuela) signed a similar arrangement known as Mercosur; Bolivia, Colombia, Ecuador and Peru formed the Andean Community; and Costa Rica, El Salvador, Guatemala, Honduras and Nicaragua joined the Central American Common Market.

ABOVE *The signing of NAFTA, 1994.*

In Mexico, neo-liberal reforms rolled back policies associated with the Revolution – notably by allowing the sale of collectively owned lands – and the ensuing popular discontent forced the one-party state, run by the Institutional Revolutionary Party (PRI) since 1929, to change direction. It now allowed greater space for the opposition to take part in elections, a democratic opening which led to changes in government in 1998, when the PRI ceded control of the legislature, and 2000, when it lost the presidency for the first time in over 60 years. Mexico also drew closer to the United States through NAFTA and the migration of millions of Mexicans who crossed the border in search of work. Relations between the two countries became frayed, however, as the flow of narcotics strengthened the power of the Mexican drug cartels, undermining the authority of the state in Mexico and driving a wave of violence which spread to many regions of the country.

Venezuela profited from its large oil reserves but little of the wealth trickled down to the poorest. In 1989, President Carlos Andrés Pérez agreed to the US Brady Plan and began instituting IMF reforms, but this resulted in mass rioting in the capital Caracas and other cities. The army stepped in to restore order. Hundreds of civilians were killed. Two years later, a group of young army officers calling themselves the Bolivarian Revolutionary Group attempted a coup to remove Pérez. They failed, and their leader, Hugo Chávez, was arrested and jailed. He was released two years later, in time to see Pérez himself imprisoned after his impeachment for corruption in 1994.

In 1998, now considered a hero representing the working classes, Chávez was voted in as president, promising a new era of democracy. While elections were held, Chávez progressively took over all of the key state institutions and suppressed critical voices. (At the same time, he aired his own views via dedicated TV and radio talk shows and two newspapers.) A new constitution was approved in 1999, introducing a single National Assembly with a number of seats allocated for

BELOW *Carlos Andrés Pérez at the World Economic Forum in 1989.*

indigenous people. Chávez set up a social-welfare programme to provide relief and education in the poorest areas. This was paid for using oil profits.

Chávez appeared to be leading Venezuela down the path of communist Cuba, particularly after he made a deal with Fidel Castro to exchange Venezuelan oil for Cuban medics and teachers. Opposition attempts to unseat him included strikes and a coup in 2002 which managed to replace him for just 47 hours. Chávez hung on to win three more elections and the result of a referendum in 2009 gave him permission to run for office indefinitely. Diagnosed with cancer, Chávez would not benefit from the vote. He died two months after re-election in 2013.

The Andean countries (Bolivia, Colombia, Ecuador, Peru) endured much political disorder towards the end of the 20th century. Rival political parties in Colombia had come to an accommodation by alternating the presidency and cabinet positions, which helped end conflict between the traditional parties (Conservative and Liberal) and stabilize the

Hugo Chávez

Hugo Chávez (1954–2013) was born in rural Sabaneta, Venezuela, the son of schoolteachers. As a teenager he entered the nation's military school in Caracas, where he developed an interest in the leftist military regimes then in power in Panama and Peru. On entering the lower echelons of the officer class, he began a double life, as a disciplined soldier and as a conspirator against the government. In 1977, he assembled a small number of like-minded soldiers into a secret revolutionary movement within the armed forces. In 1992, Chávez gathered his supporters in the army and led a coup against President Pérez. It failed and Chávez gave himself up, but the attempt turned him into a hero for the underprivileged. He would become president in 1998. While in office, Chávez instituted constitutional reforms, nationalized major industries and redistributed the country's oil wealth to support welfare programmes for Venezuela's poorest. His ties with Cuba, Iraq, Iran and Libya put him at odds with the US, which remained the largest market for Venezuela's oil. Due to his undergoing medical treatment for cancer, Chávez could not attend his fourth inauguration in January 2013. He died in Cuba that March. His vice president Nicolás Maduro then took change.

LEFT *Hugo Chávez.*

ABOVE *FARC soldiers.*

economy. Free elections were held by the 1980s, but the country was wracked by violence, with Marxist-inspired guerrilla armies and major drug cartels responsible for bombings, kidnappings and the assassinations of three presidential candidates. In 1998, President Andrés Pastrana launched peace negotiations with the largest of the guerrilla forces, the Revolutionary Armed Forces of Colombia. Known as FARC, the group was founded as a peasant defence group in 1964 and had grown into an army with more than 10,000 members, funded through kidnapping and ransom, extortion and drug trafficking. After four years without a peace agreement, Pastrana called in the army and there was a return to violence and kidnapping. Towards the end of the century, Colombia was also being torn apart by war between drug cartels and the law. The US supplied $10 billion in funds and training for the Colombian military to fight the drug lords and left-wing guerrilla groups. Efforts to stem the drug trade included the aerial spraying of coca crops with herbicides.

The interaction of guerrilla insurrection and the narcotics trade also affected Peru and Bolivia. While large areas of the eastern Andes were being used for the illegal cultivation of coca, two guerrilla movements also generated considerable disruption: the Marxist-Leninist Túpac Amaru Revolutionary Movement (MRTA) and Shining Path (Sendero Luminoso, SL) which sought to establish a Maoist state in Indian territory. Both groups gained funds through alliances with drug traffickers. Shining Path gathered support from peasantry in the highlands and from people disturbed by the brutality of the Peruvian military, but they lost sympathy following a series of civilian massacres in the mid-1980s.

RIGHT *Alberto Fujimori.*

In 1990, Alberto Fujimori became president of Peru and ordered a crackdown on the guerrilla rebels. In 1992, the leaders of both the MRTA and SL were arrested. Success in opposing revolutionaries and in boosting the Peruvian economy propelled Fujimori to further election victories in 1995 and 2000. But, accused of embezzlement, human-rights abuses and election fraud in his third win, Fujimori fled for Japan and faxed his resignation from Tokyo. He was finally extradited back to Peru in 2005, where he was convicted and sentenced to 25 years' imprisonment.

Brazil also saw its share of corruption cases in government. In the 2000s, after years of military intervention in politics, Brazil was once again holding free and fair elections. The 2002 vote saw the leftist Luiz Inácio 'Lula' da Silva take charge. Against a programme of tax and social-security reform, public investment and efforts to alleviate hunger, Lula's presidency was tarnished by accusations of bribery among his party. Lula was supportive of the rights of his country's indigenous people. In order to control unrestricted land-grabbing by farmers and loggers in the Amazon rainforest, Lula put in place a law requiring larger companies to purchase the land first.

RIGHT *'Lula' da Silva.*

Indigenous activism

In 2009, indigenous activists fought with police after Peru's President Alan García permitted foreign oil and gas companies to explore 70 per cent of the Peruvian rainforest without consultation. Similar uprisings by indigenous groups occurred in Bolivia and Ecuador, but without conflict. Protesting with strikes and public demonstrations, they demanded a fair percentage of profit from fossil fuels found on their ancestral lands. Inspired in part by the rise of Hugo Chávez and his support for Venezuela's indigenous groups, the indigenous people of Peru, Bolivia and Ecuador would build movements for greater representation in government and for the freedom to continue to practise their traditions.

CUBA IN CRISIS

The end of the Cold War and collapse of the Soviet Union in 1991 left Cuba without a supply of subsidized oil and an artificial market for its sugar. Fidel Castro responded by calling for sacrifices from the Cuban people in what he defined as a 'special period in peacetime'. Public services and food rations were reduced, fuel supplies limited and car journeys minimized. The hardship was made worse by the continuing US embargo. Among relief measures, Castro allowed limited private enterprise, such as family-run restaurants and taxi services. Forced by circumstances, Castro opened up the country to tourism, particularly from Spain and Canada (US citizens were still banned from entering Cuba). New hotel developments were built along the coast of Havana to accommodate visitors. The use of US dollars was legalized in 1994 and tens of thousands of Cubans were allowed to leave the island for the United States.

With Cuba's finances in a fragile state, Cuban exiles in Miami lobbied the US government to pile pressure on Castro's regime in the hope that it would collapse. The US toughened its embargo in 1992 and again in 1996 after Cuba shot down two small planes piloted by a Florida-based anti-Castro group. Lack of subsidized imports severely hit living standards in the country and there were reports of near famine. With food in short supply, prayers were offered; an unexpected announcement from Castro was the revival of Christmas as a national holiday in 1997 ahead of a January visit by Pope John Paul II in a historic rapprochement with the Catholic Church.

While tourism helped the struggling Cuban economy, Hugo Chávez played a key role in rescuing the regime. Chávez and Castro agreed that Venezuela would provide Cuba with subsidized oil in exchange for Cuban doctors and advisors who could help Chávez with his social reforms at home. With this new sponsor, Castro reintroduced many restrictions on foreign investment and private enterprise, and US dollars became illegal tender again in 2004.

In 2008, after 49 years in power and now in ill health, Fidel Castro stepped aside and appointed his brother Raúl president, but this did not lead to any dramatic changes in foreign policy. In the same year, the country was hit by a series of calamitous hurricanes which left 200,000 people homeless and destroyed half the annual sugar-cane crop. Raúl Castro's promise to improve living conditions took a serious blow. The island remained isolated and in financial distress.

BELOW *Horse-drawn public transport in Cuba, 1993.*

CHAPTER 10

CONTEMPORARY CHALLENGES IN THE AMERICAS

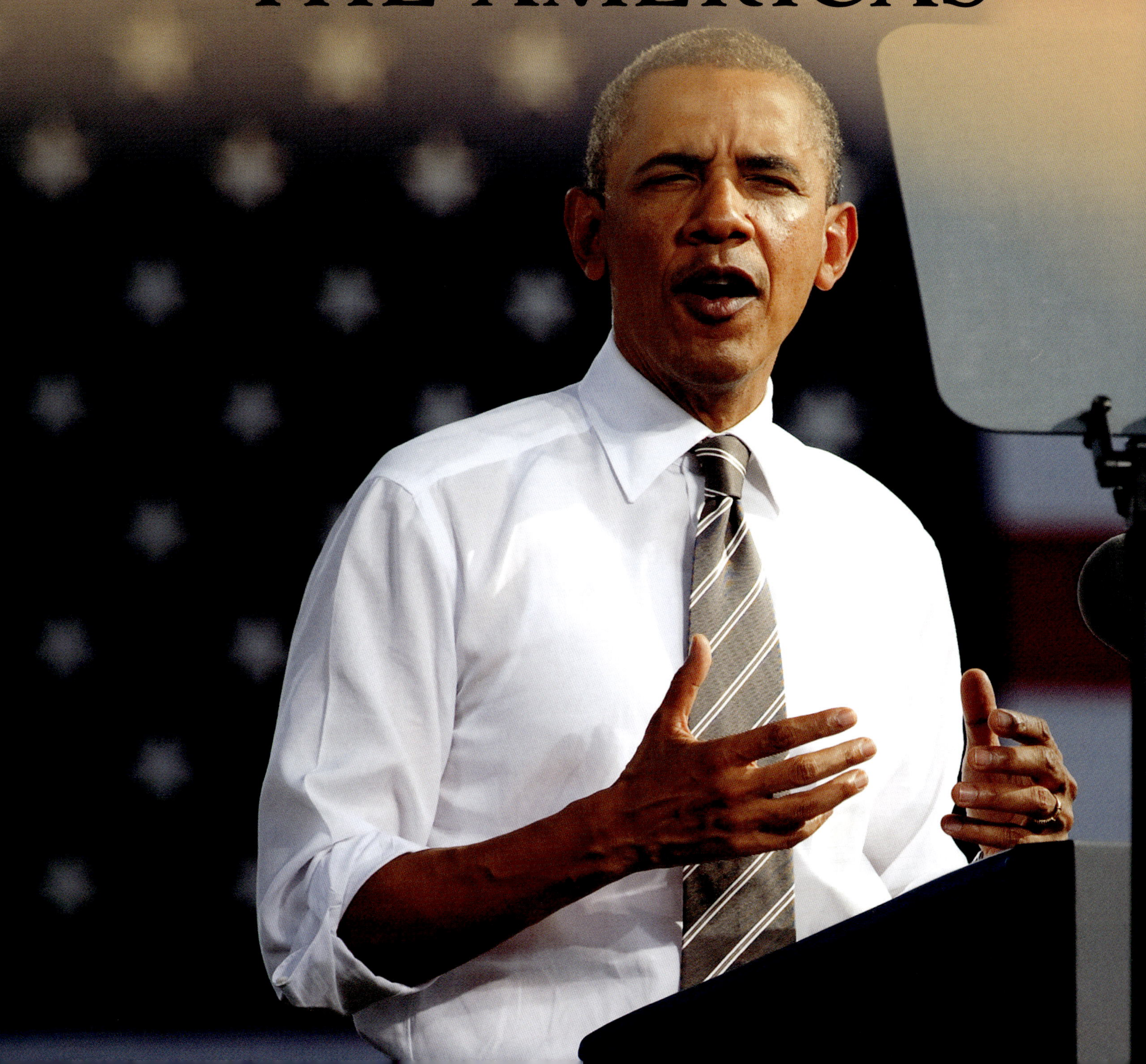

The opening decades of the 21st century have seen the United States' position as the world's dominant economic and military power challenged by the increasing commercial strength and influence of China and India. Domestically, following the election of the first African American president and first female vice president, hopes for a more diverse and tolerant nation have faced a setback. The country has become wracked by divisions over immigration, diversity programmes and climate change, with social media spreading misinformation, the rule of law being questioned and elections being challenged, sometimes with violence. Both US and Latin America voters, seeking change to the status quo or an end to governmental corruption, welcomed outspoken populists to power, with significant consequences for national welfare, the environment and international relations. In contrast, Canada has appeared more open, a haven for democracy and stability but it has been forced to hold a mirror to its past, confronting and apologizing for historic abuse of its indigenous peoples. Along with these economic and political trials, the Americas have been tested by a major pandemic. The repercussions of this and dramatic transfers of leadership continue to bear upon the destiny of the continents.

NEW REACH, NEW RIVALS

The US sustained its position as the world's leading power in the opening decades of the 21st century. In 2024, it maintained approximately 750 bases in at least 80 countries and numerous installations across the United States. Total active-duty military personnel numbered around 1.32 million. Its military capacity was unrivalled, with dominance in air, land, sea, space and cyber warfare, underpinning global power projection. AI-driven defence systems and missile defence capabilities allowed for rapid response. Its strategic priorities included the traditional commitment to NATO and maintaining its alliances in the Middle East against Iran and other sites of Islamist hostility, while becoming increasingly oriented towards countering the growth of China's military presence in the Indo-Pacific.

Great economic strength underpinned this formidable military might. At the turn of the century, the US accounted for around a quarter of the world's GDP and held a huge share of world trade. Although this share contracted from the mid-2010s – as China and other countries increased their participation in international markets – the US remains a major buyer and seller, the home of the largest banks and business corporations, and a loud voice in the international institutions that regulate global finance and business. Its economic success has created political and cultural bridgeheads across the world, through rewards for allies and aid to poor countries, through social ties built up by educational links and by migrant diasporas, especially those which originate in Latin America, and through cultural exports such as film and television.

ABOVE *US aircraft carriers in the Philippine Sea.*

New economic opportunities came with new competitors. The turn to a market economy in the Chinese People's Republic, and a similar shift in the former Soviet bloc, enlarged global productive capacity and consumer markets. This expansion gained momentum from the 'container revolution' in shipping, cheaper air travel and, above all, the application of computer technology and the internet for commerce and finance. Greater freedom for financial services and capital transfers further reinforced growth, leading to exceptional increases in the volume of international trade and the integration of economic activities across borders. These shifts all benefitted the United States. However, greater freedom for trade and the exchange of knowledge was, perhaps, ending the long divergence between the wealth of the Euro-Atlantic West and the rest of the world. The rise of China and India showed signs of a future convergence of economic power, in which

BELOW *Cargo ships arriving at Oakland, California in 2017.*

Eurasia might restore the balance in world power that prevailed before the discovery of the Americas triggered Europe's first globalization.

For the United States at the start of the 21st century, then, a key question has been how to retain its leading position as a global power when its economy, though still growing, is in relative decline. The US has also faced significant challenges in its economy and society. The presidencies of Barack Obama (2009–17), Donald Trump (2017–21) and Joe Biden (2021–4) reflected different ideological priorities and governing styles, influencing debates on health care, immigration, race relations, economic policy and the role of government. US domestic politics has, in fact, become polarized to the point where the presidential election of 2024 seemed to present a potential turning point in the history of American democracy.

THE DEMOCRATS' RESURGENCE

ABOVE *Barack Obama.*

Barack Obama's presidential election campaign made novel and effective use of social media, raising $600 million from more than 3 million supporters. His message 'Yes, we can' was one of hope and change, while his Republican opponent John McCain was burdened by his association with the party that, under George W. Bush, had led the US into a controversial war in Iraq and the worst financial crisis since the Great Depression. With major banks on the verge of bankruptcy, Bush had been forced into a major reversal of conventional policy by agreeing to a bailout for financial services (at a cost since estimated at $2,000 for every US citizen). This, along with America's troubled and prolonged involvement in Iraq, ensured that Bush left office a discredited figure.

Obama won the election by a large margin, with promises to use government power to rescue the economy and introduce social reform, notably in health care. His election also seemed to reflect a more tolerant and affirmative strand in US politics, leading away from the racism which had long made the election of a Black president unthinkable. In fact, his opponents used his origins against him during the election, with attempts from so-called 'truthers' to spread a story that he had been born in Kenya (the home of his father) rather than Hawaii, therefore making him ineligible for president. Despite clear evidence to the contrary, Obama's origin was questioned by many, including the businessman and TV celebrity Donald Trump. Thus, although his election inspired some to assert that America was entering a post-racial era in which divisions of colour would have diminishing political and social relevance, the currents of racism and nativism which surfaced during the campaign, in reference to Obama's recent African lineage, suggested that deep-rooted prejudices still suffused the country's politics.

Obama's domestic policies focused on economic recovery, the expansion of health care access, and issues of social justice. Repairing the economy was his first undertaking. His $787 billion plan consisted of expanded unemployment benefits, a middle-class tax cut, and a host of federal contracts, grants and loans extended to businesses, organizations and state governments, which in turn launched public-works projects and other pursuits that employed idle workers. He also authorized a federal rescue of the auto industry, which was on the verge of collapse. The US government assumed temporary control of General Motors and pushed Chrysler into a merger with the Italian car company Fiat. Both GM and Chrysler went into planned bankruptcy, during which they restructured their operations with the help of massive federal loans. Interest rates were cut to zero to encourage borrowing. While the economy crawled out of recession, the jobs market was in poor shape, with low-paid, low-skilled work being the norm. Meanwhile, companies being bailed out by the government, such as the insurance brokers American International Group (AIG), still found the funds to award their top executives a combined $200 million in bonuses.

ABOVE *Obama and the national security team watch the raid on Bin Laden's hideout from the White House situation room, 1 May 2011.*

From the outset of his presidency, Obama faced pressing foreign-policy issues, mostly arising from the legacy of wars started by his predecessor. In early 2009, the US still had a large presence in Iraq (140,000 soldiers) and Afghanistan (around 36,000). Obama reduced numbers in Iraq towards a final withdrawal in 2011, but doubled the number in Afghanistan, where a revitalized Taliban were pushing to regain territory from the borders. Iraq would see a new terrorist threat develop with the spread of the Islamic State of Iraq and the Levant (ISIL), to which the US responded with military force, especially

Barack Obama

Barack Obama (1961–) is the son of a Kenyan-born economist and an anthropologist from Kansas. He was raised in Hawaii, interrupted by a four-year period in Indonesia, before moving to New York in his 20s to gain experience in business. After graduating from Harvard Law School, Obama moved to Chicago to teach constitutional law. In 1996, he was elected to the Illinois Senate. Nine years later he became a US senator. In 2007, he announced his candidacy for president, beating Hillary Clinton to become the Democrat candidate and America's first Black president in 2008. Obama's presidency was defined by efforts to recover from the 2008 financial crisis, expand health care access and address issues of social justice. However, political polarization and Republican opposition constrained his agenda.

in the form of unmanned aerial drone strikes against suspected terrorist operatives in the Middle East, South Asia, and North and East Africa.

The indefinite detention of hundreds of terror suspects at Cuba's Guantánamo Bay remained a stain on America's international reputation, but Obama's attempt to close it was blocked by Republican votes. He did, however, manage to outlaw the use of torture by the US military and to reduce the number of Guantánamo detainees. One mission that

The Gun Lobby

The right to bear arms was guaranteed by the Second Amendment to the United States Constitution. The amendment was drafted to permit the formation of militias to protect the States but has been interpreted as the right of the individual to own and carry weapons. The National Rifle Association (NRA) was founded in 1871 as a sporting and firearms-training body. After the assassination of President John F. Kennedy in 1963, it had been supportive of a ban on mail-order weapons and high-risk people possessing arms. By 1981, the NRA had turned into a powerful lobby group paying millions of dollars annually in campaign contributions for pro-gun political candidates who opposed any restrictions on gun ownership. The early 21st century saw a rise in the number of mass killings by gunmen in schools, malls and even churches. In 2012, 26 people, including 20 children, were killed by a young gunman at Sandy Hook Elementary School in Newtown, Connecticut. The shooter, like many involved in mass killings, was armed with an assault weapon. Following the Newtown massacre, Barack Obama tried to pass legislation on background checks, as well as introduce a ban on the sale of military-style weapons. His efforts were defeated in the Senate by both Republicans and Democrats who supported the freedom to bear arms. The NRA's solution to the risk of school attacks was to propose that every school to employ armed guards. The US has the highest per capita gun ownership in the world, with approximately 16.7 million firearms sold in 2023 alone, one weapon sold for every 20 people. Every US state permits the carrying of concealed weapons for protection. Even in the wake of an increasing number of mass shootings, attempts at gun control face fierce resistance.

LEFT *NRA annual meeting, 2018.*

did provide Obama with a boost in domestic popularity came in 2011, when America's Public Enemy Number One was finally tracked down by US special forces. On raiding a hideout in Pakistan (without informing the country's government), a unit identified and shot dead Osama bin Laden, the mastermind behind 9/11. He was buried in secret at sea.

While approving covert missions to hunt wanted terrorists, Barack Obama also allowed greater use of surveillance. Introduced in the wake of the attack on the World Trade Center, George W. Bush's Patriot Act was intended to monitor and prevent potential terrorist activity. In 2013, former US National Security Agency (NSA) contractor and whistleblower Edward Snowden revealed that the NSA had listened in on phone calls from, among many others, the German chancellor Angela Merkel. The revelation was an embarrassment for the president. Snowden, for his part, claimed asylum in Russia.

Another problem that had been growing over previous years was that of immigration. Between October 2013 and July 2014 more than 50,000 children, many unaccompanied and mostly from Central America, had been taken into custody while trying to enter the US illegally. Obama introduced Deferred Action for Childhood Arrivals (DACA) to protect undocumented children from deportation, but Republican opposition ensured that his attempts at comprehensive immigration reform failed and left the issue of illegal immigration to become a key campaigning theme for the Republican candidate at the next election.

Perhaps Obama's greatest achievement in office was the introduction of the 2010 Affordable Health Care Act, commonly known as Obamacare, despite strong opposition from Republicans, who saw it as a form of European-style socialism. The Act required everyone to pay for health insurance or face a fine. Low-income families were provided with a subsidy, funded through taxes on the wealthy, while health-insurance companies were prohibited from capping lifetime benefits or dropping policyholders who became ill. Within its first months, upwards of 30 million people who previously had no health insurance signed up.

Obama's administration also improved the civil rights of minority groups. In 2009, the Federal Hate Crime Law was amended to protect LGBT people. In 2015, same-sex marriage was legalized (ten years after Canada passed its Civil Marriage Act and five years after Argentina became the first Latin American country to do so). African Americans still suffered unequal opportunities, however, and were more likely to be unemployed, in poverty and receiving welfare benefits. Young males were also more likely to be classified as criminals. A third of Black men in their 20s were in prison or on probation. A number of fatal shootings of Black people by law enforcement led to the founding of the Black Lives Matter movement, in 2013, which aimed to raise awareness of racial discrimination and violence against Black people. These developments were helped by advances in digital technology and changes in the media landscape. The proliferation of smartphones and of digital cameras attached to police cars and police officers made it easier to investigate police interactions with the public, while the growing popularity of social-media platforms meant that recordings of police officers in action, including ones in which they brutalized and sometimes killed African Americans, could be widely posted and shared.

Acknowledgement of social and political issues, particularly those of minorities, identity politics and slavery reparations, was pilloried by the American right who talked of a 'war on woke'. Anti-fascist activists were branded 'Antifa', which the right labelled as

a domestic terrorist organization. The period saw the emergence of many movements on the right of the Republicans, such as the Tea Party, a group opposed to big government (with John McCain's presidential running mate Sarah Palin a prominent member), and the 'alt-right', more extreme nationalists who built support through online forums such as 4chan and Reddit.

ABOVE *A Black Lives Matter protest in Minnesota, 2015.*

LEFT *A Tea Party protest in Texas, 2009.*

EXTREME AMERICA

In 2016, Hillary Clinton won the Democratic nomination as candidate for the presidency and, with it, the opportunity to become the first female president of the US. Her opponent was the New York businessman Donald Trump, who had made money in real estate and achieved public recognition due to his presence as a host of TV shows and a celebrity lifestyle. While disliked by some conservative Republicans, Trump won the election by tapping into the resentments of many Americans, especially the less educated, over a number of issues: the loss of manufacturing jobs; the perception that the United States was losing trade and production to China; the fact that much of rural America was economically stagnant and scourged by a growing opioid crisis; and, last but not least, the belief that illegal immigration was out of control. Through his TV appearances, ghost-written books and ostentatious wealth, Trump convinced his blue-collar supporters that he was the 'master of the deal', who was able to strike better trade bargains for the US and stem uncontrolled immigration from and through Mexico by building a wall between the countries.

From the start, Trump addressed his potential voters through social media, particularly

Climate Change

Since the Industrial Revolution in the early 19th century, the burning of fossil fuels (oil, gas and coal) has resulted in increased emissions of carbon dioxide and other gases, which create a greenhouse effect by trapping heat in the Earth's atmosphere. This consequent warming upsets regular weather patterns and causes loss of polar ice, rising sea levels and increasing numbers of wildfires. Of all the issues that President Obama had to deal with over his two terms, climate change was perhaps the most historically significant. In 2016, he gave US support to the Paris Agreement, an international treaty aimed at preventing climate change by curbing global warming.

The aim of the Paris Agreement was to limit the rise in global surface temperature to an average 1.5°C (2.7°F) by attaining net zero (a point when emissions balance the amount that can be absorbed by nature) by the middle of the 21st century. This required countries to set emission targets and regularly report on progress. As the second-largest emitter of greenhouse gases after China, it was crucial for the US to play its part. But, just one year later, Donald Trump was elected and promptly withdrew from the agreement. Joe Biden would re-sign in 2021, only for Trump to quit again in 2025. This see-sawing over international climate agreements was not unusual: George W. Bush abandoned a similar agreement, the Kyoto Protocol, in 2002 which his predecessor Bill Clinton had approved. However, the issue has become much more urgent as global temperatures continue to rise towards a potentially irrecoverable tipping point, after which climate change might well accelerate.

his 3 million followers on Twitter (known as X since 2023). The red caps bearing his slogan 'Make America Great Again' (also used by Ronald Reagan in his 1980 campaign) and worn by his MAGA supporters became a defining image of the election. Trump's opinions were forthright, and disregarded fact-checking. He claimed that Clinton had shared classified material using a private email account and deserved to be in prison; 'Lock her up!' was a popular chant at Trump campaign rallies. Clinton, for her part, damaged any chance of attracting Trump supporters to her side when she insulted them as a 'basket of deplorables'. She was regarded as being a part of the 'establishment' and unlikely to deliver change for the better. The election campaign was bitter and divisive, with neither candidate gaining a high approval rate. The result was close, with Trump gaining the majority of electoral votes (though not the popular vote, which totals individual ballot papers).

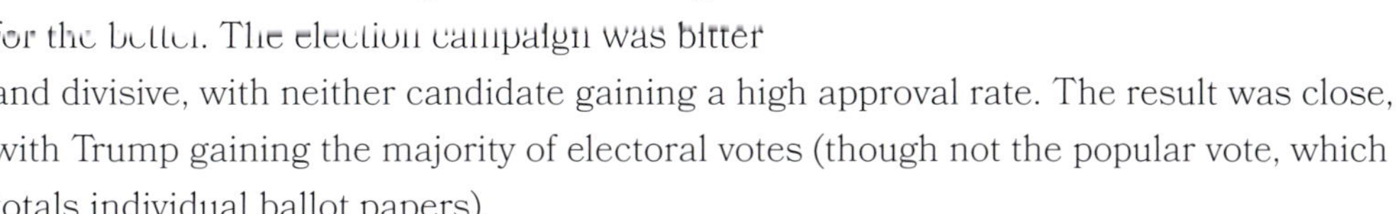

ABOVE *Hillary Clinton.*

Trump's first presidential term was an extraordinary interlude. He was the first president to serve without prior experience in political office or the military and had scant understanding of the issues of the day. On taking charge, he seemed determined to unravel every major policy put in place by his predecessor, beginning with executive orders aimed at reducing the Affordable Health Care Act and measures to protect the environment, such as the Paris Agreement. Rather than supporting initiatives to slow the global warming caused by burning fossil fuels, Trump proclaimed his support for the US fossil fuel industry and authorized new oil pipelines. He also ordered fresh efforts to arrest and deport undocumented immigrants, while giving out contracts to extend walls along the Mexican border. To pay for the wall, Trump demanded $5.7 billion in federal funding, but Democrat opposition in Congress ensured this was not forthcoming. A 35-day shutdown of the federal government began, the longest in the country's history, as both sides tried to agree a compromise. Trump's wall-building boasts fell flat, but he won support from other right-wing lobbies who sought his alliance. Among these were anti-abortion organizations and religious sects which wanted to enlarge conservative control over the Supreme Court. Trump duly seized the opportunity to nominate a conservative who might help him deliver another election pledge, to overturn the ruling on Roe v Wade and end the national right to abortion.

BELOW *Donald Trump.*

Trump pursued an 'America First' policy while courting authoritarian leaders such as Russia's Vladimir Putin and North Korea's Kim Jong Un, whom he met in June 2019. These contacts produced no result and Trump's attitude towards foreign policy was revealed by allegations that he had tried to persuade the president of Ukraine, Volodymyr Zelenskyy, to open an inquiry into his potential next election rival, former vice president Joe Biden, in exchange for $390 million in military aid. Trump hoped to discredit his rival by alleging that Biden had tried to influence an investigation into his son Hunter's work for the Ukrainian energy company Burisma. Congress believed Trump's secret phone deal was an abuse of presidential power and proceeded with impeachment proceedings against him.

PANDEMIC

Rumours of a flu-like virus spreading from China first emerged in late 2019. Later named SARs-CoV-2, or COVID-19, the virus was potentially lethal, particularly to the elderly and people with existing health conditions. As the full details of the virus became known, travel restrictions were put in place. The US imposed a ban on visitors from China at the end of January 2020 but was slow to restrict travel from Europe, where cases of the virus were already coming to light. When the virus hit America that same month it spread rapidly; hospitals and staff were overwhelmed. Trump and his supporters were initially resistant to measures that locked down businesses, but a national emergency was declared in March. By November 2020, about 10 million Americans had contracted the virus and 240,000 had died. The first vaccines became available the next month, being approved for wide use in August 2021.

BELOW *Joe Biden visits a vaccination centre in Maryland, January 2021.*

As offices were forced to close to stem the spread of the virus, the economy fell into recession. The federal government offered a $2 trillion stimulus package to help businesses survive the pandemic. While the government promoted the message that a vaccine would alleviate symptoms and potentially save lives, there was much public hesitancy in accepting it due to misinformation and conspiracy theories, such as the idea that the vaccine was used to transport tracking chips devised by Microsoft's Bill Gates. Despite the appearance of several new waves of variants, the development of vaccines and public compliance with pandemic regulations did lead to a reduction in cases.

The 2020 presidential election took place under the continuing restrictions imposed during the pandemic, with Joe Biden taking on the incumbent Donald Trump. Republicans sought to portray Biden as too old and mentally impaired to be in charge of the nation, even though, at 77, he was just three years older than Trump. Biden mostly campaigned online or else in small meetings, following pandemic guidelines while Trump shrugged off fears of the virus and rallied his supporters in large gatherings.

Due to the pandemic, mail-in voting was expected to be prevalent. Trump began suggesting the method could result in widespread fraud, preparing the ground for a potential complaint should he lose the election. As it proved, he did lose and refused

ABOVE *Attack on the Capitol building, 6 January 2021.*

to accept the outcome, alleging irregularities even before the final result had come in. Republicans issued several legal challenges to the result but the verdict stood. Biden won with a tally of 81 million votes, the largest in US history. Trump's total of 74 million votes was the second highest count on record.

On 6 January 2021, the Electoral College was scheduled to report the total number of votes to Congress. With encouragement from Trump, his supporters gathered in Washington DC to protest. Among them were right-wing extremists such as the white nationalist Proud Boys and the Oath Keepers militia group. The protest turned to violence, with hundreds of insurrectionists storming the Capitol, the building that houses both the US Senate and the House of Representatives. Lawmakers had to run for safety as groups ransacked the building, attacking police officers and disrupting the joint session of Congress. Five people, including one security officer, lost their lives in the attack on democracy. Over the coming months, having been filmed or having shared their activity on social media, most of the insurrectionists were arrested. Around 1,500 were put behind bars. Trump was impeached for a second time, for 'inciting violence against the Government of the United States'. Biden was sworn in as president on 20 January. Trump did not attend the inauguration.

One of Biden's key achievements in office was getting the Infrastructure Investment

Fake News

With news freely available online, the circulation of daily newspapers went into decline in the 21st century, along with editorial balance and fact-checking. People were getting their stories from social media. Facebook launched in 2004, YouTube in 2005, Twitter (later X) in 2006. By 2023, at its height, the latter had 368 million active users worldwide. Technology, including artificial intelligence, had advanced to allow people to create and post convincing fake photos and videos with accurate voice mimicry. By the time a video showing a presidential candidate stumbling was revealed as a fake it had already been shared a million times. Trump made many unverified claims and shrugged off criticism as 'fake news'. It was becoming harder and more important to recognize the truth.

and Jobs Act passed. At almost $1 trillion in cost, it invested in a wide range of new building projects across the country, including roads and bridge repairs, airports and rail, as well as increasing the availability of high-speed internet access. Biden's failures include the ignoble departure from Afghanistan of US troops in August 2021, when Taliban forces surged past Afghan soldiers to reclaim power. Around 100,000 people were airlifted away, but many Afghans who had helped Western efforts to reform the country were left behind in the hasty exit.

Shades of the Cold War returned in 2022, when Russia invaded Ukraine. Biden joined other countries in placing sanctions on Putin's regime while providing arms to the Kiev government. Russia claimed the land grab was in response to the threat of NATO expansion. In response, Ukraine looked towards joining NATO and the European Union as soon as possible.

BELOW
The US Air Force transport hundreds of Afghans from Kabul following the Taliban offensive of August 2021.

During his 2024 campaign for re-election, Biden appeared frail and forgetful in public, something his Republican opponents were happy to capitalize on, claiming once again that at 81 he was too old to continue as president. The first presidential debate was a disaster for Biden, when he publicly displayed a momentary loss of mental agility, confirming his critics' accusation that he was unable to discharge the responsibilities of office. Two months after confirming he would run, Biden gave in to pressure from Democrats and quit the race, allowing his vice president, Kamala Harris, to run for office in his stead. While Harris's approval ratings were higher than Biden's, she failed to express any divergence in approach to her boss. Voters felt they would just get more of the same. Even with considerable support from female voters, Harris ultimately lost to Donald Trump.

A NEW OLIGARCHY

By the early 2000s, the cost of running an election campaign was in the billions of dollars. A potential president needed a personal fortune, extremely wealthy supporters or, ideally, both. This risked leaders becoming beholden to corporations, lobby groups or individuals. In 2025, President Donald Trump invited many of his influential and affluent supporters to join his administration. Trump's new team was the richest in history, with a total wealth of around $340 billion. Eleven billionaires were invited to take positions in his cabinet. The car- and rocket-building tycoon and owner of X (formerly Twitter) Elon Musk had donated $277 million to Trump's campaign and was rewarded with his own department aimed at cutting costs and slashing federal regulations. Small wonder that in his farewell address in January 2025, outgoing president Joe Biden warned that 'an oligarchy is taking shape in America of extreme wealth, power and influence that really threatens our entire democracy, our basic rights and freedom'.

On entering the White House, Donald Trump was quick to fulfil promises made during the election, particularly those meant to reduce illegal immigration, to cut federal budgets and to end diversity programmes. He ordered the expansion of the controversial Guantánamo Bay camp to accommodate 30,000 migrants and sought to remove the automatic right to US citizenship for children born to immigrants in the country. The 1,500 people involved in the 6 January storming of Congress were all pardoned. Canada, Mexico and China were threatened with huge import tariffs, while Trump stated an interest in annexing Greenland from Denmark. All of this indicated that there would be dramatic changes in the direction of foreign as well as domestic policy. Trump's interventions in the Israel–Palestinian conflict in Gaza suggest that the US will confirm Israel as the leading regional power in the Middle East, possibly in tandem with Arab states which fear Palestinian radicalism and the Islamic Shiite regime in Iran. Trump has shown an apparent desire to reshape the world order.

ABOVE *Kamala Harris.*

ABOVE *Elon Musk.*

CANADA CONFRONTS ITS PAST

In 21st-century Canada efforts were finally made to address a major injustice against the country's indigenous people. From 1879 to 1997 the Indian Residential Schools system had seen indigenous children torn from their families and placed in Christian-led boarding schools. The system was designed to assimilate them into white-majority culture, with lessons taught only in English or French. Many of the 150,000 or so children relocated suffered abuse or neglect at the hands of their custodians; more than 4,000 died. As a result of the largest class-action settlement in Canadian history, a 1.9 billion Canadian dollar package of compensation was established and a Truth and Reconciliation Commission set up to record testimonies from those directly or indirectly affected. The conclusion of the commission in 2007 was that the government policy had been a deliberate attempt at 'cultural genocide'. A long list of recommendations were made to the government to improve the welfare and respect the rights and culture of the country's indigenous peoples.

BELOW *Justin Trudeau.*

In 2015, a familiar name returned to power in Canada. The new premier, Justin Trudeau, was the son of Pierre Trudeau, prime minister from 1968 to 1979 and 1980 to 1984. Early on, Trudeau the younger had to address an alarming number of suicides among First Nations peoples. Fewer educational and working opportunities in the country seemed to have driven young indigenous people to despair. On just one day in April 2016, 11 young members of the Attawapiskat community attempted to take their own lives, bringing the total number of suicide attempts to 100 within seven months. Suicide had become the leading cause of death for First Nations people under the age of 45. Trudeau agreed $69 million of funding towards dealing with mental health issues.

In contrast to Donald Trump's crackdown on immigration, Trudeau provided a welcome for refugees. As a result, thousands of migrants moved to Canada in 2017, including a large number fleeing Haiti and El Salvador. The country's response to the COVID pandemic was mixed, with travel restrictions implemented early on, while mask-wearing, social-distancing measures and a vaccine programme were instituted more slowly. Truck drivers objecting to a rule demanding they be vaccinated before crossing the Canada–US border protested with large roadblocks in Ottawa in January 2022. Trudeau stood his ground and ordered fines, arrests and vehicle towing to end the disruption, a stance that drew fierce criticism from the right wing in Canada and the United States. Canada has, however, avoided the swing towards nativism and populism which has swept the United States and seems set to become a shelter for liberal democracy in North America.

POPULISTS AND THE LEFT IN LATIN AMERICA

Populists were not unique to the United States. Tired of elites and often corrupt regimes that failed to balance the economy or improve their lot, Latin American voters looked to candidates outside the regular political sphere, to TV personalities and firebrands who offered radical solutions.

In 2016, the year it hosted the Olympic Games, Brazil found its economy in poor shape and its government mired in a corruption scandal. Numerous politicians and businesspeople were accused of taking kickbacks from companies who gained contracts with the national oil and gas company Petrobas. Despite President Dilma Rousseff's denials of involvement, large crowds took to the streets demanding her impeachment. She was removed from office and her mentor, the leftist former president Luiz Inácio 'Lula' da Silva, was also accused of corruption and money laundering. Locked up and awaiting an appeal, Lula was unable to run for president as planned in 2018. This opened the door for the legislator and former army captain Jair Bolsonaro to become the front runner.

During the campaign, Bolsonaro was stabbed in an assassination attempt and required life-saving surgery. He continued campaigning from his hospital bed and home, finishing ahead of the competition but requiring a run-off to clinch the presidency. He proved a controversial leader, in favour of exploiting the Amazon rainforest – some 7,600 square km (2,930 square miles) of rainforest were cut down or destroyed in just nine months – and dismissive of the serious nature of COVID-19. By May 2021, 15 million Brazilians had contracted the virus and more than 428,000 had died. Only the United States had more COVID-19-related deaths than Brazil. Like his predecessors in government, Bolsonaro also faced accusations of corruption in office.

ABOVE *Jair Bolsonaro.*

In 2022, Lula was free to contest the presidential election. Bolsonaro, following Trump's playbook, began to cast doubt on the trustworthiness of the voting system. When Lula won by a tight margin, Bolsonaro's supporters took to the streets in protest. A week after Lula's inauguration, they stormed Brazil's Congress in scenes comparable with the January 2021 attack on the US Capitol by Trump advocates.

Chile's government also became embroiled in corruption scandals. In 2015, there were allegations that President Michelle Bachelet's son had used political influence to obtain a $10 million loan for his wife, who in turn was accused of tax evasion. Further investigations led to almost 200 politicians and executives being questioned about fraud, bribery and other crimes. At the same time, the Chilean economy, which had been one

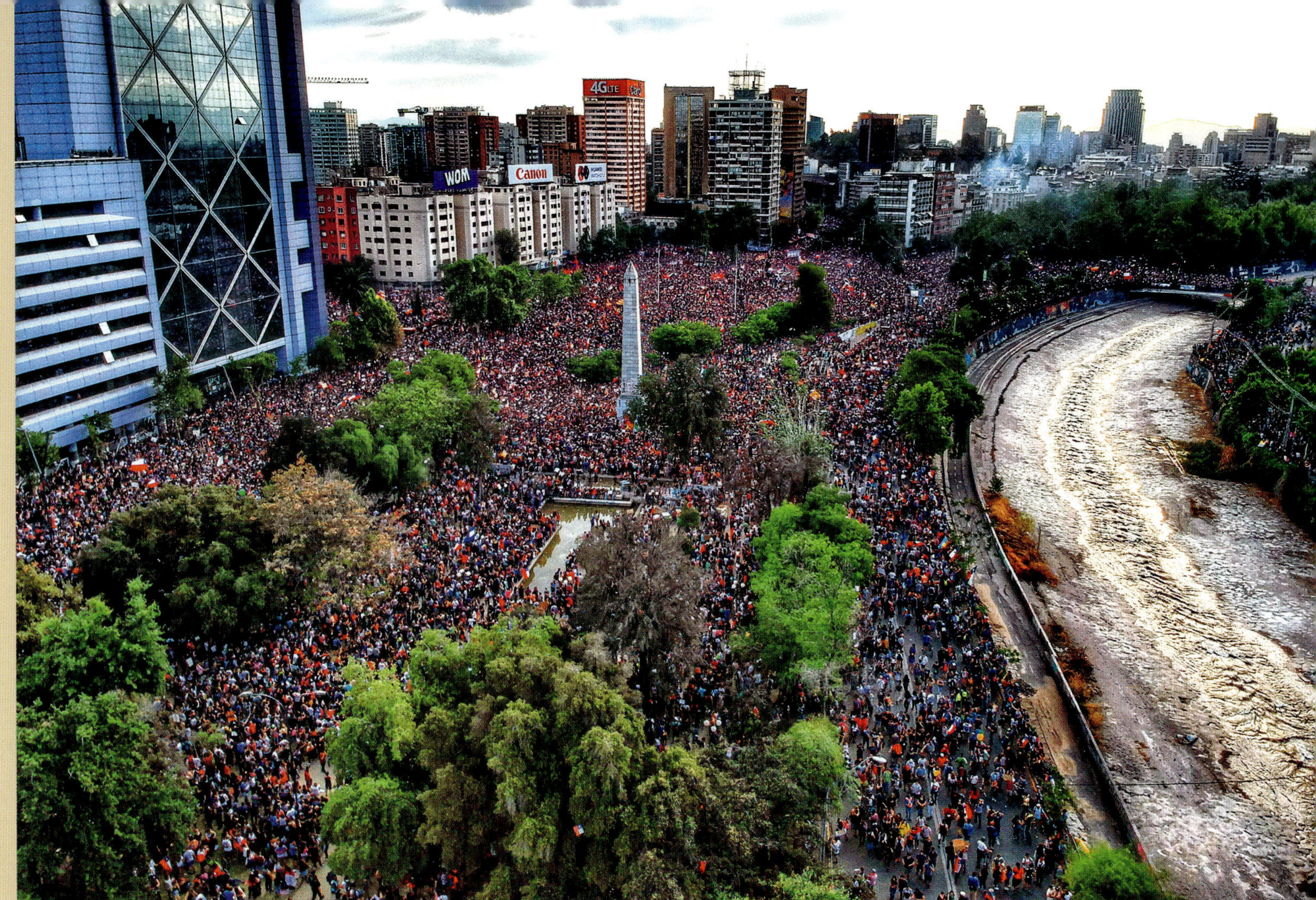

ABOVE *Protests in Santiago, Chile, 25 October 2019.*

of the strongest in Latin America over the previous decade, began to decline as copper prices slumped. The issue of social inequality became a rallying cry in 2019, with mass protests erupting following a subway fare increase in the capital, Santiago. The demonstrations turned violent with thousands wounded and more than 20 people killed. The protests led to a committee being elected to develop a new constitution in 2021. The Constitutional Convention saw an equal split of men and women (and reserved seats for indigenous peoples) but a referendum on the proposed new constitution that resulted saw it roundly rejected by the public a year later.

Argentina entered the 21st century plagued with huge foreign debt, an overvalued currency and recession. From 2014 to 2016 the country was in technical default with its debtors. The COVID pandemic badly damaged the economy too. By 2023, two-fifths of the population were in poverty and the inflation rate was one of the highest in the world. This was the stage for the next presidential election, when the Peronist economy minister Sergio Massa faced the populist libertarian and political pundit Javier Milei. A self-proclaimed anarcho-capitalist, Milei was the change candidate, an unpredictable character compared to Donald Trump in his outspoken opinions. Among his proposed policies was the deregulation of gun possession, legalization of human-organ sales and changing the national currency to the US dollar. Milei won the election and set about dissolving government ministries and devaluing the peso, the country's currency. Poverty continued to climb, reaching a peak of 57 per cent early in 2024.

In Venezuela, Nicolás Maduro, the successor to Hugo Chávez, presided over a humanitarian crisis. In his first year in office he claimed extra powers to rule by decree in order to solve the country's economic woes. He ordered the military to take over appliance stores and reduce prices. This made it possible for people to buy electronic goods but was little help against a shortage of staple foods. In 2015, the opposition won the parliamentary election but Venezuela's Supreme Court, packed with Maduro loyalists, dissolved the Congress and claimed its powers two years later. This was followed by a 15-year ban on an opposition presidential candidate being allowed to stand for election. The country was on the road to dictatorship.

As the price of oil dropped and consumer prices rose 800 per cent, people struggled to afford food. The economy was weakened further by US and EU sanctions against what they saw as an illegitimate government. Maduro would claim victory in the 2018 election, which the opposition also claimed to have won. Days after Maduro's inauguration, the opposition leader Juan Guaidó declared himself Venezuela's acting president. The US and 60 other countries agreed and recognized him as such. Russia, China, Cuba and Iran did not. A coup attempt led by Guaidó in April 2019 failed and he left for Spain. Millions of migrants fled the country too. They joined waves of people seeking escape from Haiti, Colombia and Cuba, many of them heading for the United States.

A 'NEW NEW WORLD'

Two hundred and fifty years since its independence, the United States is the world's dominant superpower. The choices made by its government affect the whole planet. The country delivers the majority of international aid. Within NATO and the United Nations, it provides vast military support for peacekeeping missions. As one of the largest trading nations on the planet it can affect, even disrupt, international markets with a change of mind or a change of tariffs. Booms and recessions in the US reverberate around the world. But, in recent years, the supremacy of the US has been countered by the rise of China and India. The two largest populations on Earth (the US has the third largest) provide the workforce for two powerful and still-growing economies. Where once developing countries looked to the United States for investment, now they look east. How the US deals with this competition will frame the next decades.

ABOVE TOP *Javier Milei.*

ABOVE *Nicolás Maduro.*

Canada and Latin America have long been out of the shadow of their former European rulers, developing their own methods of governance and economies, their own histories and cultures. Since the end of the Cold War, the relationship between the US and Latin America has become closer but has changed in balance. The US has remained the largest single trading partner for every country in the region, but US commerce and investment has declined. While the United States became more important to Latin America, the region became less important to the US. This substantially reduced Latin American economic and political bargaining power with the 'Colossus of the North'. In other respects, however, Latin America has become much more visible to the United States, as swelling flows of migrants and narcotics cross its borders.

POWER POLITICS

At the start of 2025, the United States seemed about to embark on a significant change in its internal government and its relations with the rest of the world. Donald Trump's second term began with a barrage of executive orders aimed at consolidating executive power while cutting back on the scale and cost of the federal administration. While Trump targeted the power of the bureaucracy, his election augmented the power and influence of a business oligarchy, with new allies among the chief executives of the great corporations of the digital and AI-facing world. His economic approach blended personal and national interests, on the grounds that what's good for Trump and his business allies is good for America, while at the same time he proposed a radical break with the free-trade policies followed since the end of World War II. His determination to raise tariffs against most imports (but especially from countries which export more to the US than they import from it) raised general alarm among all those countries for which America is a vital market. He focused particularly on China, which he had long portrayed as the greatest challenge to American economic and military superiority. Here, his approach began with threats to exclude China with import tariffs, while also ensuring that it did not acquire the technology or the investment capital needed to sustain its rapid development.

Trump also threatened the most significant change in US foreign policy since World War II. American policy was already shifting away from its traditional Cold War stance, which was to check Soviet power through the NATO alliance, towards an emphasis on curbing the ascent of China. On retaking office in January 2025, Trump signalled a more radical shift. By inviting Russia to negotiate with the US to end the war in Ukraine, he emphasized a major pivot away from Europe and a move to concentrate American forces on the Asian Pacific region. His view of geopolitics seemed to look back to the old days of international power politics, in which the great powers divided the world into separate spheres of influence where they exercised unchallenged hegemony.

BELOW *Donald Trump and Volodymyr Zelenskyy.*

The implications for the rest of the Americas were signalled by an intensification of pressure on American neighbours to submit to US demands.

While allowing Russia to build a sphere of influence over the lands of the old Tsarist and Soviet empires, Trump seemed intent on reaffirming US dominance in the western hemisphere, from which a new 'Fortress America' will assert its power against China in the East. For Latin America, closer connections with the United States offer dependent relations. Some, like Brazil and Mexico, might grow stronger economically, but all will be discouraged from strengthening economic ties with China. Trump's suggestions that Greenland should be removed from Danish oversight and annexed to the United States, that Canada should become part of the United States, and that Panama should renegotiate the Canal Treaty to give preference to the United States, were signs of this direction of travel in early 2025. Outcomes are, as always, uncertain, but it seems likely that the new world order will be one in which, as the ancient Athenian historian Thucydides put it, the strong do as they will and the weak do as they must, both in the Americas and beyond.

BELOW *Despite tight border restrictions, the United States remains a favoured destination for migrants seeking a safe haven and better future.*

INDEX

Picture credits

t = top, **b** = bottom, **l** = left, **r** = right

Alamy: 23tr, 38t, 49, 64, 72, 76, 129, 159, 244

Bridgeman Images: 57b, 61b, 92, 104, 107

Cleveland Museum of Art: 26b

David Woodroffe: 11, 14b, 15t, 25t, 27, 47, 56, 57t, 78, 87, 88, 98, 109b

Getty Images: 41, 51t, 58t, 59b, 81t, 109t, 140, 152, 170, 173b, 183t, 190, 196, 197b, 200, 203, 204b, 209, 211, 212t, 213, 214, 218b, 219, 220, 221, 222, 229, 231, 243, 249t

Los Angeles County Museum of Art: 54

Library of Congress: 139t, 167

Metropolitan Museum of Art: 12t, 14tl, 14tr, 16l, 18b, 20b, 21b, 25b, 26t

Public Domain: 52, 67

Science Photo Library: 34b

Shutterstock: 8, 16r, 17b, 22b, 30, 31, 60b, 61t, 70b, 82, 93, 164, 202, 228, 232, 234b, 235, 237, 241 (x2), 245t, 246, 247, 249, 250, 251

Topfoto: 46t, 75t, 106, 137, 158b

Wikimedia Commons: 12b, 15b, 17t, 18t, 19, 20t, 21t, 22t, 23tl, 23b, 24, 29, 32, 34t, 35, 36 (x2), 37 (x2), 38b, 39 (x2), 40, 42 (x2), 43, 44, 45, 46b, 48, 50, 51b, 53, 58b, 59t, 60t, 62 (x2), 63, 66, 69, 70t, 71, 73, 75b, 79, 80, 81b, 83, 84, 85, 86, 89, 90, 94, 96, 97, 99, 100, 102 (x2), 103, 108, 110, 111, 112, 113, 114, 116 (x2), 117, 118t, 118b, 119, 120, 123, 124, 127 (x3), 128, 130, 131, 132 (x2), 133 (x2), 134, 135, 136, 138 (x2), 139b, 141, 142, 143, 145, 146, 148 (x2), 149 (x2), 150, 151 (x2), 153 (x2), 154 (x2), 155 (x3), 156 (x2), 157 (x2), 158t, 160 (x2), 161, 163, 165, 166, 168, 169 (x2), 172t, 172b, 173t, 174 (x2), 175 (x2), 176, 177 (x2), 178, 179 (x2), 180, 181, 183b, 184, 185, 186 (x2), 188, 189 (x2), 192, 193 (x2), 194 (x2), 195, 197t, 198 (x2), 199, 201, 204t, 206, 207, 208 (x2), 210 (x2), 212b, 216, 217, 218t, 223, 224 (x2), 225 (x3), 226, 227 (x2), 230 (x2), 234t, 236, 239 (x2), 242, 245b, 248